T0326501

Sixth edition: June 2023

D/2017/45/314 – ISBN 978 94 014 4456 9 – NUR 801

Cover and interior design: Gert Degrande | De Witlofcompagnie

© The authors & Lannoo Publishers nv, Tielt, 2017.

LannooCampus Publishers is a subsidiary of Lannoo Publishers,
the book and multimedia division of Lannoo Publishers nv.

LannooCampus Publishers
Vaartkom 41 box 01.02
3000 Leuven
Belgium
www.lannoocampus.com

PETER DE PRINS   GEERT LETENS   KURT VERWEIRE

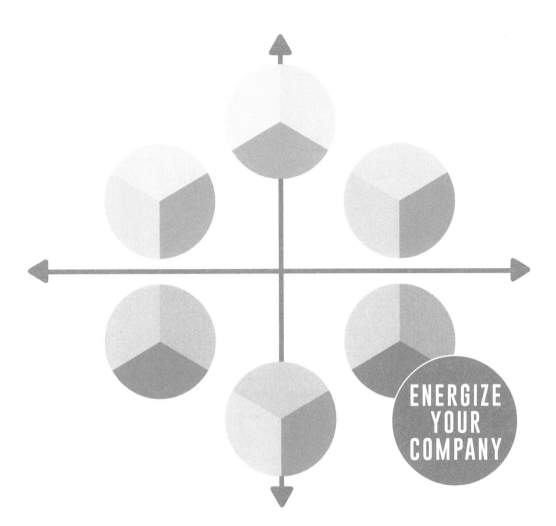

ENERGIZE
YOUR
COMPANY

SIX BATTERIES
OF CHANGE

Lannoo
Campus

TRIBUTE TO PETER PETER DE PRINS

By Kurt Verweire and Geert Letens, co-authors

It was in January 2014 that we began our search for the holy grail of change management. Initially, we each did this separately, based on our own backgrounds in the management field. However, it soon became clear that the strength of our new approach would be found in combining our knowledge and integrating our expertise. After endless hours of reading, discussing and synthesizing, we gradually began to see the contours of what would become the *Six Batteries of Change*. The book is the result of a collaboration between three very different characters, each with his own views on the theme of transformation and change. It has produced a holistic change model that brings together the best of each of us and has opened the eyes of many readers, thanks to its simplicity and strength.

Within the overall process, each of us had his own role. Peter was the man for fresh ideas, imaginative metaphors and powerful one-liners. Searching for thirty descriptions of energy loss? Only a man like Peter could actually gain energy from such a task! Our meetings to discuss the book were always inspirational and constructive. Once again, this was one of the great merits of Peter. His knowledge of the emotional side of change management and his many personal stories often gave us new perspectives on the change process and he continued non-stop to challenge a too one-sided rational approach. Sometimes uncertainly, but often with great passion and conviction.

When the book was published, Peter was the main driving force behind the ideas to more widely publicize the model. For him, the book launch had to be (and was!) a unique event. Inspiring and entertaining, but also something that touched a chord. Peter orchestrated the entire thing, right down to the smallest detail. And it was indeed a memorable experience for everyone who was there (if you want to see for yourself, have a look at the film on YouTube https://www.youtube.com/wat- ch?v=nU-ZlOe9qnKU). Even after the launch, Peter continued to be an excellent ambassador for the book. Wherever he could, he spread the 'gospel' of the six batteries in his energetic and passionate style. Together with Geert and Heidi, he even set up his own consulting company, LQ, with the aim of transforming the ideas in the book into practice.He was ready to spread the *Six Batteries of Change* ideology around the globe.

Imagine, then, our surprise and dismay, when we learnt of Peter's death in August 2020. We were already starting to think about a follow-up book... Even today, it is still hard to comprehend what has happened and to give it a place. In addition to losing a good friend and a listening ear, we also lost an enthusiastic, inspirational and energetic colleague. We miss you, Peter, but we are so grateful for our many moments of co-creation together. We continue to carry you in our memories, in our hearts and in all we do...

This edition of the book is also a tribute to Peter.

— Geert & Kurt

By Heidi Theys, colleague and business partner

For me, Peter was a good friend, colleague and mentor. He was the most intense 'people-person' that I have ever met. He really knew how to listen and how to make his conversation partners bigger and better. Peter worked very hard but at the same time he had a huge lust for life. He gave us energy and inspiration, and had a lasting impact on our 'being'.

My story with Peter starts twenty years ago, when I got to know him as a mentor in a leadership program. Peter knew how to be confrontational when he needed to be. He always gave me honest feedback, direct and straight to the point. He had the ability to turn the most complex matters into simple and powerful one-liners. During our first mentoring session, he immediately gave me two key words to remember: 'BE THERE!' He said: '*Heidi, you can always choose where you are, and with whom and why, so make sure that wherever you are and whatever you are doing you always give the full 100%! Be there ...*' This is a life lesson that I still try to put into practice every day.

Two years ago, Peter and I decided to set up the company LQ with Geert Letens. The aim was to convert the ideas in the *Six Batteries of Change* into practice. LQ stands for L 'lemniscate' and Q 'trigger'. It is our motto for continuous learning. Together with the LQ team and our customers, we intended to further perpetuate Peter's legacy. Peter always set the bar very high, both for himself and for the team. He was constantly surprising us with new strategic insights, international opportunities and creative ideas.

Peter's great passion outside of work was music. Music allowed him to find an ideal outlet for his intensity and vulnerability. With his musical stories, he wanted to make the world a pleasanter and more inclusive place. Every time he came into the office, he would say: 'Let's put some music on; you all look so serious!' He always started and finished his workshops with music and in the future he wanted to make music an integral part of our coaching sessions.

In Peter's case, there is no such thing as 'goodbye'. It is impossible to forget him. The LQ team would have loved to have worked with him for many more years to come, but it was not to be. However, he would be very proud if he could see how LQ and its customers are now making an impact worldwide. Peter continues to travel with us as we make this journey towards our dream of becoming a leading authority on business transformation and change with a global footprint. We are certainly going to do everything in our power to make this dream come true and we know that Peter's spirit and ideas will be with us every step of the way.We will honor, preserve and extend his legacy and are so grateful for the limitless passion and energy he gave us.

– Heidi

By Patrick De Greve, colleague at the Vlerick Business School

For more than ten years I had the pleasure of knowing Peter De Prins as both a colleague and as a friend. What an inspirational man! His career was varied, to say the least: entrepreneur, business coach, adviser, trainer and finally professor in leadership at the Vlerick Business School.

He was able like no one else to build the bridge between theory and practice, always finding the right synthesis that few others could see. During his lessons, Peter succeeded in working his way into the hearts, hands and heads of our students, executives and alumni, allowing him to make a lasting impact on the way they look at leadership and change.

And when he started seven years ago to dream about writing a book with Kurt Verweire and Geert Letens – the title of their book, *Six Batteries of Change*, only emerged later – you knew that it wasn't going to be just another run-of-the-mill work about leadership and change management, but would be ground-breaking and inter-disciplinary, setting new boundaries and bringing together the authors' combined years of wisdom and experience, substantiated by the most recent supportive research.

The result was indeed a powerful synthesis dealing with strategy and making choices, culture, ambition and leadership, and stability and change. It was a book that not only provided inspiration, but also offered the necessary instruments and toolkits, as well as their revolutionary model based on six forces, which the readers could use as practical guidance that could easily be translated into their own particular situation.

Many authors write their books alone or occasionally with a co-author. Books with three authors are very much the exception. Even so, *Six Batteries of Change* brought together the different and wide-ranging expertise of Peter, Kurt and Geert in a manner that created a unique book and an equally unique central model; a model with real impact and the right balance between the rational and emotional aspects of life that connect us all.

With this book, Peter continues to inspire us each and every day. Because what is written, remains. And the writer always lives on...

— Patrick

CONTENTS

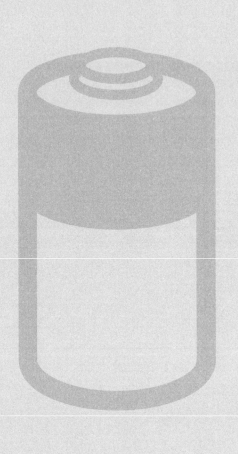

Chapter

1

AN INTRODUCTION TO THE SIX BATTERIES OF CHANGE

———

The sources of
organizational energy

Key questions

What is organizational energy and why is it key to successful change?

Why would our integrative, inclusive model of the six batteries work better than traditional change models?

Is it true that 70 percent of the change programs fail?

How do companies implement change in rapidly changing times?

Spark for reflection: The mastery of Team Sky

Cyclist Bradley Wiggins looked out of the window of his private jet, as it left the French coastline behind and headed towards England. Accompanied by his wife and two children, as well as manager of Team Sky, Sir Dave Brailsford, he was flying home for the final stages of preparation before the 2012 Summer Olympics. In 10 days he would compete for gold in the individual time trial. Wiggins reflected on what had been an incredible year for him and Team Sky. He had won three important one-week stage races and a few hours earlier he'd stood on the podium as winner of the Tour de France, the world's most prestigious cycling race.

Team Sky was a relative newcomer in the cycling peloton. It had been formed three years earlier by Brailsford, who had built credibility in Beijing 2008, where Great Britain won eight gold medals — a unique performance in British cycling history. Brailsford's goal was to have the first ever British winner of the Tour de France. Mission accomplished.

Brailsford introduced a science-led approach that bred phenomenal success in the discipline of road racing. He and his team examined every aspect of cycling in minute detail for possible improvement, and the cumulative effect of those many small gains gave the team a considerable advance on the opposition. Team Sky had rethought and worked hard on elements such as training, equipment, performance management, psychological support, nutrition, and racing tactics.

Team Sky had also established a special culture and connection among its riders. It provided individual psychological support and helped riders to deal with their emotional challenges and fears along the way

In only three years of intensive hard work, their efforts had finally paid off. Wiggins realized that he and Team Sky had shown an almost complete mastery of sport's most complex alchemy: the compelling amalgam of teamwork and individual effort...[1]

Really? Another model for change?

Getting an organization back on track and/or changing its course is always challenging. Managers try to instill new directions for their companies, but most of them fail to realize the strategic goals they have set. This is surprising, as there is plenty of help out there — including thousands of books that offer useful advice and numerous change management consultants.

Many of the traditional recipes for success have lost much of their value, though, as firms increasingly face more turbulent environments. John Kotter, Harvard Business School authority on change and inventor of the famous *Eight-Step Model For Leading Change*, acknowledges that traditional change tools can deal with tactical and strategic issues in a changing world only up to a point. These tools and approaches are effective when it is clear that you need to move from point A to a well-defined point B, and when the distance between the two points is not enormous.[2]

That linear world is gone. With that insight, it becomes dangerous to see change as a top-down, sequential process. As Figure 1 suggests, it's no longer a top team who dictates what has to happen; meaningful activity is taking place at the *grassroots level*. Managers and employees at all levels are experimenting, and their orders and instructions are increasingly ambiguous. Companies today need to be ambidextrous: *efficient* in managing today's business and *adaptive* to tomorrow's demands.

The sequential, linear approach tends to look at managing change as a primarily *rational* process, overlooking the importance of the *emotional* side — for successfully implementing or dealing with change today is largely about influencing and convincing people. Employees of today have a habit of *not* conforming to the rational arguments and orders of top managers. Change is much more unpredictable than we often take for granted.

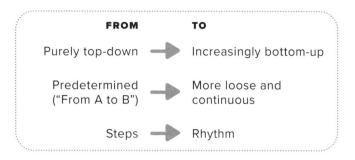

FROM → **TO**

Purely top-down → Increasingly bottom-up

Predetermined ("From A to B") → More loose and continuous

Steps → Rhythm

Figure 1 • New approaches to change management

A new change model must take into account this evolution in thinking about change. A contemporary and relevant change model needs to be *inclusive*.

- It specifies the roles of top and middle managers and employees in the change process.
- It reveals how the efforts of both top managers and lower-level employees contribute to effective change.

In addition, the new change model needs to be *integrative*.

- It reconciles rational with emotional aspects of change.

- It allows for continuous change, rather than a once-and-for-all approach to change.

We need to replace the linear and sequential approach to change with an approach where we think in terms of *rhythm*, not steps. Managers need to continuously evaluate their change efforts and processes, and adapt them as circumstances change.

At Vlerick Business School, we have developed such a model in collaboration with the Royal Military Academy of Belgium. We, the authors of this book, all with different academic backgrounds, met with change consultant Carel Boers, who has managed several corporate turnarounds, for a much-needed discussion on change models of today. The diversity of perspectives when discussing various change cases was striking. All of us had something to bring to the table — most valuable though, and especially to corporate managers, is the integration of our ideas in what follows.

Energy as the main driver of change

The starting point of our change model is that effective transformation is about managing *organizational energy*. When we look at the history of organizational change efforts, we come to the conclusion that the most common reason a company's leaders fail to reach their desired outcome is because their change efforts run out of energy... they fizzle out. Leaders who are able to tap into the existing energy for change that exists in the company's culture and in its people, and unleash this energy for the benefit of achieving organizational goals, typically get better outcomes. Building and maintaining energy for change for the long haul is a key requirement for leaders with transformational ambitions.

While the concept of energy features surprisingly little in the business press, we are all witness to its importance in the corporate world. Southwest Airlines, Apple, Google, Haier, IKEA... these are ambitious, vital and agile companies, known for being innovative and entrepreneurial, hitting the market with successful products and services, and being driven by a passionate, positive and dynamic workforce. Energy abounds in these companies; they are *energized*. Contrast this with low-energy companies, where there is a lack of challenge, lost opportunities, waste of talent, cynicism and frustration, and where mediocrity rules.[3]

Energy is an important characteristic of great leadership, too. Effective leaders are able to harness the energy of their people to create a better future. Management writer Peter Drucker claimed: "Your first and foremost job as a leader is to take charge of your own energy and then help to orchestrate the energy of those around you." Tony Schwartz and Jim Loehr, authors of the book *The Power of Full Engagement*, shared this view: "Above all else, a leader is the Chief Energy Officer. Leaders are the stewards of organizational energy; they invest energy from all the connected cells in the service of the corporate mission."[4]

But the energy of a leader is not enough to achieve great results. The entire organization needs to be energized to achieve change success or breakthrough performance; i.e. what is required is *organizational energy*.

Organizational energy can be defined as "*the extent to which an organization has mobilized its collective emotional, cognitive, and behavioral potential to pursue its goals*".[5]

- The *emotional* component is the extent to which people are passionate and enthusiastic in their pursuit of the company's goals.

- The *cognitive* component refers to the capacity to be alert to, and creative in the face of, new opportunities or threats.

- The *behavioral* component is the extent to which employees will go the extra mile, or stretch themselves to achieve shared goals.

A company's organizational energy is a collective dynamic force that is much stronger than the sum of individual forces or motivation. The intensity of energy differs from company to company; in some organizations that collective force is strong, in others it is barely present. High-energy companies have mobilized all their employees to work together to achieve great results. Low-energy companies lack such energy. Their people may feel emotionally distant from the company's goals or they may feel little excitement or hope. They are in "sleep mode", happy with the status quo. They lack the vitality and ambition to improve or to reach for something new or different.[6]

Energy, however, can be positive or negative. As a result, high energy is not always better. Some organizations have high levels of energy but use it in a destructive way: employees and managers may have internal fights; marketing fights product development; or sales is at odds with operations. Energy is wasted internally. Staff is overwhelmed by projects, without clear definitions of scope or appropriate resources. Other organizations lose energy when strategic projects fail to inspire employees. In this case, new initiatives are met with skepticism and employees oppose moving in the new strategic direction or resist adopting new so-called best practices.

It is important to create *energy that is channeled into purposeful action*. Only then is high energy productive and will it yield organizational benefits.

Although organizational energy is an emerging concept in the academic and business literature, there is evidence that productive energy is positively correlated with company performance. Productive energy affects profitability and productivity, and has a significant effect on customer loyalty and employee commitment.[7] Our research confirms that *energy today drives tomorrow's performance*. Companies with high levels of (productive) energy are better performers but are also better at change.

Six sources of organizational energy

Having established that organizational energy is a critical factor in successful adaptation, we were led to ask: why do certain companies have such low or negative energy levels, and what are the sources of energy loss that make strategic change projects fail? We found multiple sources of energy loss in organizations (see Figure 2), which we grouped according to meaningful themes that we've come to call our 'six batteries of change'.

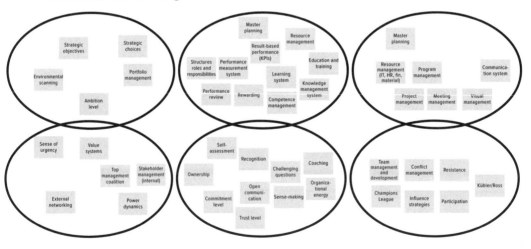

Figure 2 • Sources of energy loss in change[8]

These themes help us to explain *why change efforts fail or succeed*. If you charge the 'batteries', they generate enough energy to get the change project moving in the right direction. Change management is about managing the batteries of change.

Specifically, we contend that these batteries help to explain two key change dilemmas faced by managers.

The first is the *distinction between top and bottom*. Change tends to be initiated at the top, where senior executives create visions for their organization and develop strategic plans to realize those visions. Having both a purpose and a plan are undoubtedly important. However, many change projects fail because there is a gap between top management's announcements and action plans at the bottom.[9] Executives need to be aware that a change plan is often translated into many local initiatives that need to be managed in turn by *local change agents*. In reality, top executives don't always spend enough energy translating their visions and blueprints into concrete actions to be launched within different departments and sub-units of the organization. Conversely, many change projects cannot surpass the operational level. Change is initiated at a local level by enthusiastic individuals who want to improve the functioning of the organization, but is never taken to a more strategic level. The result is change initiatives that remain local initiatives with limited impact. In other cases, local change initiatives conflict with one another, leading to internal fights and destructive energy. Successful change requires that change occurs both at the *strategic level* and at the *operational level*.

A second change dilemma occurs when change leaders are unable to connect what we describe as the 'formal' and 'informal' sides of change. Specifically, they prioritize the rational over the emotional. Change strategies, project management, and change management infrastructure must of course be sound – this is the hardware of change. But even the best hardware cannot work properly without adequate software – the people and culture of an organization.

Many organizations are too focused on the formal (rational) aspect of change at the expense of the informal (emotional). We contend that these are equally important. In *The Happiness Hypothesis*,[10] Jonathan Haidt illustrates the battle between emotions and rationality with a metaphor based on a (fictitious) premise that elephants love ice cream. The riders on the elephants symbolize the rationality of the mind and expect to go from point A to point B. The six-ton animal symbolizes the emotions of people. If someone would stand along your path holding an ice cream cone, your elephant would be very tempted to get it. As a rider you would be pretty helpless and have little chance of getting the elephant to move in any direction but towards the ice cream. The conclusion is that the rider is an advisor or servant, not a king. The emotions of the elephant make it reach for short-term satisfaction (getting the ice cream), which momentarily blocks the long-term goal of getting to B. Put differently, change leaders need to be aware of the emotional aspects of the organization and master these often hidden dynamics of organizational change in order to succeed.[11]

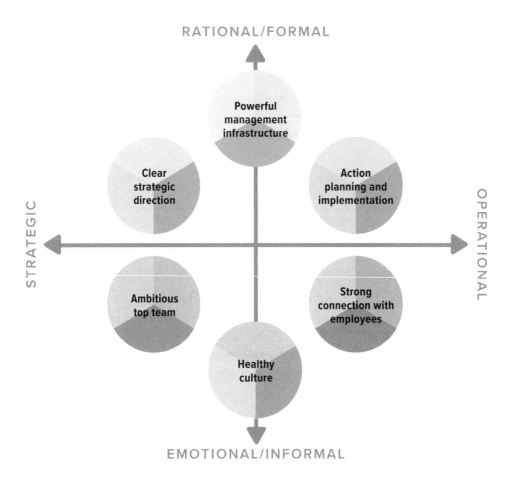

Figure 3 • The Six Batteries Model

The resulting framework in Figure 3 illustrates an ideal balancing of the formal and the informal and the strategic and the operational:

- *Battery 'Clear strategic direction'*: provides focus and ensures that change energy is oriented in the right direction.

- *Battery 'Powerful management infrastructure'*: comprises the organization's structures and systems needed to balance *running* and *building* the business as well as *maintaining* and *improving* performance. It is the energy control system that bridges the high-level strategy and the many operational projects and processes undertaken in the organization.

- *Battery 'Action planning and implementation'*: covers project and process management; this is where energy is transformed into clear customer benefits or improved organizational capabilities.

- *Battery 'Ambitious top team'*: covers the top team that generates energy for change; a cohesive top team inspires with vision and aspiration. This team brings passion, purpose and meaning to the table while serving as a role model for change.

- *Battery 'Healthy culture'*: amplifies change energy by building an open and transparent environment that brings people closer together. This drives the organization to stretch its goals and to seek opportunities for individual and organizational growth.

- *Battery 'Strong connection with employees'*: focuses on the connection with the people in the organization. There is no organizational change without individual change. Connecting with the emotions of employees gradually increases their desire and ability to embrace change and become fully committed to it.

Each battery of change is in turn associated with six energy domains:[12]

- *'Clear strategic direction'* is the source of *intellectual energy*. It is the company's choice of direction based on analysis, insight, thinking and synthesis. It is the energy generated by understanding your internal and external environment, planning ahead, and making consequent strategic decisions.

- *'Powerful management infrastructure'* contributes to the organization's *systemic energy*. It is derived from the company's systems, structures and procedures that prioritize and support change efforts while improving on them continuously. It is about figuring out how to get more out of the whole rather than out of the constituent parts.

- *'Action planning and implementation'* provides *physical energy*. It is the drive to make things happen, by way of sound data analysis and thoughtful experimentation that identifies the best way forward. It is also about making progress visible and the vitality this creates. Here lies the kinetic force of change.

- *'Ambitious top team'* is the source of *spiritual energy*. It is the commitment of the company's leaders to build a common vision and to create confidence in a compelling and meaningful ambition.

- *'Healthy culture'* is the source of *social energy*. It is the energy people get from positive relationships with others, their feeling of 'us' instead of 'I' and their common search for victory.

- *'Strong connection with employees'* generates *psychological energy*. It is the trust among employees and leaders, and the courage to embrace the change. It is the feeling of safety and support when making changes that ultimately translates into a belief in the power of 'self', 'team' and 'organization'.

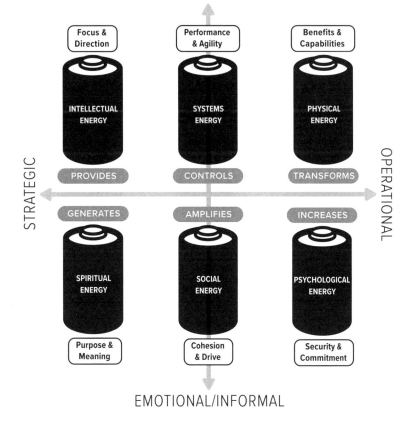

Figure 4 • The six batteries and their associated types of energy

We started this research project in the winter of 2012, three academics and one change manager. We had different backgrounds, but all of us had had regular contact with the business world – whether as a teacher, consultant, or business manager. What drove us together was the realization that we all looked at change from a fragmented perspective. If we brought our ideas together, we believed, we could bring something more valuable to the table.

When we developed our batteries model in 2014, we presented it to hundreds of managers in talks, in our classes, and in our consulting meetings. We received positive feedback: the model was simple, but not simplistic. It helped managers to discover the blind spots in their change approaches. Often they brought examples of how they had tackled particular change problems. We started to document these cases to show how the batteries of change could be used to explain successful change.

In 2016, realizing it was time to empirically validate whether the concept of organizational energy was linked to change success and change effectiveness, we approached managers who had been exposed to the batteries model, asking them and their executive colleagues to fill out a questionnaire. We collected information from 112 companies: subsidiaries of famous international companies — like Medtronic, Merck, Yusen, KBC and ING — and many smaller local firms; companies from different industries, including construction, financial services, logistics, automotive, postal services, technology, and professional services. We collected information on their batteries of change, but also on the characteristics of their change projects and the effectiveness of their change journeys. For example, some change projects helped companies to improve their performance. Other change projects helped companies to get ready for a digital world. With some of the companies from our sample, we had follow-up meetings to discuss the findings and validity of the results.

TEAM SKY AND THE BATTERIES OF CHANGE

Being successful in cycling — as in most sports — is about more than attracting a bunch of top athletes and paying them well. Our batteries model helps to better understand why Team Sky has been able to achieve such remarkable success over the last couple of years.

Sir David Brailsford had an ambition for Team Sky that was inspiring and motivating: to have a British rider win the Tour de France within five years. Brailsford then went one step further in a sport mired in doping scandals: he added that he wanted a clean (drug-free) winner. He attracted not only great riders, but also top sport experts, such as Rod Ellingworth, Tim Kerrison and Steve Peters, to rally behind that aspiration. He built an *ambitious top team* that worked towards realizing a shared ambition.

After a disastrous Tour de France in 2010, Team Sky analyzed where it had gone wrong. Their conclusion was that Bradley Wiggins and Team Sky needed a different game plan, one that meant a break with cycling tradition. Kerrison was the mastermind behind the new strategy: intense training at high altitude and reverse periodization – less racing and more training – turning the idea of gradual build-up to the Tour on its head. In the races, Team Sky adopted a defensive racing style, especially in the mountain stages. This racing style leveraged Wiggins' strengths as a time trial specialist and allowed him to cope better with the acceleration of the star climbers of the peloton. Team Sky's *strategy* was clear to everybody in the organization.

But strategy without action is merely a daydream. Team Sky needed an overview of their action portfolio as well as a sound performance management system to keep track of progress on actions. For Team Sky, the aggregation of marginal gains principle unified all efforts to make the dream come true. Brailsford and his team put performance and training programs in place, worked on nutrition, and introduced technological innovations to boost rider performance, among several other initiatives: the grouping of all those initiatives becomes a program, that needs to be monitored and screened. (Just like a strategy map groups all activities, this is a program for all Team Sky's activities). In other words, Team Sky developed *a powerful management infrastructure* to turn the strategy into results. Ellingworth, Sky's performance manager, was responsible for recording what everybody was doing and monitoring how it was done. There was also commitment to discussing the lessons learned along the way.

Ellingworth and Kerrison put together a method of internal communication, essential (though often neglected) if your team is spread across Europe. The pair also put advanced planning and logistics systems in place.[13] Whether rider or member of staff, each individual had absolute clarity concerning roles, responsibilities, structure and tactics — a rigorous application of *action planning and implementation.*

It's important to note that the application of the marginal gains principle was also a cultural thing. In an interview in *Harvard Business Review*, Brailsford commented: "Perhaps the most powerful benefit [of marginal gains] is that it creates a contagious enthusiasm. Everyone starts looking for ways to improve. People want to identify opportunities and share them with the group. Our team became a very positive place to be. One caveat is that the whole marginal gains approach doesn't work if only half the team buy in. In that case, the search for small improvements will cause resentment. If everyone is committed, in my experience it removes the fear of being singled out — there's mutual accountability, which is the basis of great teamwork."[14] As we will show later, teamwork, accountability and a strong drive to achieve excellence are key elements of a *healthy culture.*

Finally, Brailsford realized that more was needed than a healthy culture and top support. He chose to spend a significant amount of time and resources on individual coaching, investing heavily in supporting the athletes. This included employing the best technology and providing psychological support from Peters, Team Sky's psychiatrist. Specifically, Peters taught Wiggins and the other riders to control their 'chimp', the emotional and irrational part of the brain, which has the potential to inhibit performance. No other cycling team invested so heavily in this kind of coaching. Arguably no team had a *stronger connection with its employees* than Team Sky.

Of course, Team Sky had the money to invest in all this, and clearly Wiggins had, and today Froome has, the legs of a champion. But we believe that it takes more than money and stars to build a successful organization. The six batteries of change help to explain why Team Sky has been so successful. As in other successful organizations we have worked with, we believe their success is largely determined by design, not by chance. Team Sky has consistently built an organization that continuously feeds energy into all six batteries of change.

New insights on change management

Our change model offers new insights on how to manage change in rapidly evolving times. This is how our model differs from other change models:

Change involves marshaling energy throughout the organization

Transforming organizations is about creating energy in your organization so that it becomes a better organization, able to produce better results for your customers. You create energy by *charging the six batteries of change*.

Change is multidimensional

It's important to develop a comprehensive view of the energy status of your company. The six batteries, with their different focus points, help you to get a more detailed and nuanced view of your *level of organizational energy*. Some concern the rational aspects and have an impact on the formal side ('the hardware') of the organization. Others touch on the informal and deal with the software of the organization. Some of the batteries are charged at the top; others deal with operational issues and are charged by lower-level employees at the bottom of the organization.

Change is integrative

The batteries are connected and interdependent. They are mutually supportive or destructive: the energy or lack of energy in one battery affects other batteries. For example, if you launch new performance initiatives and set up an appropriate management infrastructure, you will only generate great results if you also possess a healthy culture. It's not sufficient to focus all your efforts on charging one change battery. Working for two years on a strategic masterplan won't work if you're not starting to translate it into concrete projects, or if the strategy is not supported by every member of the top team. Effective change requires *charging a series of connected batteries*.

Change is not one-size-fits-all

We don't believe in managing change with a predetermined step-by-step model. There is no standard approach to tackling change. Organizations differ in how their change batteries are charged. Companies have a legacy; they all have their own *change history*. Managers need to know which batteries generate energy and which drain energy. The content of your change program and your change process varies depending on the energy status of your six batteries. Where or what is the engine of your change? This differs from company to company.

Change is inclusive

Successful change is never the result of the Herculean efforts of one person. A change leader is crucial, but successful change requires that you build a critical mass of change leaders at all levels in the organization. Top-down change does not generate long-term results — neither does pure bottom-up change. Successful change requires that top managers, middle managers and employees all have a role to play in the change process. Top executives are the *sponsors* of the change program; they create awareness and set the pace and the direction of the change. *Change managers* ensure that the program helps to realize the intended goals and control whether projects are delivered in time and within budget constraints. They also manage conflicts, provide feedback, recognize and reward. The *champions* coach their team members to actively contribute and support the change as individual projects are delivered.

The mythical 70%

It is a commonly held belief, and one frequently reported in literature, that 70 percent of all change initiatives fail. We contest this figure, which our research shows is inflated. We developed a measure for overall change success, which included measures of *initial performance dips, project timing, whether desired benefits were achieved*, and whether *change results were sustained*. We also examined the impact of the change program on hard performance items, such as financial performance, customer benefits, and operational measures, as well as on soft performance measures, such as employee satisfaction and leadership-related measures.[15]

Depending on the change effectiveness measure, we see failure rates ranging from 30 to 58 percent, far lower than the traditional 70 percent predictions. Of course, concluding that more than 30 percent of change initiatives therefore succeed is too bold a statement. While more than 30 percent of the initiatives don't fail, only a minority of firms report overall success. Most firms have 'low positive' change success scores. This means that while they may have done well on some of the change effectiveness criteria, they may not be fully satisfied with the performance on some of the other criteria.

Executives do report, however, that charging the batteries of change is correlated significantly with change success. The higher the number of batteries charged, the more likely executives are to rate the transformation a success.

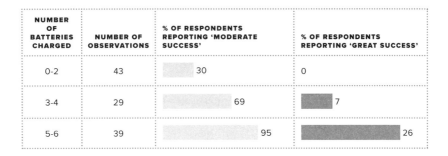

NUMBER OF BATTERIES CHARGED	NUMBER OF OBSERVATIONS	% OF RESPONDENTS REPORTING 'MODERATE SUCCESS'	% OF RESPONDENTS REPORTING 'GREAT SUCCESS'
0-2	43	30	0
3-4	29	69	7
5-6	39	95	26

Figure 5 • Number of batteries charged and change success

How to read this book?

The following six chapters are dedicated to each of the six change batteries and aim at understanding the energy status of each battery. The chapters also offer recommendations on how to charge each change battery. You might want to consider spending more time on the chapter that details the battery of most concern in your organization. Note that we will discuss the batteries from left to right, alternating rational with emotional batteries. We emphasize that this sequence is *not* our recipe for successful change, but resembles a top-down approach that many readers will be familiar with. Each of the battery chapters includes a quick scan that allows assessing your energy level in this particular battery. The main purpose of these chapters is therefore twofold: first, to provide you with a quick energy health check of your organization, and secondly to inspire you with ideas to recharge the various batteries.

The final three chapters discuss what to do next. Chapter 8 describes the components of a good organizational energy analysis. It examines why it is important to look at the most significant energy drainers and gainers in your company. It provides an overview of the most common change pathologies and shows why it makes sense to have a look at your change context and history. This 'diagnosis' will provide valuable insights in preparation for chapters 9 and 10 as you build a customized roadmap to charge all of your batteries.

Chapter 9 moves from analysis to launching change interventions. It helps you to design change interventions that manage both the rational and emotional side of change, and that span the spectrum from strategic to operational. This chapter presents two major energy design principles: balance and flow... both useful concepts when building a portfolio of change initiatives.

The last chapter examines your change ambition level. Are you considering setting up a change project just to get your organization back on track? Or do you aspire to develop change capabilities that help you to deal with fast-changing and turbulent environments? If the latter, arguably the only way to survive and secure sustained performance is to build capabilities that allow you to renew yourself faster than the competition does. We finish this chapter with a case study of a large financial institution, KBC, which transformed itself into an entity capable of dealing with the digital disruptions in its industry.

Chapter

2

AN AMBITIOUS TOP TEAM

——

The spiritual energy

Key questions

What is a 'good' ambition?

What is the importance of the top team as role models for change?

How do you create a strong top team? How do you enable this team to act with one voice, bringing one message?

What can you do if the top team is disconnected from the rest of the organization, or stuck in its ways?

HOW WELL IS *YOUR* TOP TEAM BATTERY CHARGED?

Tick whether you agree or disagree with each of the following statements.

		AGREE	DISAGREE
1	In our organization, top managers' needs are more important than collective goals.		
2	Our top executives are role models for change.		
3	Our organization has a cohesive top team in which members trust each other.		
4	The top team has no clear mandate and lacks support from major stakeholders to transform the organization.		
5	The top team has allocated significant budgets to fund our change initiatives.		
6	Our change vision is uninspiring: it does not generate energy within the organization.		
7	Our top team radiates an inspiring and motivating ambition within the organization.		
8	Our top team periodically assesses the gap between current and desired change capabilities of our organization.		

Give yourself one point each time you agreed with the following statements:

2   3   5   7   8

Give yourself one point each time you disagreed with the following statements:

1   4   6

What is your total score on eight?

INTERPRETING YOUR RESULT

Score	Implications
0-2	The top team battery is an energy drainer. There's insufficient energy to inspire the rest of the organization, because employees don't believe in the change story – either because top team members are not the role models for change, either because the message lacks inspiration and ambition. There may be a lack of trust among top team members, potentially because they serve their own agenda.
3-4	Your top team battery is weak. Your top team is not acting as a team yet, or they lack budgets and resources to support the change ambition. You need to put extra energy into building and communicating a credible and inspiring ambition.
5-6	Your top team generates energy for the change project. To fully benefit from the power of this battery, you should work on one or two focused criteria. The organization should periodically assess the gap between current and desired change capabilities.
7-8	Your top team battery is fully charged. You have a great team that supports an inspiring change vision. The top team has a clear mandate from the major stakeholders and you have the means and energy to change the organization.

Spark for reflection: Marissa Mayer's leadership at Yahoo[16]

Yahoo is facing turbulent times. The original Internet media giant is failing at its core business as it is outcompeted by Google and Facebook, as well as new kids on the block such as Instagram and Snapchat. Although Yahoo owns a $30 billion stake in Alibaba and an $8 billion stake in Yahoo Japan, it's considered a liability by many in the industry. Its business model is built for an era that has long since passed and financial analysts agree that breathing life back into the company will be no easy task. Yahoo has gone through five CEOs in five years.

In July 2012, Yahoo announced that Marissa Mayer would take the helm. Given her experience as a top executive in a leading technology firm — she was Google's twentieth hire and spent years in its inner circle — Mayer was optimistic that she could turn Yahoo around. By 2016, however, more than a third of Yahoo's employees had left and financial results had not improved.

Business publications like *Forbes*, *Fortune* and *The New York Times* attribute the problems at Yahoo to Mayer's poor leadership. "Mayer's leadership seems to be more about Mayer than those she is responsible for leading," writes *Forbes* journalist Mike Myatt. "Mayer loves the spotlight and she seems more concerned with building her own brand image than working on Yahoo's problems."[17] One journalist called her "the queen of excess" and reported that Mayer was under fire by a Yahoo investor for her excessive spending habits, including reportedly spending $7 million on a Great Gatsby-themed holiday party in San Francisco.

Mayer is also accused of micromanagement. She reportedly wanted to keep close control, and consistently rebuffed dissenting and differing opinions. One commenter noted: "She exhibits a close-mindedness that rarely serves a leader well. Having strong convictions is a healthy thing so long as you're convicted by the truth and not your pride or your ego."[18]

She clearly had problems building a strong top team. Senior executives have left at an alarming rate since 2015; new executives have been hired without fully vetting them with her team. Some had to leave shortly afterwards, sometimes with a huge bonus.

Finally, Mayer has been criticized for some of her strategic decisions. For example, she embarked on the process of reorganizing Yahoo's product teams without presenting a grand vision. "Instead, she began sketching out different scenarios in one-on-one meetings with various executives, floating one plan by one exec and a different by another. Unable to make up her mind, the process dragged on for months."[19] The result has been a company in strategic and financial limbo. In March 2017, Mayer announced that Yahoo would be sold to Verizon.

Top team: unity is strength, unity is energy

The strength and vibrancy of an organization starts in the C-Suite. The CEO of an organization of course plays a crucial role, driving change together with a well-aligned top team. A divided top team, focused on playing political games, drains energy and infects the rest of the organization. As the case of former Yahoo CEO and president Marissa Mayer illustrates, being an ego leader with all the attention on you does not do the job. Without the support of the leaders in your company, implementing strategic change becomes a mission impossible.

Characteristics of an empty top team battery

A top team can be a liability rather than an asset to a change program. We list some of the typical characteristics of an empty top team battery.

 Energy ruled by the ego

Arguably no one is immune to power, but how management deals with that power makes all the difference. Some of the more typical signs that ego is hijacking management:

- A need to keep control
- Surrounding themselves with people who resemble them ('clones')
- Being afraid to allow diversity in the team
- Ignoring or avoiding feedback
- Avoiding conflicts
- Interrupting before others can make their point
- Using their status or position as an argument to make their point of view appear more valuable
- Avoiding others with the argument of 'no time'

Destructive energy output due to a dysfunctional team

Change requires a lot of energy from a whole set of people, not just from an enthusiastic change leader. Successful change requires a cohesive top team, not 'a genius with a thousand helpers'. Patty McManus from Interaction Associates, an organizational development consulting firm, sees three common types of dysfunctional teams:[20]

- In the 'war zone', top team members watch their backs, form factions, and maneuver behind closed doors. Team members are primarily competitive with one another and fight for resources and influence for their business line. In this environment, the CEO may use a 'divide et impera' dynamic to maintain control. Such a dynamic proliferates the rest of the organization and leaders fail to act in concert, sending contradictory messages to their staff.

- In the 'love fest', team members focus on getting along, often believing they are superior to the rest of the organization. You might hear comments like: "If only our people could get along as well as we do." Top teams like this assume that they have all the knowledge and skills to tackle change, which separates them from the rest of the organization. They can also be inclined to avoid tough issues in the interest of maintaining good feelings.

- In the 'un-team', top team members have little connection to one another. Feeling responsible first for their department, they function independently, with their main connection being to the CEO. Meetings are used for status updates and functional performance reviews, not to build a shared perspective on the broader organization or industry. Top team meetings are seen as a waste of time.

Blocked energy: no licence to operate

In our executive training and workshops, we regularly hear from participants that their successfully launched change projects are blocked either by a corporate manager or by a member of the Board. This is true in smaller entrepreneurial organizations as well as in larger international corporations.

In smaller companies, for instance, managers are asked by a founder to get the company ready for the next stage of growth. Those managers develop new strategies and new organizational structures in line with this ambition. Then the founder intervenes, usually via cronies: first to get informed, and later to sabotage the managers' plans if they entail a new style that the founder cannot adapt to.

In larger organizations business managers do not always get the freedom and support to launch a strategic change program. Sometimes the business manager succeeds but when the results deviate from what was expected, the manager loses a licence to operate, or gets fired.

Lack of change energy: no drive for change

JP Morgan, founder of the well-known American investment bank with the same name, said it best: "The first step towards getting somewhere is to decide you're not going to stay where you are." Is your top team convinced that the status quo is no longer acceptable? How committed to change is the top team?

Organizations should be especially wary of falling into the 'success trap', which arises when a firm looks at the present and the future with a mindset of the past. Firms that have been successful in the past owe their prosperity to a distinctive combination of strategies, processes, relationships and values that set them apart from the rest of the industry. Success leads to more customers, more talented people, and increasing profits. They are doing the right thing and they do it well. And then change knocks at the door. The outside world sends signals that the old 'right thing' is no longer right – it may even be very wrong; your business model may have become outdated.

The innovative thinking that once made the organization a success is now replaced with a rigid dedication to the status quo. We call this *blind fairness*: leaders of the company justify their blindness to the existing changes in the outside world, not because they don't know of them, but because they underestimate the strength of the new threat. They wipe any attempt of actions for change under the carpet with statements like: "Why change? The bad years are only temporary"; "Something new? We've seen all this before"; or "Yes, we have created a task force, led by a member of the Executive Team, but not the CEO. He has other things on his plate right now."

Sometimes executives *are* ready to change, but they use the wrong recipes to address the change. In that case, top teams are too confident about their old recipes. Don Sull, a professor at London Business School, calls this *active inertia*. "Active inertia," he explains, "is management's tendency to respond to the most disruptive changes by accelerating activities that succeeded in the past."[21]

Dragging energy: goals without aspiration

What do you want to achieve in life? How do you want to be remembered after you've left the stage? The answers to those questions – your aspirations – tell a lot about you. Aspirations are more than goals; aspirations are *ambitions*. They guide you in making decisions that contribute to a meaningful life. A personal aspiration is enduring and is based on a deep motivation; it is the force that keeps you going after a setback or failure. An aspiration is a prerequisite for a strategy. Conversely, developing a strategy without an aspiration begs the question: "a strategy to achieve *what*?"[22]

Companies also need to clarify their ambitions, and especially if they're about to embark on a change program. They need to provide a compelling answer to *why we need to change*. In most organizations, however, the decision to change leads to a set of goals, such as an increase in profits, or lowered costs, or fewer levels of management. Though important, these kinds of goals are not aspirations. They don't inspire employees.

What are the aspirations of your company within the change project? Are your people connected to these aspirations? Do you touch your people with your change aspiration? Do you inspire? Are your people motivated to help you realize your goals by financial rewards only? Or will the change lead to a better future for most stakeholders?

Overview of dischargers

Figure 6 • Why your top team battery is running empty

The top team battery and change effectiveness: What does our research say?

An analysis of the 20 percent most successful transformers ('Top 20') and the 20 percent most unsuccessful transformers ('Bottom 20') from our research database indicates that companies with high change effectiveness have higher energy scores for the top team battery than companies that struggle with their change initiatives.

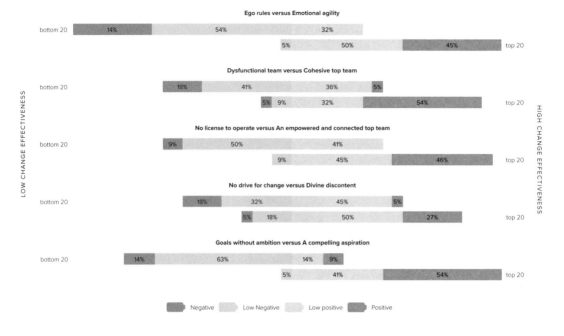

Figure 7 • How successful and unsuccessful transformers score on the top team battery[23]

Figure 7 shows that the unsuccessful transformers have a top team battery that generates negative energy, while in the top performers the top team generates positive energy. For four of the five criteria of the top team battery, bottom performers have more negative scores than positive ones. Nevertheless, there's a significant group of bottom performers that have (low) positive scores on some criteria.

Almost all top performers have a top team battery that generates a lot of positive energy. They all have (low) positive scores on each of the five top team criteria. At least 77 percent of the top performers score positive on all five dimensions of the top team battery.

The top team battery is the battery with on average the highest score of all batteries. Nevertheless, our research indicates that a significant number of companies still have room for improvement in this area.

How to charge your top team battery?

When you are confronted with a malfunctioning top team, the question is how to turn the situation around. Having a fully charged top team battery generates a lot of energy to start the change process. The role of the top team goes beyond initiating the change, though; a cohesive and ambitious top team is needed during the *entire* change journey. Our research demonstrates that an energetic top team is essential to assure the *sustainability* of change results. Change creates friction between people and between departments: not everyone will buy into it, some may even give up. Therefore, it's crucial that the top remains united and keeps on pushing and pulling, motivating, and inspiring the rest of the organization. In turbulent times and when change is continuous, the role of the top team is ever more important. So what can you do to get this battery fully charged?

In our discussions with managers, we've noted that top teams struggle with the following when tackling the top team battery:

- How much involvement is needed from the top in a successful change program?

- How do we approach change when your executive team lacks trust or is a dinosaur?

- How do we create a top team that speaks and acts with one voice?

- How do we create a compelling aspiration? What does an inspiring and energizing change vision look like? And how can we make sure our aspiration appeals to all stakeholders, not only our employees?

These questions can be grouped into three major sets of activities (see Figure 8). First, top managers need to be aware that change starts at the top. They should therefore take actions role model the desired change. Second, successful change requires the top team to be a true team, not a working group or a pseudo team. And thirdly, top managers need to spend significant time to create a compelling aspiration for the entire organization.

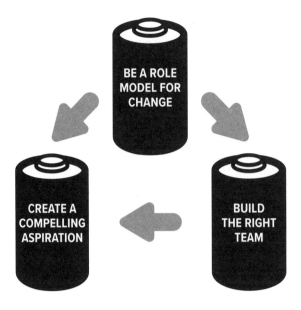

Figure 8 · Charging the top team battery

Be the change energy role model

Most managers would agree with Gandhi's famous statement: "Be the change you want to see in the world." If you can't be a good example, then you may well be a horrible warning. For change to happen, each individual member of the top team needs to demonstrate the desired behavior. Leaders often assume that they already exhibit the right behavior to be a role model. They rarely count themselves among those who need to change.

Build emotional agility

Being a role model requires that you have a high level of emotional intelligence. Most executives have a well-developed rational brain. They are smart, and able to tackle problems efficiently and effectively. And that's mostly how they got promoted. But it is also important to have a well-developed emotional brain. *Emotional agility* is a crucial trait of effective change leaders[24].

Many companies organize leadership trainings in which executives get better insight in their personality traits. These trainings help them in developing their emotional intelligence -- the ability to accurately perceive your own and others' emotions.[25] However, emotional intelligence in itself is not enough. An equally important trait is emotional agility, which is the *ability to manage your thoughts and feelings, especially the negative ones.* Our Vlerick colleague and leadership professor Katleen De Stobbeleir meets many leaders who struggle with their 'negative' emotions, such as criticism, doubt or fear. How well you deal with these has a significant impact on your leadership style. Executives are not always aware of the consequences of their leadership style. For example, an executive may lose his temper often, but is then frustrated that employees are afraid to talk openly.

Senior leaders are not always aware of the implications of their inappropriate coping strategies on the rest of the organization. They often ignore or suppress their negative feelings. They believe that difficult thoughts have no place at the office: leaders should be stoic or cheerful, they must project confidence and damp down any negativity bubbling up inside them. However, minimizing or ignoring emotions only amplifies them.[26] Worse, emotions are copied by colleagues or by your employees in an emotional contagion. Before you know it, one executive's ineffective behavior ripples through the entire organization, resulting in a macho culture or toxic culture. That's also role modeling... but not the kind you want.

Talk openly about negative emotions

Individual as well as group coaching and mentoring sessions, led by an expert, are a good way to create emotional awareness in your top team and to convince executives of the dramatic consequences of a lack of emotional agility. When executives give (and receive) honest feedback and dare to challenge each other on how they cope with negative emotions, they build emotional capabilities that also benefit the organization. These sessions can be tough, and it's important that executives support each other to understand how and why they react in particular ways. Those sessions won't fundamentally change a personality but help to make some essential adaptations to behavior. However, there are many examples of executives reporting to have changed their leadership style to the benefit of the organization.

Create a 'band of brothers and sisters'

There is a general belief that teamwork is beneficial: teams can tap into more knowledge, they can bring a variety of perspectives and judgments to the situation, and team dynamics result in higher performance than the sum of the individual effort. A good team can bring better ideas to the table and can work more efficiently. *Then why is it so difficult to find good cohesive teams at the top?*

A working group is not a team

Jon Katzenbach, a former McKinsey director and author of several books on teams and the 'informal organization', argues that teaming at the top is an unnatural act for leaders. Most executive councils function as an efficient and effective working group with a single leader, but seldom apply the discipline of team basics to their group. Top teams often have rather general goals – not the specific goals that operations or sales teams have. Membership in the top team is not always based on skills, but rather on formal position. Top leaders are also used to individual accountability – that's how they've grown to the top ranks – making *mutual accountability* hard to develop.[27]

When business is running as usual, this set-up can work. However, profound change requires *teamwork at the top*. A strategic transformation involves so many decisions and actions in different units that it can never be managed with a traditional leadership model, where a leader dictates and other members follow and execute orders. The involvement and commitment of the entire leadership team is desperately needed. Change leaders need to spend time and effort on building a strong, cohesive top team. Only then can this team focus its energy and attention on the job at hand, and avoid being drawn into being strategically disingenuous or political with one another.

Digitization is a potential major threat for most financial institutions. Erik is a member of the executive team of one of the larger European banks and responsible for the bank's successful digital transformation. He and his management team worked towards creating a band of brothers and sisters[28]. "If you are not aligned and not prepared to back each other up, then your projects will suffer," he says. "There will be arguments among your people. As a result, they will wait for decisions, and this will delay your projects. All that extra time and the extra costs will hinder achieving your objectives and results. Before you engage in a massive encounter that will transform your entire business, you need to be sure that the top team is aligned and ready to go the extra mile for each other. The first required attitude for top managers is to get rid of their ego. And then to dare to stand in for each other, to dare to take risks for one another. Support your colleagues' ideas, even if they are not fully in line with yours. If your staff sees that the top team is not aligned, change will never work."

So how do you create a 'band of brothers and sisters' in your top team? Here are some of our recommendations.

Define the team

Determine who is part of the top team and who is not. This is not as obvious as it sounds. Top team members need to be committed to defining the strategic ambitions and priorities of the firm. They need to energize and empower people and ensure that the right structures and systems are in place to move the organization forward. Are all team members ready to take up a role in this process? Is your CFO up to the job? Your COO? The rest of your executive team? This is usually a decision for the chief executive to make. Yet, fearful of seeming exclusionary or determined to put people on the team for purely political reasons, a CEO can create a dysfunctional team. We recommend being ruthless when it comes to deciding who is on the team and who is off. Professor Leigh Thompson from Kellogg School of

Management remarks that teams are not cocktail parties. Trying to be overly inclusive inevitably leads to a team that is too large. A strategy she recommends for managing team size is to consult specialists only when their expertise is required, rather than keeping them on full time.[29]

Find the time to build a team
It takes time to build a great team. Top teams too often neglect to question how they are functioning as a team.

DARE TO ASK THE QUESTION!

"Frank" was a manager at a large industrial organization. His company had some strategic challenges ahead that required input from the entire top team. "At a certain point I asked the managers: 'How well do you feel we act as a team?' They were somewhat surprised by the question, but agreed that we had a fairly well-functioning team. Then I asked them to rate our team's functioning out of 10. Now they were more hesitant. The result? A disappointing average of 4 out of 10." It took Frank more than six months to create a high-performing, strong top team. Afterwards they realized how inefficient and ego-centered they had been before.

Ask yourself: how much time does your top team spend on addressing team dynamics and on building a cohesive team? All too often we hear comments from top managers such as "Emotional intelligence is for softies," or "Business managers have more urgent issues to tackle..." We disagree. Building a cohesive team is one of the best investments you can make as a top team member. It's hard, but it pays off. There is a lot of help out there to support and inspire you to build a better team. A good start is Patrick Lencioni's *The Five Dysfunctions of a Team*, in which he describes what it takes to build a cohesive team that is committed, accountable and focused on results.[30] He also identifies five major dysfunctions of a team and how to go about solving them.

DYSFUNCTION	FIXING IT
Absence of trust	Dare to be vulnerable; become trustworthy
Fear of conflict	Take time for genuine opinion sharing without judgement
Lack of commitment	Agree to disagree. Be clear on what the final decision is, make sure everyone understands this, and acts on it
Avoidance of accountability	Create a culture of feedback and responsibility; dare to refer to the commitments made
Inattention to (team) results	Create team objectives as well as individual objectives

Figure 9 • Working on team dysfunctions (Lencioni)

PSEUDO TEAMS DON'T WORK

"John", a top manager at a global pharmaceutical corporation, shared the following with us: "Building a top team is crucial and I spend a lot of time on it. One element of team building is to have shared goals. As a team, we always have a team goal to work on and I insist that my team members put the shared goal before their individual goals. If they are not able to do that, there is only one option: leave the team. So I set goals for every top team member. The first goal is shared by everyone in the team. And I often – sometimes weekly – ask: 'What have you done to realize the team's goals?' It's important not to have too many goals per team. The more goals set for each team, the more your executive colleagues can deviate from the core team goal. I don't believe in goals per calendar year either. We may change goals after 3 months – as long as the goals fit the larger, longer-term vision.

Managing the dynamics in my top team is one of my core activities. And that's not always straightforward. For me, the worst thing is having pseudo alignment in the team – when everybody agrees and when there are no conflicts, but there is no commitment either. Pseudo teams cannot handle conflict; it makes team members uncomfortable. I hate it when everybody agrees. When I meet a new top team, I ask them to read Lencioni's book and we take half a day to discuss it. I pay explicit attention to discussing how we function as a team. And in team meetings, I regularly refer to key messages in the book. For example, if a team member has not contributed to the team meeting, I dare to ask: 'Are you really committed to what we've agreed?' A good top team manages itself — the final stage in Lencioni's framework.

I also coach my team members in one-on-one discussions. I have feed-forward meetings with them and ask questions like: 'This was a missed opportunity to bring up your point. How could you handle this situation better next time?'

It's my experience that a well-functioning team attracts good people and resources. Everybody *wants* to work for a good team where issues are communicated well and the vision is clear."[31]

Increase potential energy with a compelling aspiration

When individual top team members are seen as credible and trustworthy and when the top team is acting as a cohesive group, the next step is to create a compelling aspiration.

Divine discontent gets you moving

An aspiration is a hope or ambition of achieving something. With change, you want to create a better future for your company. Profound change requires that you challenge the status quo and that you instill an ambition to move forward. Being in the game is not enough; the ambition should be to win the game. Every top team member needs to be infused with the desire to win and a passion to serve a common purpose, a *raison d'être*. *Divine discontent* among the top members — an attitude to learning and growth that is never satisfied with past achievements and always searching for the next challenge — ensures that your organization feels the need to keep moving. It avoids the state of blind fairness. This is a continuous search for the tiniest possible increment of improvement. Divine discontent over the limits of current performance is balanced with a healthy dose of confidence in the ability to improve.[32]

Your key stakeholders also need to understand where this divine discontent comes from. Check to what extent your stakeholders — your board, the unions — understand and agree that something needs to change. Try to figure out how much freedom you have to change what ought to be changed. What can absolutely not be changed? How much time do you have for the change?

How can you create this sense of divine discontent in your top team? Creating discontent means that you confront your top team colleagues with two questions:

1 Why do we need to change?

2 What should we change?

Only when you agree on the answers to these key questions you are ready to move ahead. Executives in a top team should spend sufficient time tackling these questions. Smart executives are connected and take the time to discuss and influence key stakeholders to ensure that they have the necessary freedom to change. It's our experience that this process can take months. One business manager told us he regularly spent one or two days per week talking to and informing managers at the corporate level in order to obtain resources and the freedom to formulate and implement a change vision and strategy. Our research indicates this is one of the most differentiating factors between successful and unsuccessful transformers.

Starting from this divine discontent principle, the next questions to ask are:

- Is everybody convinced that the status quo is no longer acceptable?

- Is everybody convinced that, for example, changing regulations will have an enormous impact on your firm's success?

- Are technological revolutions really eating your profits?

- How will all this impact your organization?

How urgent is the threat (or the opportunity)?

What needs to be done to deal with the changes?

Define *where* you're going

Divine discontent gets you moving, but a compelling and energizing aspiration tells you where to move to. It is the answer to how you want to address both the internal and external challenges that your company is facing. It doesn't matter whether you call this aspiration a vision, ambition, strategic intent or 'big hairy audacious goal'. What's important is that you sketch a desirable picture of a shared future. An aspiration generates energy and motivates employees as it clarifies the direction for change.

CREATING A POSITIVE FUTURE FOR YOUR COMPANY

"Francis" was the founder of an importer of healthcare materials for end-users and professionals in hospitals, nursing homes and pharmacies. As an importer Francis was stuck in an endless cost-cutting game. His suppliers were asking him to sell higher volumes at lower margins. And his customers saw him as a box mover, a necessary evil that increased the costs of basically standard products. In order to escape the commodity game, Francis realized he needed to tackle this challenge differently. His vision was to turn his company into a solutions builder. He was convinced that he could escape the price pressures by establishing a house of knowledge for his suppliers and customers. By adding extra services, Francis believed he could provide more added value to his customers. He would also be a better partner to his suppliers as he began to understand the evolving needs of hospitals and nursing homes. This aspiration had significant implications for his organization. Francis and his team had to rework their strategy, invest in training and knowledge development, and build a more proactive sales and service culture. The aspiration to become a service provider was appealing because it implied a better and more positive future for his company.

Create an inspiring aspiration

The more your change aspiration is embedded in a shared purpose and a clear identity, the more your aspiration inspires.

ING DIRECT'S MISSION STATEMENT

When Arkadi Kuhlmann, former CEO of ING Direct USA and Canada, was interviewed about ING Direct's success, he didn't talk about financials – unusual for a banker – but about the company's core purpose and mission. "ING Direct was born in an age of broken promises. The last thing America needed was another bank, but that didn't mean America didn't need us. We are unconventional. We aren't like other banks. We've not only developed a unique business model, but the way we look at the business is different to how our competitors look at it. Our purpose is to be a servant of the average person. Rather than getting people to spend more – which is what most banks do – our approach is to get Americans to save more, to return to the values of thrift, self-reliance and building a nest egg. How do we do that? We make it easy to save by offering the same great values to all Americans."[33]

Building an energizing aspiration is far from easy. Take the necessary time to shake your colleagues from entrenched mindsets and get agreement on a common future. In order to make the discussions vivid and relevant, interrogate which differences in the new world matter most. Use imagination to enhance, or even exaggerate, the differences between the past and the future. Sticking only to the rational is why business cases are not sufficient to bring about real change.[34] Aim for the heart and the mind!

Tips for reimagining and communicating
a change vision that resonates:

- Invite your customers to your top team meetings.

- Bring specialists in, or send your people out.

- Create experiences and make stories that appeal to all senses.

- Turn your change aspiration into a story, not a PowerPoint slide of bullet points.

- Build a story in the language of your audience (not in the language of your top team colleagues).

- Avoid including too many financials. Avoid management jargon.

- Use videos to convey your messages.

- Come back to your compelling aspiration in every meeting.

Kotter calls this the 'See-Feel-Change approach' to change. When you are able to create a sensory experience for people about the change that you have in mind, the change in behavior you require from them will come about much easier.[35] Explore what needs to change but also explain why people should strive to create that future. Martin Luther King said "I have a dream", not "I have a plan". Dreams touch people, plans don't.

A change vision should be ambitious. It should not be easy to attain. The company will need to put energy into realizing the change vision. Once realized, the change vision should appeal to a broad set of stakeholders, not just your shareholders.

THE ASPIRATIONAL STORY OF INTERPOLIS

In the early 1990s, Dutch insurance company Interpolis had massive financial challenges and was required to reduce costs by 40 percent. The top team realized that reducing staff was not enough. Piet van Schijndel, a member of the top team and one of the architects behind the company's successful transition explains the approach they took: "We did reduce the number of employees and our company reduced in size. Our profitability increased, but our fundamental problem remained the same: our customers remained unhappy with our way of working. It was not just us — customers were unhappy with the whole insurance industry. We realized the problem was trust. The whole industry was — and still is — based on checks, audits, and controls. Insurers see and treat their customers as crooks. We wondered: what if we build an insurance company where trust is the main pillar in that relationship? What if we assume that customers can be trusted? So we made insurance crystal clear. That required a transformation from us, and from our customers, but it worked. We were one of the most successful insurers in the late 1990s and early 2000s — because we developed a change vision that was compelling and inspiring, not just for our shareholders, but also for our customers and employees."[36]

Key messages of this chapter

Building an ambitious top team is one of the most important challenges in a successful transformation. This battery largely generates the energy at the top of the organization that is essential for any change.

In this chapter, we've outlined what an empty and a fully charged top team battery look like. Our research reveals that companies score relatively well on this battery. The top team battery is the battery with the highest average scores of all six batteries.

An empty top team battery	A fully charged top team battery
FROM...	TO...
Ego rules	Emotional agility
Dysfunctional team	A cohesive top team
No licence to operate	An empowered and connected top team
No drive for change	Divine discontent
Goals without aspiration	An energizing aspiration

Figure 10 · From an empty to a fully charged top team battery

There are significant differences between winners and losers on each of the five dimensions of this battery (see Figure 10). How do you create an ambitious top team that emanates spiritual energy and generates purpose and meaning? What do winners do to get this battery charged?

- First, top managers of successful transformers realize that change starts with *them*. Top executives are role models for change. If they don't show the desired behavior, there's a high chance that your change will lead nowhere.

- Second, executives of successful top teams spend sufficient time on building a real team, not a pseudo team.

- Third, winning top teams create a feeling of divine discontent that gets the organization moving. At the same time, they build a compelling aspiration that energizes and motivates the rest of the entire organization to change course.

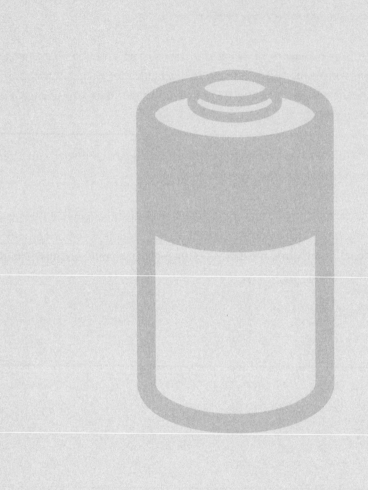

Chapter

3

A CLEAR STRATEGIC DIRECTION

The intellectual energy

Key questions

Why is strategy an energy drainer or driver in change?

What is a 'clear' strategic direction?

How is a change strategy linked with a business and corporate strategy?

How do you develop a clear strategy? Who should be involved?

To what extent is the concept of strategy still relevant in today's turbulent times? Is it strategic not to have a strategy at all?

HOW WELL IS *YOUR* STRATEGY BATTERY CHARGED?

Tick whether you agree or disagree with each of the following statements.

		AGREE	DISAGREE
1	Our organization systematically collects information on performance and actions taken by the competition.		
2	We are always late in detecting and responding to new industry developments.		
3	Our organization systematically collects information on how well we meet the changing needs of our customers.		
4	Our organization has set up a portfolio of initiatives to renew the organization.		
5	Our employees have a clear idea of where and how we make the difference with competitors.		
6	Our strategy clearly outlines whom not to serve and what not to provide.		
7	Our business strategy is a compilation of our departments' action plans.		
8	We have set up strategic experiments to come up with radically new products or business models.		

Give yourself one point each time you agreed with the following statements:

1   3   4   5   6   8

Give yourself one point each time you disagreed with the following statements:

2   7

What is your total score on eight?

INTERPRETING YOUR RESULT

Score	Implications
0-2	Your strategy battery is leaking energy badly. You have no clear priorities and your organization appears directionless and uncertain about what's going to happen.
3-4	Your strategy battery is weak. Although your organization performs a few strategic activities, the direction for these is not well founded nor clearly articulated. You are likely unprepared for changes initiated by your competitors or by strategic disruptors.
5-6	Your strategy battery generates positive energy for your change process, though you may need to take extra actions to charge it further. For example, systematically collect information on changing customers' needs, competitors' actions, and on what is happening on the periphery of your market. To ensure you are ready for disruption, create experiments to test new business models in your market.
7-8	Your strategy battery is well charged. Your strategy is grounded in reality and well defined. You have built strong antennae to scan what is going on in your market, and you are ready to act to build the future.

Spark for reflection: Newell's deal from heaven[37]

John McDonough was appointed CEO of the Newell Company in January 1998. Newell was a large manufacturer of basic home, office and hardware products. Newell offered its products through mass retailers, office superstores and home centers, such as Walmart, Staples, and Home Depot.

Since the 1960s, the company had embarked on an aggressive growth path by acquiring smaller underperforming competitors. These companies were 'Newellized', which meant that they were integrated into Newell's financial, manufacturing and logistics systems and were then challenged to improve their performance. That strategy had paid off well: throughout 1997 Newell had a 10-year average ROI of 31 percent, compared to an 18 percent yearly average for the S&P 500, and revenues had grown to more than $3 billion.

But McDonough believed that the company needed to grow further. Financial analysts had argued that companies with more than $10 billion in market capitalization commanded higher price/earnings multiples. In the face of the increasing market power of Newell's main customers, McDonough believed he needed to develop or buy stronger brands. Rubbermaid, a manufacturer of plastic consumer and commercial products with revenues of $2.4 billion seemed like an excellent opportunity to help realize the company's growth ambitions. McDonough hailed the acquisition as a terrific strategic fit, and in 1999, the Newell Rubbermaid company was formed.

However, in November 2000 McDonough was fired only one year after the mega-merger. The deal from heaven had turned into a merger from hell, as *Business Week* dubbed it. Newell shareholders lost 50 percent of their value in the two years after the closing, while Rubbermaid shareholders lost 35 percent. In 2002, Newell wrote off $500 million in goodwill.

Was the failure a matter of paying too much? Or was the so-called 'strategic fit' not that strategic at all? From the outside, everything looked fine: both companies sold household products through essentially the same channels and there were significant economies of scale to be gained by combining operations. Newell could also help Rubbermaid with its supply chain problems.

Looking at a deeper level, the deal did not fit. While both companies operated in the same competitive arena, their bases of competition were fundamentally different. In essence, Rubbermaid competed on innovation and brand, while Newell emphasized low-cost production and efficiency in the supply chain. Their operating models were very different, as were their value propositions. Newell didn't have an appropriate answer to Rubbermaid's strategic problems and underestimated the major differences in their strategic approaches.

The role of strategy in change

In the previous chapter, we stressed that it is important to have an inspiring change vision, an ambition to create a future that is better than what exists now. It is equally important to translate that aspiration into a *well-defined direction and strategy*. An aspiration without a strategy is little more than a dream. In too many organizations, the 'how' of change is as unclear as the 'why' of change.

Strategy is complex. Everyone agrees that strategy is important, but almost no one agrees what it is. One of the reasons for this is that strategy occurs at different levels: there is corporate strategy and there is business (unit) strategy. The core of the latter is how a firm can achieve a competitive advantage over its competitors.

Many companies, however, are multi-business firms. For example, Disney is a multinational entertainment conglomerate with a film studio, theme parks, and television networks. The company even had a professional ice hockey team at one stage – the Mighty Ducks of Anaheim. Apple is a technology company with a computer business, phone business, tablet business, and much more. Those firms need a business strategy for their individual business units, as well as a corporate strategy that specifies what businesses should be part of the corporate portfolio and how synergies can be achieved within the corporation. In other words, corporate strategy answers why the whole is worth more than the sum of the parts.

In the remainder of the book, our focus is on *business strategy* and on how it can be a major driver of change... or a major barrier to change.

Three touch points to find out how clear your strategic direction is:

- Do you have endless meetings about setting the right priorities for the company and the different departments? Or is the direction of change in your organization clear?

- Is the strategy based on deep analysis?

- Are you ready to deal with disruptive threats?

Characteristics of an empty strategy battery

In most change projects, managers spend significant amounts of money and time defining a change direction. Our research reveals, however, that few can claim to have a clear and robust strategy that boosts energy to efficiently tackle their change problems. How do you know when your strategy battery is leaking energy?

SWOT energy (Strategic Waste of Time) of a quick fix

What is the proposed solution to your change challenge? Another restructuring exercise? More cost cutting? Good luck. We doubt these will be effective. Quick fixes don't work. In the best case they provide some breathing room for another year, perhaps two. They are often solutions that fail to address the core issue: how to deliver value to your customers in a profitable way. We often see managers grab to a standard package of recipes and solutions for any strategic problem. But will restructuring help you to make a difference in the market? And will further centralization help you to create a more convincing value proposition?

Many managers launch change projects that address the wrong problem. They barely take an internal cost/profit perspective. This leaves the rest of the organization confused. There is no buy-in if your employees don't believe that the proposed solution will make the company better. This requires a deep analysis of the root causes of the company's problems. A drop in profitability can be caused by many factors: such as an increase in the price of your supplies, or a drop in revenues because your products and services are no longer competitive. Do you really know why your company ran into trouble? Maybe you've lost touch with your customers? Have you taken the time to explore where it went wrong and to understand how you can make a real difference compared to the competition? Can you honestly say that you know how your strengths and weaknesses connect to the opportunities and threats of the environment? Or is your SWOT analysis just a Strategic Waste of Time?

🔋 Short-sighted energy

Companies need to assess the current situation and ensure they are adequately prepared for tomorrow. Predicting the future, of course, has never been more challenging. But that's no excuse for not identifying change drivers in your industry. Kodak, Motorola, and the traditional European airline companies that were challenged by low-cost competitors, are famous examples of market leaders who got into serious trouble because they were unable to keep up with new developments in their industry.

Jim Lovell, a NASA astronaut and former commander of the Apollo 13 mission, once said: "There are people who make things happen, there are people who watch things happen, and there are people who wonder what happened." Managers should ensure that their company is not situated in the last category. But that's easier said than done. A survey of 140 corporate strategists conducted by the Fuld-Gilad-Herring Academy of Competitive Intelligence found that two-thirds had been surprised by as many as three high-impact competitive events in the past five years.[38] One of the major problems was that firms lacked an early warning system: they didn't see it coming. And when they finally understood what was going on, it took them a long time to adapt to the moves of the major disruptors in their market (remember the 'blind fairness' we discussed in the previous chapter).

🔋 'Everything is important'energy: strategy-obesity

Many organizations have too many strategies. They call everything that is important 'strategy'. So they have a strategy for sales, one for marketing, one for operations, and one for IT. But they often lack an overall business strategy. The consequence is that different parts of the organization try to implement different – often conflicting – strategies.

In these organizations, the enemies are not competitors, but the enemy is within. For production, this may be sales: "They keep accepting offers from customers that don't fit our profile". For product development, this may be marketing: "They keep projecting an image that doesn't align with the products and services that we design".

Silver bullet energy: a slogan parade

We were recently invited by the CEO of a large European bank for feedback on a new change program. The bank was facing the aftermath of the 2008 financial crisis and was working on the roll-out of a new strategy program. The strategy program consisted of twenty large projects, each with clear deliverables and deadlines, and high-level project sponsors and project managers. Each of those programs focused on cost reductions, simplification of organizational structures, activities to get closer to the customer, creation of a more innovative and agile organization, being a better corporate citizen, rethinking internationalization, and the development of a better culture. When we asked what the bank would no longer do, they had no answer.

In some organizations, every couple of years or so, somebody in the executive team, like clockwork, decides that what is needed to make the organization successful again is a new silver bullet. Companies with an empty strategy battery jump from one management fad to another. 'Lean', 'dual-purpose organizations', 'customer centricity', 'blue oceans', 'agility', 'strategic innovation'... these all come with their own vocabulary, which of course needs to be reflected in the new strategic recipes of the organization as well. Organizations try it for one or two years, then get bored, and move on to the next one. Consultants love it!

This approach does not lead to long-term success. Even in turbulent industries, *companies don't win by constantly changing their strategies*. Strategy authors Paul Leinwand and Cesare Mainardi have found that companies that are good in strategy and execution are clear-minded about what they do best. They develop a solid value proposition and build distinctive capabilities that support that value proposition.[39] Here too, Newell made a mistake: the company forgot that its distinctive capabilities were in supply chain management and operational excellence, not in innovation and brand management. Strategy, in other words, is *not* about buying into the latest hype.

Why is the 'slogan parade' so popular in so many larger organizations? Mainly because strategy discussions are often tough and painful. Strategy is choice. All too often top managers don't want to make those hard choices and in that case, strategy slogans soften the blow and feel like a gift from heaven. Find a nice slogan that everyone embraces and there you go. Who can be against 'customer centricity' or 'agility'? But when slogans mask a lack of clear strategic choices, they make things worse as they drain energy from your strategy battery.

🔋 Slumbering energy of bureaucratic goal setting and planning

For many managers, strategy has become a tedious annual planning exercise. A strategic plan typically consists of the following set list of ingredients.

First comes the definition of a mission statement, which sets lofty goals, like "We want to be #1 or #2 in our market," or "Our goal is to be the best in our industry". Second is a list of initiatives to pursue the goals. The length of the list is only constrained by the size of the flipchart. The third ingredient, usually the most extensive part of the plan, is the conversion of the initiatives into financials. The emphasis is on having a rigid, data-driven process dominated by the production of budgets and financial forecasts. Managers make extensive plans on cost planning, and replicate this exercise on the revenue side of the equation, where they make revenue plans per salesperson, per product, per channel, per region, and so on.[40]

This exercise is valuable because it helps to set goals. But goals are not strategy. Goals say what the company wants to be, not *how* it will become that. This is like an athlete who says: "I am going to win the 400 meters in the next Olympics by running faster than anyone else." Great, but *how*?[41] Goals are important but they do not substitute for strategy. If the planned revenues don't show up, managers wonder, "What could we have done more of?" But here's where strategy pops in. Strategy is about making choices on where to play and how to win. It is about building recipes to get good customers and keep them.

Great strategies provide guidance and coherence to the organization. Financials, unfortunately, do not. This is also the trap that Newell fell into. McDonough appears to have been blinded by an obsession with top-line growth, and diverted from a strategy that had fine-tuned over more than 30 years.

Planning is even more dangerous in turbulent industries, where it's near-impossible to make accurate and durable plans. In those markets, it is no longer about being accurate and precise, but about being quick and agile. Effective top managers set direction, explore what is happening in the market, and research by managing a portfolio of experiments that aim to get a better understanding of emerging needs and technological game changers. They select the promising opportunities and roll them out when they become successful. This is very different from the typical strategic planning ritual you still see today.

Overview of dischargers

Figure 11 • Why your strategy battery is empty

The strategy battery and change effectiveness: What does our research say?

Figure 11 summarizes the typical characteristics of an empty strategy battery. But how important is the strategy battery in getting your organization energized for change? How differently do successful transformers score on this particular battery compared to unsuccessful transformers? Again, we selected the top 20 percent performers and compared them with the bottom 20 percent performers, comparing their scores on each of the five criteria of the strategy battery.

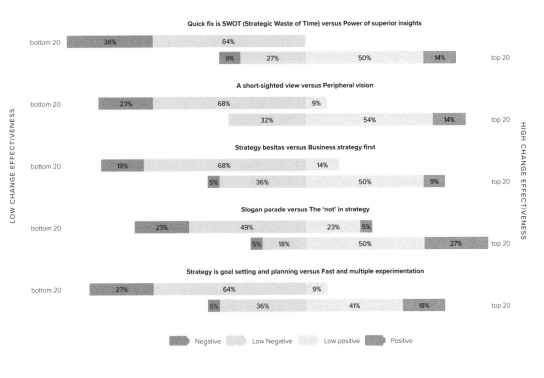

Figure 12 • Strategy scores for successful and unsuccessful transformers[42]

As with the top team battery, we find significant differences between the 20 percent companies with the highest change effectiveness (Top 20) and the 20 percent companies with the lowest change effectiveness (Bottom 20). As with the top team battery, bottom performers generate mostly negative energy on this battery, while most top performers generate positive energy.

The results indicate that bottom performers struggle with doing sound strategy analyses, they fail to make clear choices, strategy tends to be a slogan parade, and they see strategy mainly as goal setting and planning.

Top performers do on average much better on all five of the strategy criteria. But it's worth mentioning that a significant number of these top performers struggle with the strategy battery as well. For most criteria, the number of top performers that struggle is higher than 30 percent. More than 40 percent of the best transformers suffer from strategy-obesity. Many face difficulties in preparing for success under fast-changing conditions. Too many companies still follow the 'old' paradigm of strategic planning.

How to charge your strategy battery?

Now that you know what a bad or mediocre strategy looks like, and you've got a better view on the energy level of the strategy battery of your company, the next question is how to get your strategy battery fully charged. The typical questions we receive from managers who want to charge their strategy battery can be summarized as follows:

- What is a clear strategic direction? When is your change strategy really clear?

- How do you develop such a strategy? How many people should be involved in setting the strategic direction?

- Where does a good strategy come from? Does strategy come from a visionary or from a lot of hard work?

- And last but not least, how relevant is the concept of strategy in today's turbulent times?

Create clarity

What is a clear strategic direction? We already argued that this consists of more than precise financial targets. Above all, it needs to specify *how* you will reach those targets. A clear strategic direction provides specific answers to the following questions:

- Who do we serve? Who are our core customer segments?

- What do we provide? Do all our product or services fit in our product portfolio?

- What is our value proposition? Why do customers choose us rather than the competitors?

- And what is our core operating model? How are we organized to make our value proposition come true?

The first two sets of questions tell you *where to play*; they outline your 'competitive arena'. The latter two sets of questions specify *how you win*; i.e. they outline your 'competitive theme'.

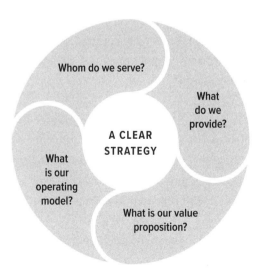

Figure 13 · The four essential strategic questions every company should address

Strategy is choice

It is our experience that managers are afraid to make clear decisions on these four essential strategy questions. The essence of strategy is also choosing whom *not* to serve, and what *not* to provide. Winning means accepting your limits, saying no to some customers in order to serve others better. Focusing on high-end products, not on the low end of the market.

Setting direction means setting clear boundaries, first for the business, then for the departments. The 'not' in strategy is crucially important. Many companies try to address too many customer segments, which can lead to costly compromises – what you do well for one segment hurts another. The result is that the company's offering is gray, dull, and undifferentiated from what competitors are offering.

Companies struggle with delineating their competitive arena – they are afraid to lose customers. But customers who are not adequately served will move anyway.

Answer these questions to help clearly define your competitive arena:

- Do we have a clear view of who our main customers are?

- Who are the good and the bad customers in our portfolio? Are there some customer segments we'd be better off not serving?

- How many bad customers do we have in our customer portfolio?

- How can we discourage these bad customers from buying from us?

- Are our products/services focused on the high-end market, or are we more low-end? (Note: there's nothing wrong with targeting low-end customers. Think IKEA.)

An equally important element of a clear strategy is a compelling competitive theme. Where do you make the difference with your competitors? How do you win? What is your value proposition? In their inspiring book *The Myth of Excellence: Why Great Companies Never Try to Be the Best at Everything*, Fred Crawford and Ryan Mathews argue that many companies suffer from a desire to achieve across-the-board superiority, trying to outperform competitors simultaneously on too broad an array of benefits, such as low price, better service and more attractive products. We support their view that companies should overcome the constant temptation to strive for universal excellence.[43]

Answer these questions to determine your competitive theme:

- On which of the five value attributes – product, price, access, service, and connectivity[44] – do you want to lead your industry? Where do you want to be: the 'number 1'?

- In which area do you want to be 'top 3' in the customer's mind?

- On which attributes do you want to be at par?

- To what extent do all departments support that value proposition?

Choose and align

Answering these questions about your competitive arena and your competitive theme can lead to some tough discussions. But developing answers aligned to these questions is an essential step to get your strategy battery charged. Choosing 'where to play' and 'how to win' is critical to provide direction for the rest of the organization. If no choices are made, energy is wasted on working on conflicting priorities. If you don't make firm decisions, you create a perfect battlefield over resources in your company.

THE IMPORTANCE OF MAKING CLEAR CHOICES

"Tom" was an executive at a process consulting firm in the utility industry. The company was growing fast and had built a successful software product that helped energy providers and utility companies to better manage their performance and processes. The company had built an extensive network of global partnerships with business consultants, systems integrators and solutions providers to sell the software module across the globe. At the same time, the company had become a system integrator itself in three European countries, where it moved beyond selling the product and offered advanced control and IT solutions.

However, Tom felt that his company was stuck and initiated a strategy work-shop for his organization. The top team members found it difficult to provide clear answers to his strategic questions. Was the core of the company its software product? Or should the company be concentrating on its solutions offering? Who would then be the core customers? Should the focus be on conquering the world, or should they focus their efforts on becoming a regional service provider? It took several management meetings before a decision was taken to split the company in two parts: a global software product company and a regional service provider. These were not straightforward discussions and the stakes were high. The CEO, who had favored an integrated company, lost his job. The new company now has two CEOs — Tom is one of them. The revenue and profit growth for the last two years has been impressive. Tom says: "Now it is clear to everyone what the company stands for, and how we are positioned in the market. It is amazing to see how much energy this clarity creates."

The example above shows that reaching aligned answers is not a given and that forcing executives to think about what *not* to do creates a very different dynamic in the boardroom. Managers often have different opinions on which customers to serve or not to serve. They frequently disagree on what the company's value proposition should be. It is, however, crucial that executives take the necessary time to sort this out.

Generally, these discussions tend to converge to two or three key decisions. For example, the discussion in one company boiled down to a choice between being flexible for its top 20 customers, or to give a fast and hassle-free experience to all its customers. If there are major differences of opinion like this, it is advisable to take some time to develop the different scenarios. Split the executive team into two groups, and let them work out a solution for each. However, after some time – depending on the case, this can take three to six months – the team will need to make a clear decision. Once those decisions are made, there is no turning back.

A strategy expert can be valuable in coaching the team to answer these questions. If the discussions continue without end, the CEO should ultimately decide.

Several executives told us that having those discussions was not easy, but that making the final decisions generated a lot of energy within the top team. In this way, the strategy discussions can also help to create a more cohesive top team.

Use three phases to build strategic energy

How do you develop a clear strategy? How many people should be involved in setting the strategic direction?

Organize several strategy sessions

Creating a strategy is not a linear process, whereby you collect input, make decisions, and then communicate the strategy to the rest of the organization. Figure 14 shows that we distinguish several phases in the strategy development process.

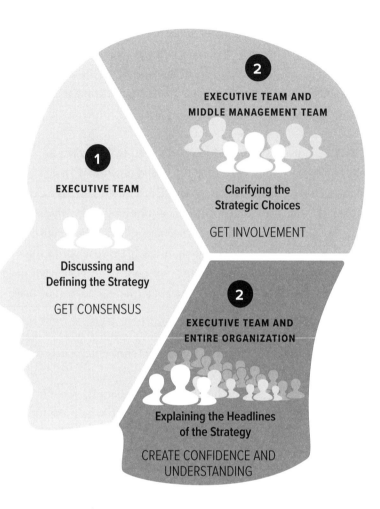

Figure 14 • Different strategy discussions

Step 1 is to start the strategy discussions in the executive team. This team and possibly a few influential board members, reflect on the strategic questions presented in the previous section. We believe it is best not to include middle managers or high potentials in these discussions. Especially if you anticipate disagreements among top executives on strategy, it is best to sort them out in a separate strategy retreat. Middle managers should not be exposed to the tensions that exist at the top. The goal of this first step is to get consensus among top executives about the strategic choices and the strategic direction, and to get support from the shareholders or board members.

The next step is to communicate the strategy to your middle managers. A common practice is to repeat the session you did with the top team, but now involve the middle management team and some high potentials — those you consider crucial in helping to roll out the change. The major strategic direction has been set, but by exposing middle managers to the same strategic dilemmas that top managers addressed, these middle managers better understand why those particular choices were made. Middle managers do not expect to set the strategy, but being included in key strategic issues builds confidence and trust. They are also likely to offer extra input and new insights that help to improve the quality of the strategy. In this way, the strategy gets sharper and more robust.

In step 3, you summarize the main strategic conclusions in a strategy story that you communicate to all employees, using language appropriate to your audience (see chapter 2: 'Tips for reimagining and communicating a change vision that resonates'). We believe it makes no sense to involve other employees in the *definition* of the strategy. Involve employees in the operationalization and translation of the strategy, or even in a strategy analysis exercise, but not in the strategy formulation.

Understand the past to create the future

Where does a good strategy come from? Does strategy come from a bright insight from a visionary in your company or from a lot of hard work? Mostly it is the latter. Each great strategy rests on a couple of unique insights, gathered through a good and deep strategy analysis. The quality of these insights has a direct impact on the quality of your strategy. Many companies are so focused on daily operational issues that they forget to observe and analyze what is happening in the world outside.

A good strategy analysis should provide you with unique and superior insights on your past and current performance, and on the trends of tomorrow and thereafter. Like the god Janus, you need to look back and forward. But what does that entail?

Looking back: understanding your past and current performance

Why do you change your organization? Essentially because performance is no longer up to standard or because it will suffer tomorrow. In the latter case, you believe your organization is ill-equipped to deal with the challenges of tomorrow.

If your organization is underperforming, the key is to understand where it is doing so and what the root causes are. It is important that you develop a good understanding of why your performance is lagging or does not meet expectations. Is your drop in performance an industry-wide phenomenon? Or are you struggling more than your competitors?

In order to answer these 'simple' questions, you need to collect more detailed information about:

- Your company situation: Where are you making money? Where are you losing money? How has your performance changed over time? Where do you gain market share? Where do you lose it? What is your cost position relative to that of your competitors? What are your key strengths? What are weaknesses that you should monitor closely?

- Your competitors: Where do your competitors compete? What particular markets do they serve? What do they offer in each market? What is their strategy? How successful are they in each of these markets? Is their market share growing? Are they making money? What are their margins?

- Your customers: Which customer segments are profitable? Which are not? What do your good customers expect from you? What are their major needs? And how well do you currently serve those needs? Who do your customers see as your main competitors to fulfil these needs?

It is not always easy to find the right data to answer these questions and sometimes it is difficult to discern patterns in the data and to agree on key trends. Doing a good strategy analysis is a lot of hard work, but it is worth the effort. It requires competencies and network connections that may not be abundantly available in your organization. Consulting firms can be very helpful in this process by providing benchmarks and good methodologies for analysis, but we also recommend engaging your people. A sound strategy analysis is a learning process with an *outside-in focus*, conducted by cross-functional teams. Only then will you be able to come up with rich data that allows you to outsmart the competition.[45]

A strategic analysis should provide you with *information your competitors don't have*. To generate powerful plans and make real impact, a strategy analysis needs to reveal new, unfamiliar, uncomfortable and unanticipated insights that none of your competitors have.[46] A strategic analysis is *not* a confirmation of the action plans you already had in mind.

OUTSMARTING THE COMPETITION

"Wim" was a manager at a small business unit of a larger consumer finance group. His company was looking for new growth paths and Wim had been tasked with exploring the attractiveness of the Belgian mortgage market. He looked at consulting reports and collected data about the mortgage activities of the major Belgian financial institutions. His conclusion was that this was a saturated market with powerful competitors who would react aggressively to any newcomers trying to muscle in on their market share. In other words, this was not an attractive market and the newcomer had no chance of victory.

However, in talks with industry experts, Wim learned that the subprime mortgage market offered opportunities for growth. This was a market arena neglected by the incumbent financial institutions; only smaller players offered special mortgage products for this niche segment. There was no data, however, on the size and the growth potential of the segment, nor on its profitability. So Wim engaged in more discussions with experts, interviewed customers and was creative in finding unique data to help him get a better grip on the market. Together with his marketing and sales colleagues, he also found out more about the needs of this particular customer segment. His efforts paid off: after six months he had compiled enough data to make a well-informed decision... Ultimately the company entered the market.

Looking forward: From managing the present to creating the future

A good analysis yields insights into trends in past and current performance – but it should also look forward. Industries evolve, customers' needs change, and competitors will surprise you with new tactics and strategic moves. A good strategy analysis helps you to get ready for tomorrow's challenges. As a result, it is a prerequisite to understand how your future performance will evolve.

The following questions help you to get a better grip on what you might expect in the near future:

- Your company situation: What markets offer great growth opportunities for the future? Which markets should be milked? What investments can you make to improve your competitive situation? Which strengths should you leverage in new markets?

- Your competitors: Where do you expect your competitors to play in the future? What have they done to get ready for the future? Who do you expect to be a winner tomorrow, and why?

- Your customers: How are customers' needs evolving? How will tomorrow be different for your customers?

The importance of looking forward and building foresight is getting more important in the turbulent times we are facing today. It is no longer sufficient to get ready for tomorrow, but also to spend some time thinking about the 'day after tomorrow', as trend-watcher Peter Hinssen has called it.

Volatility or disruption?

Turbulence is a hot topic in management today and means different things to different people. A turbulent environment is an environment in which rapid and unpredictable changes influence a firm's ability to create value; in this case turbulence refers to *volatility*. When macroeconomic changes occur rapidly – for example, when exchange rates drop by half – companies might see their revenues decrease significantly. Other people use the term turbulence as a synonym for *strategic disruption*. When companies face strategic disruption, the most significant threat does not come from traditional competitors, but from disruptors, those strange 'animals' that invade your territory at speed. Think Uber, or Airbnb, or Alibaba.... companies that were not on your radar five years ago but are now growing rapidly towards market leadership.

Disruption can be technological; smart phones that replace the traditional mobile phones. Or it can come from companies who have a different business model. Can you predict who will be the winners the day after tomorrow in, for example, the financial services industry? Will it be a leading bank, or a 'Fintech' with a superior new financial platform?

Technological disruption is a major challenge for established companies. Incumbents realize that their arsenal of strategic tools and maneuvers to beat existing competitors is not appropriate to fight the strategic disruptors. This is not 'competition as usual'. It is a kind of competition that established companies have never faced. There's a lot of buzz – and uncertainty – around these new business models. Still, we don't know yet which will be successful. Uber's business model looks attractive, but the company has to defend case after case in court. In turbulent times, there is no proven formula for success. There's no clear answer how to react best. Companies will need to experiment and even explore fundamentally different growth paths for the future. They should do so when newcomers pose a direct threat to core source of profits. Traditional print media companies have seen their advertising and circulation profits dry up with the arrival of online media companies. You should be even more cautious when newcomers have business models that make your current assets obsolete. Again, think financial services: what's the use of a branch network if everybody is banking mobile?

When the disruptors begin to grow faster than your traditional competitors, it is time to investigate and analyze the new game. The focus of your strategy analysis is no longer on your immediate customers and competitors but shifts to what's happening on the periphery of your industry; i.e. you have to develop peripheral vision.[47] You need to set up an early warning system to detect, interpret and act on distant, even fuzzy signals. It is easy to spot the big evolutions in your market once they have reached a considerable size, but really you should be alert long before that so you can respond appropriately and in time.[48] The goal of an analysis of the day after tomorrow is to distinguish the buzz from fundamental trends:

- In what direction do the new trends point? What is really going on? For example, what does digital disruption in your industry mean? Is it just a change of the distribution model, or does it affect other parts of your value chain as well?

- How is your business model different from these new business models?

- How likely is it that the disruptor will conquer the market, and how soon? What time horizon are you looking at?

- How much of your customer base will consider changing suppliers? And what is the effect on your revenues and profits if they do?

- What are the options to protect your business?

- Are you challenging your current business model? Are you running small-scale experiments that are very different from what you usually do?

Use strategic energy as innovative energy

Today's world is VUCA: *volatile, uncertain, complex* and *ambiguous*. How relevant, then, is the concept of strategy? In our sessions with executives we often hear: "In today's turbulent times, our strategy is to have no strategy." If you can no longer predict the future, does it make sense to have a strategy? Are unlimited innovation and unfettered entrepreneurship the new mantras? Does the new competitive environment demand a new strategy… for strategy?

Exploit and explore

The answer: definitely, yes. The key feature of new strategic thinking is that *innovation* and *entrepreneurship* have become much more important. This does not mean that you should forget about strategy – Having a good strategy and continually exploring the core remain essential aspects.

At the same time, to get ready for disruption, you should be exploring and reinventing yourself by setting up experiments that challenge your current business model. Amazon, for example, has reinvented itself several times. It started out as an online bookstore and evolved into an online superstore (1994–2000). By the early 2000s, Amazon was not only selling its own products but also provided other retailers with an online sales platform. Since 2005, Amazon has turned itself into a cloud computing company, developing new skills and capabilities, and buying companies like Zappos, ClusterK, NICE, Curse, and others to expand its capability base.[49]

Often, companies build a portfolio of growth initiatives, some more focused on *exploitation*, others more focused on *exploration*. Figure 15, a popular graph called the 'Horizons of Growth' developed by consulting firm McKinsey, captures this idea. As well as funding growth initiatives for their core business (horizon 1), firms should launch initiatives to grow the business in new markets (horizon 2) and to validate new business concepts through pilots with potential customers (horizon 3). Consultants recommend distributing the growth budget as follows: 70 percent – horizon 1; 20 percent – horizon 2; 10 percent – horizon 3.

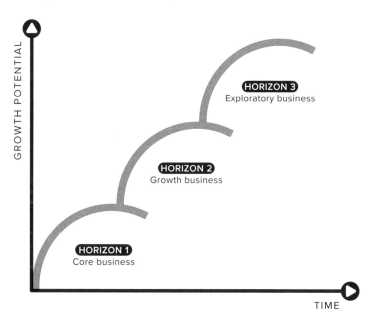

Figure 15 • Horizons of growth (Baghai, Coley and White, 1999)[50]

Separate, but don't isolate

Setting up new growth platforms is not difficult. What seems to be more challenging is how you organize for innovation. There is strong academic evidence that many growth initiatives from horizon 3 fail and never become a viable business. Organizations struggle when trying to manage a mature business (the tanker) and a new strategic experiment from horizon 3 (a speedboat) at the same time. There are many potential conflicts between the old and the new venture, including cannibalization, brand destruction, and destruction of established relationships with distribution partners or customers.

That is why researchers like Clay Christensen of Harvard Business School (and many others) recommend separating the new business from the traditional core. Too close involvement from the managers of the core does not give enough breathing space to the new unit. All too often, managers of the core business apply old recipes that are not applicable to the new business. *Separation* guarantees that managers from the old core resist the urge to meddle. The new ventures need to create their own recipe for success: they need to find *their* competitive arena and competitive theme, which is typically very different from the original core. American savings bank ING Direct had a different business model than the traditional businesses of ING; Nespresso is different from Nestlé, and so on.

However, there is evidence that *rigid separation does not work either*. Xerox PARC is known to be the birthplace of some cutting-edge inventions in the technology world. Unfortunately, it wasn't Xerox who benefited from these inventions. Xerox had made a significant mistake: it isolated PARC too far from the traditional core, geographically, culturally and commercially. And it was Steve Jobs who commercialized most of the inventions.[51]

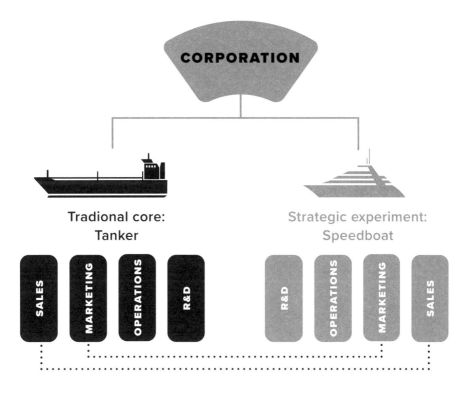

Figure 16 • Dual-purpose/ambidextrous organization (Govindarajan & Trimble, 2005)[52]

It is important that the new businesses can benefit from the strengths of the core business. Figure 16 illustrates linkages that are crucial to explore and nurture between the traditional core and the strategic experiment (Sales and Marketing, in this example). A great example is New York Times Digital (NYTD): NYTD used content provided by the journalists of the *New York Times*. Advertising teams of the traditional core collaborated with advertising teams of the digital unit, and the new unit could benefit from a well-established brand.

Our colleague Marion Debruyne recommends combining *separation* with *mechanisms that link the new venture and the parent firm*. According to her, by exchanging shared resources, the parent company and the new venture live together and share their strengths. This facilitates the level of operational integration required to give the new venture maximum opportunities to succeed by using any parent firm resources that fit their business model. One caveat: the operational integration should not be dictated by the parent company. Neither should it be inspired by the desire to create operational synergies that lead to lower costs. The only valid reason to create operational linkages is to help grow the new venture and make it more competitive.

In conclusion, the major recommendation to win in turbulent and disruptive times is to go for some *connected isolation*. Placing your day-after-tomorrow efforts in a separate unit inside your corporation is a good idea — but never have it entirely disconnected. If it is too far removed — like PARC was from Xerox — your efforts may backfire.[53]

Key messages of this chapter

Charging the strategy battery is a tough job for any management team, but crucial for successfully managing change. Figure 17 shows what an empty and a fully charged strategy battery look like. A charged strategy battery helps you with your change program because it focuses and directs the energy that comes from the top team. It ensures that this energy does not get diffused because the company is working on too many unrelated, even conflicting projects. A good strategy provides the kind of cohesion and direction that lead to *coherent action*.

| **An empty strategy battery** | **A fully charged strategy battery** |
FROM...	TO...
Quick fix is SWOT (Strategic Waste of Time)	Power of superior insights
Short-sighted view	Peripheral vision
Strategy-obeslty	Business strategy first
Slogan parade	The 'not' in strategy
Bureaucratic goal-setting and planning	Exploit and explore

Figure 17 • From an empty to a fully charged strategy battery

How do you move from an empty to a fully charged battery? How do you generate intellectual energy that provides strategic focus and attention?

- Make *clear choices* on your competitive arena and your competitive theme.

- Take the necessary time to have a *sound strategy development process*. Involve different layers at different times.

- Complement strategy formulation sessions with *strategy analysis sessions*. Try to get input on customers, competitors, and your internal situation.

- Be aware that the future is not just an extrapolation of the past. When your company is facing turbulent times, set up *experiments* to develop new business models.

Chapter

4

A POWERFUL MANAGEMENT INFRASTRUCTURE

———

The systemic energy

Key questions

What is a powerful management infrastructure?

How can you set up a powerful management infrastructure that doesn't turn into a rigid bureaucratic monster?

How important is it to invest in the creation of a powerful management infrastructure?

How can your management systems help you to implement your strategy?

What can you do if your systems are old-fashioned and inappropriate for realizing your change vision?

HOW WELL IS *YOUR* MANAGEMENT INFRASTRUCTURE BATTERY CHARGED?

Tick whether you agree or disagree with each of the following statements.

		AGREE	DISAGREE
1	Our management infrastructure and processes assure that we focus on what matters for our customers.		
2	Due to a lack of time or experience, we tend to outsource important change initiatives to external specialists.		
3	Our organization communicates well between every level of management.		
4	We struggle to complete our change initiatives due to the sheer number of projects that we try to implement concurrently.		
5	We periodically assess progress and results and link this to how this was achieved.		
6	Reporting on change projects is an overly complex bureaucratic activity in our organization with little added value – or it is rather non-inexistent.		
7	We share lessons learned and best practices through systematic knowledge management to avoid reinventing the wheel.		
8	We systematically identify best practices and opportunities to simplify our change approach.		

Give yourself one point each time you agreed with the following statements:

1   3   5   7   8

Give yourself one point each time you disagreed with the following statements:

2   4   6

What is your total score on eight?

INTERPRETING YOUR RESULT

Score	Implications
0-2	Your management infrastructure battery is an energy drainer for your change project. You lack most critical processes and structures to complete your change journey successfully.
3-4	Your management infrastructure battery is weak. You either miss critical resource allocation or steering processes, or you fail to measure progress. The result is that your projects lack direction, people and budgets.
5-6	Your management infrastructure helps to drive change. You might have installed a program management office to keep track of your strategic projects. But are you providing enough resources to each project? And do you make sure that you learn from the successes and failures of each project?
7-8	Your management infrastructure is a powerful driver for change. You have an exceptionally strong infrastructure that is clearly linked to your strategy and is an anchor point for individual projects. Your infrastructure is a powerful tool to get your culture battery charged as well.

Spark for reflection: How a market leader lost it[54]

Medtronic, today a leading medical technology firm and at the forefront of the pacemaker industry, had lost much of its appeal by the 1980s. Its market share had dropped from 70 percent in 1970 to 29 percent in 1986, and many good people had left the company. The company had also experienced quality issues, problematic for a company known for its high-quality products. What went wrong — and how did it get so bad?

Innovation had always been the main driver of Medtronic: it was a first mover and had built a strong technological lead. Though it had continued to invest heavily in technology and product development, much of that investment had been unproductive.

Many innovative companies suffer from a lack of good ideas — that wasn't Medtronic's problem. As one executive indicated: "In our situation — with rapidly changing technological possibilities, some darned good competitors and thousands of cardiologists out there with ideas for all kinds of new features — the opposite was true. We've always had too many ideas for new products. In our functional organization, without a single, coordinated process or person to articulate a product plan or strategy, development projects started everywhere." Another manager confirmed: "We were trying to do too many things, and no project got the focus and attention needed to get it done right. It took too long to get anything to market."

Speed-to-market is important for any product leader. But you can only be fast when departments work together on a common project. Here Medtronic failed too. "The development people would tell me that they could never get anything to market because marketing kept changing the product description in the middle of the projects. And the marketing people would say that it took so long for engineering to get things done that by the time they completed something, the market demands would have changed." Between 1970 and 1986, it was almost always a competitor, not Medtronic, that introduced major new improvements to the market.

In 1987, Mike Stevens was appointed as vice president for product development of the Pulse Generator & Programming Systems (PGPS) Division. This division manufactured the pacemaker and its programming unit. When asked what he saw as Medtronic's key problem, he answered: "I saw much of Medtronic's problem as Management 101. We had very strong functional roles yet there was no accountability for the delay or failure of a new product. I felt the basic values and ethics of the company were still strong, but what needed work were its *processes*."

Change and management infrastructure

Stevens realized that Medtronic's challenge was not its strategy so much as a management infrastructure problem. He realized that successful innovation is about more than having a bunch of creative employees come up with great ideas, but requires a seamless process with appropriate resources and structures.

Any discussion about organizational change needs to pay careful attention to the role of the company's management structures, systems and processes. Many change initiatives fail because the company lacks appropriate systems and processes, or because these systems and processes impede a successful implementation of the change vision. They often are not aligned at all with the messages communicated. Therefore, changing any systems and structures that undermine the change vision and strategy is a crucial step in every change process.[55]

Characteristics of an empty infrastructure battery

In our research, we have identified some typical patterns that indicate that your management infrastructure battery is running empty. Do you recognize some of these patterns in your organization?

Bouncing ball energy: 'running' the business

Many organizations launch initiatives to improve their performance, with many activities going on at the same time, drifting from one operational issue to the other. New or similar problems pop up again and again. The organization is fighting a multi-headed performance monster that generates more heads (problems) just as quickly as heads get chopped off.

These companies don't lack the energy to tackle problems, but like Medtronic, their efforts are unproductive because they move in too many directions. In our management programs, we meet many managers who proudly cultivate this kind of 'do mentality'. Their motto is: "Do, then think," or "Roll up your sleeves and tackle the next issue". They don't see the need to look for systematic answers to business problems and their initiatives rarely lead to solutions that are embedded in the infrastructure of the organization. They tend to resist building an appropriate change management infrastructure, fearing this would lead to a bureaucratic organization, dominated by rules, procedures and systems.

What they don't realize is that, in change, it's about finding a balance between 'running the business' and 'building the business'. Your management infrastructure is the backbone of your change that helps to guide priorities, decision making and performance management.

'Managing-the-holes' energy

Do all your action plans lead to clear and specific customer benefits? Are they aligned with the strategic direction of the organization? In our experience some companies prefer to 'manage the holes' rather than 'managing the whole'. In those firms, the action plans of the various departments contradict each other. Supporting functions pretty much operate independently from the core business. This lack of alignment with the strategic orientation of the organization leads to conflicting improvements and functional strategies; e.g. cost-reducing efforts of purchasing increase operational lead times and endanger operational flexibility.

Why do companies struggle to manage the whole? One of the major reasons is that they lack an *overall framework* – a compass or a map – that helps to translate the strategy into operational goals and action plans. They've defined a set of strategic priorities but then leave implementation to functional managers. Managers then lack an overview of the business system as well as all change that is going on in parallel. Nobody knows who's working on what, or why. Conflicts between departments and functions become the norm. And when you celebrate the success of one area, you realize that you've introduced a new problem to a different part of the organization.

This lack of overview also affects the effectiveness of *communication* in change projects. Poor communication is often listed as a primary source of failure related to change. Successful change requires that strategy is not just communicated, but translated to the rest of the organization. Translation requires a two-way communication. Contrast this with the typical one-way communication from the top to the bottom. Change is announced by the CEO at a single event at the end of the day or end of the week. Of course, you are allowed to ask questions at the end of the session, in front of the whole crowd... but who has the confidence to do this?

Direct and more frequent communication is often considered a primary role of middle managers, who unfortunately already have a lot on their plate. Perhaps your company decided to cut back on emails and paperwork: you can find it all on the web, after all. If you do send out emails, you copy everyone. This is the fastest way to make sure your email lands in the trash bin of already overloaded workers – or spam filters automatically filter out these broadcasted messages. Outsiders, customers and suppliers don't hear about the change until they are confronted directly with it. Though organizations tend to believe that the overall awareness of their employees has increased through the use of technology, they may in fact have created an organization that is comfortably numb until it is too late.

'Hell's-kitchen' energy: cooking without ingredients

Another reason that change fails in organizations is that people feel overwhelmed by the sheer volume and speed of change initiatives. Are you running several projects at the same time? And do you feel like you are constantly switching your attention between them?

When organizations primarily operate in a *reactive* change mode, they rarely make arrangements to attract the required financial, human and material resources. As a result, they start to cook without ingredients and produce only steam. The result is that levels of anxiety among personnel and uncertainty rise. By the time any real steps are unveiled or resources made available, employee desire or need for change has evaporated.

Successful change does not only require your organization to devote enough resources to the change, but also that you have a clear view on which projects to prioritize. Many organizations lack an overview of ongoing change initiatives or daily tasks that managers have to perform and therefore neglect to do a *capacity check* before assigning targets and milestones. 'Stretch' becomes 'overwhelm', which leads to dramatic quality and lead time performance of change and improvement projects. The result is often that 'management by decibels' decides what gets done and what has to wait – the loudest voice gets priority. Very often this leads to frustration and a perception that 'management doesn't know what they want'.

As a result, the organization fails to move. People also fail to move if they need to learn new capabilities to perform the change – not an easy thing to acknowledge or admit. Black and Gregersen taught us that "[many] people would rather be competent at the wrong thing than incompetent at the right thing."[56] Are your people equipped for the change? How much do you invest in training and coaching as part of your change project? How do you ensure that people feel confident to learn and develop new skills? Do you give your people the tools to get better in the new job? Do you ensure that your people have sufficient *change capacity* to implement the critical strategic changes?

'Checking-the-box' energy

Change is tough and requires a lot of energy. If you don't track progress, your people get tired and lost. They get impatient or they give up, which all leads to lower levels of commitment. Most change managers know that measurement is important, but sometimes they need to understand better *how* measures should be used to help frame and guide the change.

Defining appropriate KPIs is one thing, but what do you *do* with these measures? A healthy number of effective and efficient meetings and reports can be significant drivers of change; too much can lead to low energy levels, though. Some organizations require so much reporting and detailed data collection that employees start to merely check boxes after a while. Even the best standards can become meaningless in this scenario.

Meetings can also become forums to impress management with fancy Power-Points or extensive reports. Often they are limited to activity reporting: what we have done over the last month. But what about the effect of these activities? Is there any reflection on the methods used? What about the spirit in your team? These are important aspects to include in your meetings.

Wasted energy of reinventing the wheel

Does your organization fail to systematically identify important insights worth sharing with others? Do new employees have to go through long learning curves? Is everyone presenting solutions and results in their preferred way? Do you end up with reports that have a myriad Excel sheets and graphs with different portrayals? If so, there may be a lot of time and energy wasted reinventing the wheel. Many companies struggle with documenting knowledge from both positive and negative change, and as a result they keep repeating errors, or spend way more time on analyzing problems, identifying alternatives and proposing solutions than needed. Effective change requires a *systematic approach to knowledge management*. This is, however, more than the creation of a database or website which stores hundreds of reports. This only leads to an information overflow. Knowledge management is as much about knowledge creation as it is about knowledge transfer. Do you have any structured approach for that?

Overview of dischargers

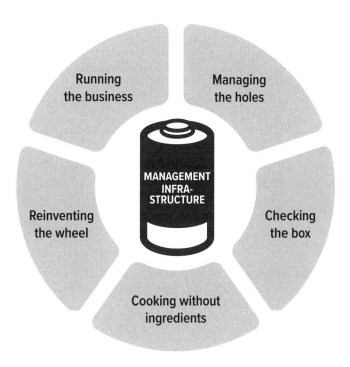

Figure 18 • Why your management infrastructure battery is empty

A powerful change management infrastructure and change effectiveness: What does our research say?

Building a powerful change management infrastructure is critical but charging this battery is not easy. Our research demonstrates that successful transformers have a powerful management infrastructure that translates strategy into action plans and initiatives. This, however, is the battery with the lowest average scores. More than 40 percent of our respondents indicate they have a weak management infrastructure.

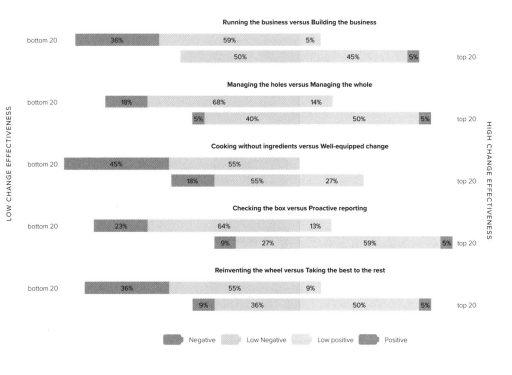

Figure 19 • The management infrastructure of successful and unsuccessful transformers

Companies that struggle with change – the 'Bottom 20' – struggle heavily with the management infrastructure battery. With regard to 'cooking without ingredients', there is not a single unsuccessful transformer with a low positive or positive score. On two other criteria, 'running the business' and 'reinventing the wheel', less than 10 percent of the bottom performers have a low positive score.

The scores for successful transformers — the 'Top 20' companies — are better. But it's fair to say that successful transformers also show generally low scores on the management infrastructure battery. For example, half of the successful transformers have negative scores for 'running the business versus building the business' for the item 'cooking without ingredients', the number of successful transformers that score positively is roughly 1 in 4. Despite all management recommendations to prioritize initiatives to allocate enough resources and ensure proper training, in reality even top performers struggle with this criterion.

How to charge your management infrastructure battery?

In the opening case, we referred to Medtronic, a leading medical technology company that lost its leading position over the 1970s and 1980s. Medtronic is also known, however, for its strong recovery in the late 1980s under the leadership of Mike Stevens.[57] Stevens was brought in to restore discipline in the organization and to get the organizational processes back on track. Given Medtronic's focus on innovation as a cornerstone of its competitive advantage, Stevens' focus was on restoring the company's *innovation processes*.

Build a sound management infrastructure

Define the essential elements of a powerful management infrastructure
What is a powerful management infrastructure? What are its building blocks? We adopt a process-oriented view and have identified the following sets of essential business processes.

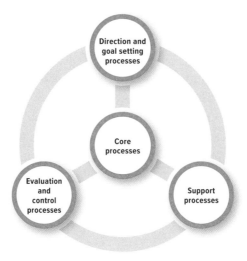

Figure 20 • Defining the building blocks of a powerful management infrastructure

Core processes are those processes that create immediate value for the customer. They create, build and sell the products or services of a company, and help to generate revenues for the company. *Support processes* constitute activities that provide the resources for creating those goods and services, such as buildings, information, people and technical applications. In our model, we make a distinction between the resource allocation processes and the processes that ensure you have the right human resources to do a good job. Steering processes are needed to set direction for the company and to evaluate and control whether the organization is on the right track (for example, your performance management system is an important steering process). We make an explicit distinction between *direction and goal-setting processes* on the one hand and *evaluation and control processes* on the other hand.

Dare to invest in a sound management infrastructure

Some managers appear to be allergic to the words 'management infrastructure'. They immediately think about bureaucracies or hierarchical and political organizations that are rigid and inflexible, with no personal relationships allowed. These managers believe in informal structures and light organizational processes or even in no management infrastructure at all. Sure, smaller organizations typically do have a less-developed management infrastructure. They focus more on exploring new opportunities than on exploiting the existing business. However, as these organizations grow, there is an increased need to manage the exploitation side of the business too. There is a need for more clarity, consistency and reliability across the organization. That is where a management infrastructure comes in. As organizations grow, they also specialize, creating departments that are responsible for specific tasks. As a result, they have to develop ways to allocate resources based on clear goals, and set clear performance targets. That's a natural and logical evolution towards a more sustainable growth path.

Our research finds that successful companies have a clear strategy *and* a well-elaborated management infrastructure that supports the implementation of that strategy.[58] A powerful management infrastructure is an essential ingredient of a successful change program. Building a powerful management infrastructure shifts the attention from purely 'running the business' to 'building the business'.

Manage the whole

Clear strategic goals: the power of strategy mapping

How do you make strategy operational? How do you ensure that individual change initiatives are linked to the overall strategy? For an organization to become successful, it's important to translate strategy into measurable and clear objectives that can be systematically evaluated, based on well defined milestones. Only then will strategies be translated into projects and results. Only then is it possible to manage the whole rather than the holes.

There are several tools available to help translate your strategy into strategic objectives. One of the best-known is *strategy mapping*. A strategy map is a diagram that depicts various sets of strategic objectives — financial objectives, customer objectives, process objectives, and people objectives — into a coherent whole by connecting them through explicit cause and effect relationships. Robert Kaplan and David Norton, the inventors of the strategy map and the Balanced Scorecard, offer a good methodology on how a strategy can be linked to the most important value-creating processes. As Figure 21 shows, companies need to define explicit financial objectives. But these can only be achieved if targeted customers are satisfied with a convincing value proposition. This is captured by your customer perspective objectives. Internal processes create and deliver the customer value proposition and the elements of the learning and growth perspective ensure that the human capital, the information capital and the organization capital is present to have good internal processes. As such, a strategy map forces an organization to clarify the logic of how it will create value and for whom.[59]

Define measures, targets and initiatives for your strategic goals

A strategy mapping exercise forces you to define the most important strategic objectives that will support your company to thrive in the future explicitly, and to link measures, targets and initiatives for it. A strategy map incorporates both leading and lagging indicators. For example, the financial outcomes tell you how you performed yesterday. But measures on culture, teamwork and alignment are predictors of your future performance. Obviously, you need to launch initiatives to reach those targets.

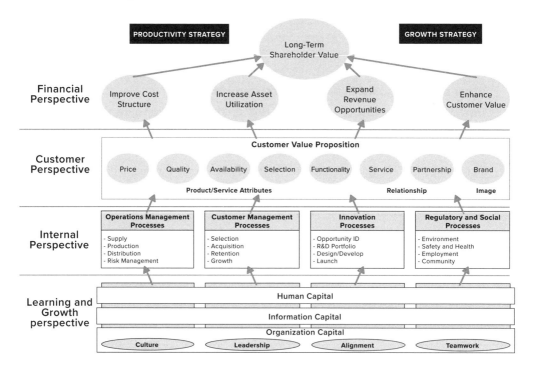

Figure 21 • Example of a strategy map (Kaplan & Norton 2004) [60]

Make it a core element of your communication

Strategy mapping does not only translate strategy into more specific strategic objectives, it's also a great communication tool. Your strategy is summarized on one page and when you have identified the appropriate performance indicators you see where you've made progress. It visualizes what matters and how you are making progress on it.

It's important not just to concentrate solely on your strategy map, but to build stories around it and to develop unusual strategy communication channels. One manager even made placemats with the strategy map in the restaurant so that the staff could even see the strategy during their lunch breaks. Another recommendation is to use simple language. Avoid management jargon. And sell it by building colorful visuals around it so that recognition will be boosted immediately.

Dedicate time for change

How do you 'make time' for change? How do you deal with change fatigue? This is the 'big one'. Cooking without ingredients is the number one problem for both companies that do well in change and for companies that struggle with change. It remains a constant battle to proactively manage time and resources for all ongoing change initiatives. Sometimes this is linked to tight budgets, which generally results in significant (and frustrating) delays. Most of the time however, it really boils down to managing resource bottlenecks: managers at various levels of the organization and IT or technology specialists, for example, who are overloaded and often lack skills to deliver effective and efficient change initiatives. As Peter Drucker said: "Time is the scarcest resource, and unless it is managed nothing else can be managed." Organizations that can't find a solution to this problem create hotbeds of change fatigue and burnout. In this case, not just delays but complete change failure ensues.

Change portfolio management, pipeline management and *capacity planning* are the answers to this challenge. Or in short: basic rules for priority and capacity management will enable you to be well-equipped for change. There is no one-size-fits-all solution, but applying the following *basic principles* can lead to breakthrough results for most organizations.

Start by listing all your change initiatives

Your first step is to clean up the portfolio of all your change initiatives, and we mean *all* initiatives: strategic initiatives at the cross-functional level, tactical projects at the department or functional level, and local operational initiatives. For larger organizations, this also includes projects that are initiated at the corporate level and that require time from managers in your organization. The majority of organizations have little overview of what is going on and even less understanding of the dependencies between initiatives at various levels. Too many organizations underestimate the workload of less strategic initiatives. The reality is that even local projects can be very demanding on management time or critical IT resources during certain periods of the year.

Our advice is to ask managers at all levels to list their involvement in change initiatives of all kinds, then bring the managers together and help them to create an overview of the interdependencies. This exercise will be an eye-opener as it facilitates shared understanding for change at all levels of the organization. The picture that emerges from this is generally overwhelming. Cleaning up this mess implies defining larger families of change programs that align with your strategic goals. You have to create *the big picture of change*. This exercise will also allow you to integrate some of the local or tactical initiatives with the strategic initiatives. Initiatives that don't align with the strategic picture need to be killed. Smaller ongoing initiatives need to be cleared from the table. An approach that often works to accomplish this is to postpone major initiatives by two months – allow everyone to finish what they are working on. Be firm about the boundaries; in other words, timebox the initiative and get the most value out of it within the granted period of time. Three man-days of work often go a long way, provided that participants can focus on what needs to be done and do not have to continue to juggle several balls. What remains is a clear view of what is strategically needed – and strongly connected with local issues or needs. You are now able to connect every initiative with your strategy map.

Manage the pipeline of the selected initiatives

This second step necessitates that you segment larger initiatives in buckets of a maximum of three months and that you clearly specify the deliverables within that time period. If you aim for annual goals only, chances are that you will be confronted with the 'student syndrome': your people postponing the real work until the end of the year. Not because they are irresponsible, but because people who feel overwhelmed are more attracted to focusing on 'urgent' tasks. Come up with some rules to control the amount of concurrent projects. Organizations that apply lean thinking in their production environment know that a high amount of 'work in process' (WIP) is deadly for your process lead times. The same principle goes for 'projects in process' (PIP). If your PIP is too high, it has a disastrous effect on the lead times of all your initiatives. Visual management (such as the Kanban board in Figure 22) can help you to apply simple rules with regard to how many initiatives you want to run in parallel.

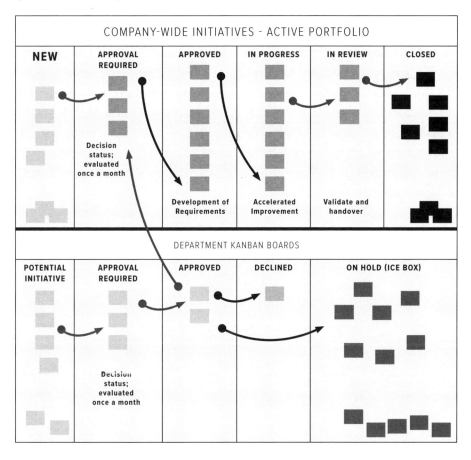

Figure 22 • Example of a Kanban Board for managing initiatives, adapted from Reiner Grau (2015)[130]

Especially for organizations with a low change maturity, there is one golden rule: less is more! Focusing on three to four projects for the following three months will allow you to make sound progress on the selected projects. It will also allow you to work together as a team in this period, rather than having to continuously defend your agenda. Additionally, it will also allow you to develop change capabilities for your change leaders.

Check whether you have capable change leaders

This third step is essential for avoiding 'cooking without ingredients'. Change needs *change leadership*. We will clarify some of the critical roles — such as change sponsor, change coach and change project leader — later on. When you decide on the prioritization of your change initiatives it is essential to check on the capability of your change leaders: they need to have the *ability* (know-how, experience) to pick up their roles as well as the *capacity* (bandwidth, availability) to do so. We will clarify later in this chapter how knowledge management systems can help you to systematically increase the abilities of change leaders. To manage the capacity of your change leaders, we recommend that you build a matrix that clarifies the roles of your personnel in the selected projects of your portfolio and pipeline (see Figure 23 for an example).

	Leadership Team	Strategic Projects	Competence Management	Service Management	ERP Platform	Planning Process	Relocation Support	Centralise Purchasing	Central Helpdesk	Local Initiatives	Loss of Power Risk	Service Catalog	Security	5S Mechanical Dept	Score card Maint	Total Involvement	>=3 Sponsor	>=2 Project Champion	>=3 Team member	OVERALL TOTAL
Internal participants																	S	P	T	TOTAL
Verheijen	T			S	P							S					2	1	1	4
Rotsaert	S	S				S						S					4	0	0	4
Hardy			T		S				S					S			3	0	1	4
Herrezeel	T						P	S				P		T	S		2	2	2	6
Vandendorpe	T																0	0	1	1
Jacobs E							T							S			1	0	1	2
Huybrechts																	0	0	0	0
Markham								P	P					P	T		0	3	1	4
Hugelier	T		T				T					T					0	0	4	4
Konigs			T				T								P		0	1	2	3
Gerard								T	T								0	0	2	2
Oeyen				T		T						T	P	T			0	1	4	5
Pinoy	T				S						T						1	0	2	3
Herregodts	T					P			T					T			0	1	3	4
Van Wittenberghe	T		P											T			0	1	2	3
De Meulemeester				P		T					T						0	1	2	3
Moesen			T				T		T		T	T			T		0	0	6	6
Flament				T													0	0	1	1
Boschman				T		T	T				T						0	0	4	4
Hemeleers			T											T			0	0	2	2
Dethier																	0	0	0	0
Danzin			T	T	T				T		P		T				0	1	5	6
Putseys		T			T		T				T	T	T		T		0	0	7	7
Deman			T														0	0	1	1
TOTAL # OF PARTICIPANTS			7	6	5	6	6	6	6		5	7	6	6	5		13	12	54	79

Figure 23 · Change projects and roles

There are many insights that can come from this type of matrix. For example, if it becomes clear that some people are over-allocated (e.g. they sponsor three initiatives and lead two others, or they participate as team members in four initiatives), this overview will help you to protect them against over-commitment. Assuring the involvement and coaching of your personnel in change initiatives is essential to energize your connection battery, which we will discuss later on in this book.

This can be a pitfall as well, as there is a limit to the amount of good you can do. We recommend creating simple rules as to the number of projects individuals can serve on depending on their roles; e.g. a maximum of three sponsoring roles; or one sponsoring and one leading; two participating, and so on. How you allocate this may also depend on the functional role of the individual for running the business. It comes down to identifying and managing the constraints. If people are over-allocated, you either have to identify alternative staff, or you have to reprioritize certain initiatives and delay or prevent some of them from entering the pipeline. You will notice that while there are always ringleaders whom you need to protect against themselves, there are also folks who are good at hide-and-seek! The visibility that this type of matrix creates can be a strong incentive for leaders to step up as well.

Install proactive reporting

Do measure change progress...

Assessing where and how you are performing in your change program is key to successful change management, but many companies are swamped by reporting or drown in follow-up meetings. Change then puts even more pressure on an already overloaded agenda.

When your management infrastructure turns into a bureaucratic reporting monster, this is often a reflection of an unhealthy culture. When there is overemphasis on conformance, reports tend to become thicker. When your culture is toxic and the distance between employees and superiors becomes larger, more and longer meetings are often the expression of a need for control. You cannot change this type of culture, however, without intentionally redesigning the way you handle reporting and meetings.

... but do it efficiently and effectively

Unfortunately, a lot of meetings are more about impression management than they are about decision-making and knowledge generation. "The more I write in my reports and the more I talk during meetings, the more my superiors will think highly of my efforts", seems to be the general perception. Good reports and meetings however, connect *efforts* with *results*, or *insights* with *next steps*. They evaluate good and bad performance in order to learn from it, and seek advice for things that remain unclear. Do your reports provide an honest assessment of how things are going? Sound meeting and reporting should stimulate *ownership*. It needs to create a dialogue based on evaluation and questioning, not reporting and approving. Effective meetings and reporting stimulate discussion and integration across projects, not just alignment with the top.

Standardize where possible

Many organizations benefit from developing standards for types of meetings and types of reports. These include basic project management variance reporting as well as reporting based on problem-solving cycles such as Define, Measure, Analyze, Improve, Manage (Six Sigma[61]); Look, Ask, Model, Discuss, Act (rapid learning cycles[62]); or A3 reporting (Toyota production system[63]). The combination of an evaluation of results with an assessment of the approach stimulates reflection and ownership. It also creates common mental models for change and therefore supports cross-functional discussion and joint meaning-making.

Assess your reporting and meeting efforts periodically

What we typically see is that organizations have to go through a learning curve to achieve effective and efficient reporting and meeting efforts. When their culture doesn't support collaboration, they develop structures that collect *too much information*. If not addressed, this can develop into rigid bureaucratic structures that inhibit change. Especially when they don't receive decent feedback on reports or reporting, people will start limiting their efforts to conformity and checking the box. Many organizations that went through ISO 9000 certification witnessed this tendency. Where initially nothing is documented on paper, the first two years the number of paperwork only seems to increase. It is only after a few years that they manage to reduce their quality management to the essential minimum. To avoid this, high maturity organizations don't limit questions to content discussions. They also seek to identify how to improve the way that they have handled their change. A key element of this reporting is to evaluate the motivation of the team members involved. In other words, so you have achieved the results that you wanted – did you also like the way you obtained the results? This refines both the hard and soft approaches used to handle your change. It lays a strong foundation for learning about how to run the business as well as how to build the business. That is the essence of what we call 'proactive reporting'.

Take the best to the rest

Einstein said it best: insanity is doing the same thing over and over and expecting different results. Change isn't a crystal ball — it is a journey in which we learn. You have to take the time to figure out what works versus what doesn't and learn from your mistakes to avoid repeating unsuccessful behavior. There are many pitfalls to this. For many companies, when there is a red light reported on their scorecard, they understand that some kind of action is needed. The good news is that this triggers reflection. The bad news: if they don't develop knowledge about the core problem, a quick fix results in a temporary green light. Learning should take us deeper and fundamentally change our processes and behavior. If not, it is foolish to expect systematic better performance.

The biggest mistake organizations make, however, is to act only on failure. The 'real' insanity of many change projects is that they don't repeat *successful* behavior. When an area is working, they may feel quite comfortable abandoning it and moving on to the next item on the agenda. The result: they don't learn from what *does* work. They don't see their own best practices. Or if they do, they assume that since they know something, everyone in the organization knows this as well.

There is a lot you can do to improve your learning from mistakes, and we will share more details on how to do this in the action planning and implementation battery. But when it comes to creating a powerful management infrastructure, what really matters is building sound knowledge management systems. This starts with asking individuals behind successful initiatives to document what works, so that you can share it with others. Nonaka and Takeuchi,[64] global experts on knowledge management systems and proponents of the 'SECI Model', call this step 'externalization'. You try to convert the *experience* (tacit knowledge) of a worker *onto paper* (explicit knowledge). The better organizations make sure best practices are documented in a systematic way and make them available to a wide audience — on their intranet, for instance. That is just one part of the *SECI model*, though.

Build a knowledge base and spread the message

If you have documented a number of lessons learned, the bigger question be-comes: *What is the message behind the message?* In other words, '*combination*' looks for systematic lessons from multiple projects. This is an important step often ig-nored by organizations. Without combination you typically get information over-flow – there is so much information available that nobody knows where to get it when needed. It's all on the Net... but where? And how do I filter the many hits of an important search or query? Combination uses various approaches (e.g. big data analysis) to create knowledge that cuts down to the essence.

However, even the deeper knowledge that is obtained through combination is worth nothing if it is not passed on to new employees through '*internalization*': *training needs to assure that knowledge is embedded in routines of behavior.* However, even the best training will not be able to address all the details of a specific context that may be important to successfully implement a best practice in a particular environment. '*Socialization*' assures that employees are supported by more experi-enced colleagues when they want to apply best practices to their project.[65]

Create a social system for learning

Building a knowledge management system based on the SECI knowledge manage-ment cycle often implies some investment in technology (e.g. website, a 'lessons learned' database, advanced analysis tools). Above all, it implies building a social system that leverages individual and team learning. Building knowledge manage-ment systems is as much about building communities as it is about developing technical solutions to store and share valuable information. We have three major recommendations.

First, *turn your managers into teachers*. There are multiple benefits to this. You don't pay a fortune on external experts and consultants. You may need them to get started, but relying on external sources is far too expensive to be sustainable. If you expect your managers to teach their colleagues and employees, you also trig-ger a new learning loop in them. This loop goes far beyond the knowledge that they gained by practice. People learn a lot if they have to *do* something, but they learn even more if they have to *teach* others. Many will overcome any initial dis-comfort they may feel as they begin to enjoy the recognition they will receive for their expertise.

Second, *create room for discussion* — literally create spaces where people can learn. The different SECI dimensions of knowledge creation require different types of rooms to support learning and knowledge creation. Cockpit rooms for example, can be great places to learn to see the whole picture with your teams and to combine knowledge across projects. Bring your classroom to the shop floor too, so that institutionalization and learning can take place where actions are taken. Many organizational teams can benefit from walls that are turned into white boards. Add a couch to your workspace, where people can sit next to each other with their laptops and socialize to share knowledge and feedback in more informal ways.

SPOTIFY AND KNOWLEDGE SPREADING

Spotify, the Swedish music streaming company, is known for its agility and adaptability as much as it is known for its service. The company is split up in many small teams, called 'squads'. Each of these squads focuses on a specific function — say, creating the radio experience or providing payment solutions — and iterates on minimum viable product, releasing updates early and often. These squads have an inspiring workspace, including a desk area, lounge area and personal 'huddle' room. Almost all walls are white boards, ideal for collaboration and knowledge exchange.

But the organization doesn't limit knowledge exchange to the squads. It has also created tribes, which consist of several squads. Tribes and squads work autonomously, but there is a lot of knowledge sharing between them. That's why Spotify has also created chapters and guilds — groupings of people from different tribes and squads — that meet regularly to discuss challenges and solutions in their areas of expertise. You could say that the whole organization is focused on fast knowledge spreading across different parts of the organization and has built an appropriate organization structure, as well as an appropriate management infrastructure.[66]

Our third recommendation is to *align your HR training and development initiatives with knowledge creation*. Many organizations use training as an incentive to motivate people, but hardly ever use it in a systemic way to support knowledge creation. Specifically, we recommend providing internal basic training on a systematic basis with internal experts/trainers. Keep it short (maximum two days) and allow a lot of time for exercises and examples from your organization. Expect people to then practice what they have learned in their environments – support them with ad hoc two-hour sessions with a trainer-coach. Encourage them to continue to practice what they have learned, in at least two new projects, so that they can grow to become experts. When they reach this stage, you may want to include them in an internal learning group on this topic, so that they further share experiences and combine knowledge with other experts. When they feel a need for more external knowledge, you can support them with external training – then take advantage of the unique learning that occurs from this, and ask them to share their insights with the learning group. Good knowledge management systems are built on good competence management systems. Many organizations that invest in Lean or Six Sigma Belt Training (e.g. General Electric, DuPont, Intel, Caterpillar) follow this competence management process.

Key messages of this chapter

Charging the management infrastructure battery may be one of the toughest challenges of your change journey. Our research reveals that building a powerful change management infrastructure is difficult but critical. This battery stores and distributes the energy of the organization in meaningful projects so that the overall goals of the organization are reached. The management infrastructure battery ensures that all parts of the organization are fueled with energy. If this energy is not distributed properly, some departments will be full of energy, while others will lack the energy to proceed.

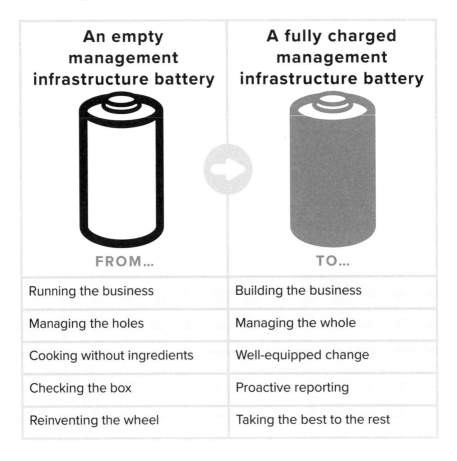

An empty management infrastructure battery	A fully charged management infrastructure battery
FROM...	TO...
Running the business	Building the business
Managing the holes	Managing the whole
Cooking without ingredients	Well-equipped change
Checking the box	Proactive reporting
Reinventing the wheel	Taking the best to the rest

Figure 24 · From an empty to a fully charged management infrastructure battery

What are the key triggers to get your management battery charged? How can you trigger systemic energy, able to manage both day-to-day performance and breakthrough improvement? It all starts with acknowledging the importance of a well-functioning, powerful management infrastructure and with paying special attention to four sets of activities:

- 'Manage the whole' by developing a strategy map that clarifies the logic of how value for the customer and shareholder is created.

- Vigorously manage time through sound capacity and priority management.

- Develop an appropriate reporting and meeting infrastructure. Don't concentrate on the 'control' function only, but ask what your collaborators and colleagues have learned so that they are stimulated to take ownership for further projects.

- Build a knowledge management system that helps you to continuously improve.

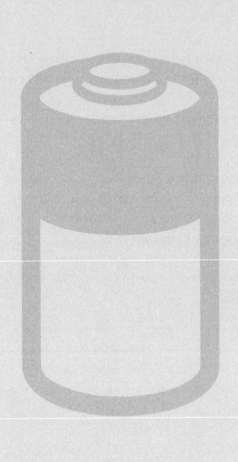

Chapter

5

A HEALTHY CULTURE

———

The social energy

Key questions

How can
you measure
culture?

How does one turn
an unhealthy culture
into a healthy one?

What is a healthy
culture?

How can you create
cultural competence
in your organization?

HOW WELL IS *YOUR* CULTURE BATTERY CHARGED?

Tick whether you agree or disagree with each of the following statements.

		AGREE	DISAGREE
1	Our values are more than words or slogans on wall posters: they guide us in our daily work.		
2	In our organization, we continuously challenge and stretch our goals.		
3	When errors occur, employees and managers blame their colleagues or find excuses in the company's management systems.		
4	In our organization, we focus attention on building relationships with key people across functions at all levels.		
5	In our organization, change communication is mostly a one-way top-down street following the structure/hierarchy of the organization.		
6	We openly share information that allows us to discuss individual and team performance and behavior.		
7	When new initiatives are proposed, 'no' is the norm, 'yes' the exception.		
8	Most people believe that change happens too quickly and causes too much disruption.		

Give yourself one point each time you agreed with the following statements:

1   2   4   6

Give yourself one point each time you disagreed with the following statements:

3   5   7   8

What is your total score on eight?

INTERPRETING YOUR RESULT

Score	Implications
0-2	Your culture battery is (almost) empty. Your culture is not just weak, it's unhealthy. This has a significant negative effect for the progress of your change journey.
3-4	Your culture battery is weak and needs extra charging. There is a high probability that your culture is defensive, non-collaborative, toxic and risk avoiding. These cultural traits limit change success.
5-6	Your culture battery contains strong elements that generate energy for your change process. Your organization is aware that culture is important and you've actively worked on a healthy culture: a performance-driven organization, a collaborative culture, and/or an opportunity-seeking culture. Check out which element in particular of your culture needs to be improved.
7-8	Your culture battery is well charged and helps to drive change. Your culture is a source of competitive advantage that few companies have.

Spark for reflection: Who killed Nokia? Nokia did[67]

The competitive battles in the smartphone industry have attracted a lot of attention in the business press. The industry is considered to be one of the toughest and most competitive, where winners become losers, and newcomers lead the industry within a short time. Nokia, once heralded as an example of strategic agility and a successful global market leader at the end of the 1990s, ended up selling its phone business to Microsoft in 2013. The company's market value had declined by about 90% in just six years, the loss hovering around a dazzling $100 billion. Business analysts have attributed Nokia's fall in the mobile phone market to a failure to react appropriately to Apple's iPhone.

But according to Quy Huy, a strategy professor at INSEAD, Nokia's tumble can be put down more to internal politics.[68] Nokia lost the smartphone battle because divergent shared fears among the company's middle and top managers led to company-wide inertia that left it powerless to respond to Apple's iPhone. Nokia did not fail to see the new threat, as many people argue, but a toxic culture made the company vulnerable to competitive forces.

Nokia's culture in the period between 2005 and 2010 was characterized by one word: *fear*. Top managers were afraid of the external threaths and not meeting their quarterly targets. In this unhealthy environment, where there was so much pressure to perform, top managers became intolerant of bad news. Indeed, these managers were described as "extremely temperamental" and "regularly shouting at people at the top of their lungs".

As a result, middle managers became afraid of disappointing top managers, who intimated that the former were not ambitious enough to meet the tough new goals. In response, these middle managers remained silent or filtered overly optimistic information to the top. When several middle managers were fired for bringing bad news or because they were not 'bold enough', many of those remaining turned inward to protect resources, themselves and their units, giving little away because they feared damage to their careers.

In the end, middle managers overpromised and underdelivered. They knew that Nokia had to invest in a new operating system – theirs was inferior – but nobody wanted to be the bearer of bad news. Nokia therefore ended up allocating disproportionate attention and resources to the development of new phone services for short-term market demands, at the expense of much-needed investment in a new operating system. Top managers were left in the dark about what was going on and were unable to implement the strategic solutions required to recapture market share.

Lessons learned from Baywatch

Although the immensely popular television series ended in 2001[69], the image of trained bodies running around in red bikinis and red swimming shorts is iconic. While it has probably not contributed to the overall increase of public IQ, it did reveal the hidden dangers of the ocean. On rare moments during the series, marine scientists were giving us some insights into the secrets of the ocean's currents: a continuous directed flow of ocean water capable of traveling thousands of kilometers. Surface currents move water at the surface of the ocean, while submarine river currents flow deep below, able to significantly influence the climate of coastal areas.

A corporate culture is no different. There are elements visible at the surface, and parts that flow deep within the organization; both are able to significantly influence the culture of your company. The wind will affect the surface of the ocean, as the outside world will impact organizational behavior on a day-to-day basis. Deeper water currents are not as quickly or easily affected by the external, although they are the most impactful.

Edgar Schein, a specialist in organizational culture, taught us: "The only thing of real importance that leaders do is to create and manage culture. If you do not manage culture, it manages you, and you may not even be aware of the extent to which this is happening".[70] His definition of culture is "a pattern of shared basic assumptions, beliefs and values that the group has learned as it solved its problems of external adaptation and internal integration, that has worked well enough to be considered valid and, therefore, to be taught to new members as the right habit, the correct way to perceive, think, behave and feel in relation to those problems".[71]

According to Schein, to understand a corporate culture, you need to analyze three layers:

- *Artefacts* are the most visible and tangible manifestations of a culture. Artefacts include the various attributes of the physical workplace, but also the language and style of an organization. They can be easily discerned, but are often hard to understand.

- *Espoused values and behaviors* are the conscious and explicit philosophies and strategies that an organization believes in. They characterize the preferences and aspirations shared within the organization and which contribute to a shared sense of identity and meaning.

- *Basic assumptions and values* are the unconscious, taken for granted beliefs, perceptions, thoughts and feelings that shape the culture at a fundamental level and influence its manifestation at all other layers.

Research shows that culture can either be an *enabler* or a *barrier* to change within organizations and that, ultimately, culture is a key driver of business performance.[72] The story of Nokia confirms that culture is as critical to an organization as ambition, vision, and strategy.

Characteristics of an empty culture battery

Some cultures generate energy throughout the organization while others drain energy from it. C-levels understand the impact of culture on the success of change implementation and continue to put effort into managing it. However, these efforts often fail. Let's look at some indications that your culture battery is running empty.

 ### Misty energy: a fluffy culture with lifeless values

Many managers think of culture as something obscure, difficult to understand and to define, and therefore probably less important. Little effort is put into trying to understand it, let alone manage it. It remains a soft, almost mythical aspect of the organization, limited to a few defined values visible on a framed poster on the wall. The result is a misalignment between the actual work environment and the messages that are communicated. The message might be 'simplicity', but the daily perception is of complexity. The message might be 'entrepreneurship', but employees feel they are punished and blamed for every mistake made.

In the long run this lack of synergy creates employees with low organizational pride. There is little allegiance to the DNA of the company. Employees don't understand why the company was founded at all, let alone what challenges it had to overcome to get to where it is; how these challenges were tackled; and what the impact was on the evolution of the organization. Overall, there is little to no emotional commitment to anything that the company tries to achieve. The only thing employees really care about is their paycheck.

Regulated energy: a conformance-oriented culture

Conformance-driven organizations are obsessed with regulations, rules and procedures. Conformance is appreciated above performance. Those who don't make mistakes because they stick closely to the rules are promoted. Regulation is standard. Setting ambitious targets and proposing innovative projects is inherently seen as an attempt to attack the company.

Destabilizing energy: a toxic culture

In toxic organizations, fear is all-present. Energy is sucked away from employees, who do only what they are told to do. Employees' perception is that their emotional, physical and/or financial wellbeing is at stake. Negativity and fear are enhanced due to the lack of transparency in communication. There is no open dialogue between (top) managers and employees. Different opinions are barely tolerated or heavily challenged. The apparently cooperative meeting in which nodding heads are the majority masks a wave of resistance. Genuine feedback, especially negative, is rare. You hear about the true feelings of employees during informal gatherings in the corridors, where gossip and rumors flourish. Employees act in silent disagreement.

Office politics and back-stabbing are the norm. Leaders show favoritism; those who are liked are publicly praised. The silent achievers are never mentioned and get demotivated. Political players create confusion and demotivation, often for their own benefits. It's not what you know or how you do it, it's *who you know* (and who likes you) that makes or breaks your success and impact. Double standards are part of the game. Those closest to the power holders get preferential treatment. Meetings become a fake ritual, and backdoor tactics and meddling become the norm.

 Egocentric energy: a defensive culture of 'me'

Another characteristic of a dysfunctional culture is when middle managers and employees are unable to see the big picture and concentrate solely on the goals of their own departments. A silo mentality is the result of a top management that is unable to create a shared ambition for the whole organization. Departmental managers pursue their own goals and interests, often at the expense of the goals of other departments. Lack of information and knowledge sharing between departments leads to sub-optimization. Managers use their energy not to collaborate but to prohibit collaboration. What ensues is a culture of finding excuses for bad performance and blaming, especially when some departments fail to meet their goals.

Departments fight over budgets and putting their own house in order is everyone's priority. They care little for other departments. Very few cross-functional projects are launched, let alone become successful. Every organizational challenge is ripped to sub-project pieces, sculpted to the competences and expectations of the different departments. It's more like competing entities trying to win the 'who is the best department' competition.

Meetings tend to be intra-departmental only and the majority of these gatherings are unnecessary, keeping everyone busy with mostly the wrong priorities. These meetings are often platforms for satisfying the urge to showcase expertise and superiority. Each department considers itself the most important or the most crucial to the everyday operations of the company. Departments use their own systems and approaches and are generally unwilling to share it for others to adapt. Overall, the organization lacks common views or commonly supported models. The image of the organization is that of an organization chart, not a value stream map.

Inertia energy: a risk-avoidant culture

Especially in turbulent times, risk avoidance can hamper an organization from being agile and responding appropriately to disruptive threats. It's mainly successful firms that find it difficult to be honest about the current reality. Michael Tushman and Charles O'Reilly, two innovation professors from Harvard and Stanford, call this the 'tyranny of success': "As long as there is no gap between expectations and performance, a successful system will actively attempt to remain stable. Managers of successful organizations learn what works and are able to incorporate their learning into the firm's formal and informal structures and processes. Yet, if the learning emphasizes today and yesterday, the organization runs the risk of being trapped in the present."[73]

Success can breed inertia. Successful companies become arrogant and inwardly focused. They are overconfident in their ability to outperform the competition and don't see the need to look outside. There is hostility towards change. In these risk-avoidant companies, there is always a reason why *not* to do things. When this group of naysayers builds momentum, the culture becomes one of criticism and cynicism, two 'weapons' that are frequently wielded in meetings and discussions on how and why to change. Organizations suffering from naysaying-culture have often put complex decision-making processes in place, requiring multiple approvals from different management levels, in which anybody can say 'no' but nobody can say 'yes'.

People tend to become apathetic, change-fatigued and distrustful because prior leaders repeatedly proclaimed a 'state of urgency' and 'need for change' but made few substantive changes. Employees develop a heads-down mentality and a reluctance to respond to management directives. They become BOHICA ('Bend Over Here It Comes Again') people: they believe that the wisest course of action is to do the absolute minimum, or ignore new initiatives and work around them, or wait things out.

Overview of dischargers

Figure 25 • Why your culture battery is empty

We have described five characteristics that point to an empty culture battery. In most organizations with an unhealthy and dysfunctional culture, you typically find a combination of these characteristics.

The culture battery and change effectiveness: What does our research say?

Our research reveals significant differences between the successful and unsuccessful transformers on the culture battery. As with the previous batteries, unsuccessful transformers – the Bottom 20 – have mostly negative energy on this battery. That's the case for more than 75 percent of them.

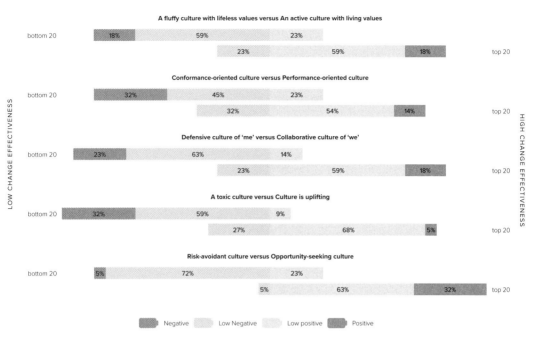

LOW CHANGE EFFECTIVENESS

HIGH CHANGE EFFECTIVENESS

A fluffy culture with lifeless values versus An active culture with living values

bottom 20 — 18% | 59% | 23%
23% | 59% | 18% — top 20

Conformance-oriented culture versus Performance-oriented culture

bottom 20 — 32% | 45% | 23%
32% | 54% | 14% — top 20

Defensive culture of 'me' versus Collaborative culture of 'we'

bottom 20 — 23% | 63% | 14%
23% | 59% | 18% — top 20

A toxic culture versus Culture is uplifting

bottom 20 — 32% | 59% | 9%
27% | 68% | 5% — top 20

Risk-avoidant culture versus Opportunity-seeking culture

bottom 20 — 5% | 72% | 23%
5% | 63% | 32% — top 20

Negative   Low Negative   Low positive   Positive

Figure 26 • How successful and unsuccessful transformers score on the culture battery

The picture is very different for the top performers. The top performers — the companies that enjoyed change success — have mostly positive scores on all five items. For example, only 5 percent of the top performers do not have an opportunity-seeking culture. What is striking is that the large portion of top performers that have a slight (low negative) tendency towards a conformity-driven culture (32 percent) and even a toxic culture (27 percent).

How to charge the culture battery?

Managing culture should be one of the top priorities of any manager. It's a continuous process; long-term success is dependent on a culture that is nurtured. Culture is the environment in which your strategy and your brand thrives, or dies a slow death. Think about it as a *nurturing habitat for success*. Culture cannot be manufactured. It has to be genuinely cultivated by everyone from the CEO down.

Ignoring the health of your culture is like letting an aquarium's water get dirty.[74] In the remainder of this chapter, we elaborate on how to keep the water in your 'aquarium' clean.

Become culturally competent

Organizations are cultural competent when they have a thorough awareness of their culture and consequently put this awareness into action. Let's look at each of these components.

Create cultural awareness — measure it!

Culture needs to be reinforced at every opportunity through word and deed. But what can you do if one of the key challenges in your change process is an unhealthy culture, and where do you start?

Transforming an unhealthy culture into a healthy one takes time. In companies with a few hundred people, the transformation process can take two to five years. Transforming a culture involves more than changing the values and behaviors of a small group of managers. Even when executives try to reform a problem culture through a series of well-intended actions, they are likely to fail at weeding out embedded cultural traits, especially if widespread employee skepticism about a new strategy and culture-change efforts spawns covert resistance.[75] You have to involve your employees in this process and that inevitably takes time.

A crucial first step in charging your culture battery is to have a thorough understanding of your existing culture, recognize which traits are preeminent and consistent, and discern under what conditions these traits are likely to be a help or a hindrance.[76] Find out what is "the smell of your place".[77] Build cultural competence by creating cultural awareness, but first make sure you understand the existing culture at a deep enough level.[78]

Start by *measuring* your culture. There are many cultural measurement tools around. We highly recommend *Corporate Transformation Tools* (CTT), by Richard Barrett, for its ease of use, clear visual representations, and high level of practicality.

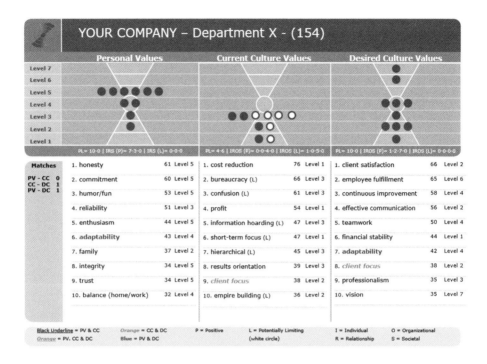

Figure 27 • Output of Barrett's Corporate Transformation Tool (Barrett 2006)[79]

In Barrett's tool, respondents are asked to select ten personal values that resonate, ten values that represent how their current culture operates, and ten values that constitute the desired culture. These three sets of values are mapped to seven levels of personal and organizational consciousness. The results create a thorough understanding of the degree of alignment between participants' personal values and the current culture, as well as the current culture and the desired culture. The model also calculates a *cultural entropy score*, which is a measure of the degree of disorder and dysfunction in a company. Too much disorder will negatively affect the company's performance.

Another popular and useful toolkit is Quinn and Rohrbaugh's *Competing Values Framework* (see Figure 28). While Barrett's model is oriented towards the *values of employees and the organization*, this model helps to assess the *behavior of managers*. These authors built a model based on two dimensions:

- organizational focus, from an internal emphasis on people in the organization to an external focus of the organization itself

- contrast between stability and control, and flexibility and change.

These two dimensions make up four quadrants and the framework allows firms to position themselves on these quadrants (see Figure 28).

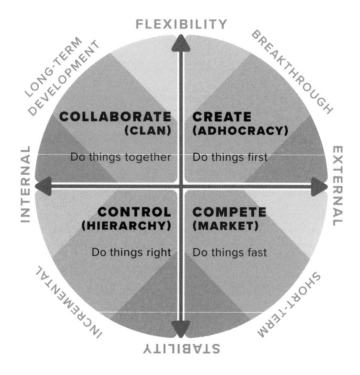

Figure 28 • Quinn and Rohrbaugh's Competing Values (Cameron & Quinn 2011)[80]

Use the results of your cultural assessment to discuss how your culture needs to change and to create more cultural awareness in the organization. Share them with your employees and discuss them, whatever the scores. The advantage of a cultural assessment is that employees easily recognize the results, so the buy-in to work on the results is usually high. This also strengthens the willingness to discuss and act upon the results.

Changing your culture

'Knowing' your culture is one thing, acting upon that knowledge is another. Let's look at some concrete actions, you can take to transform your culture and to influence your organizational context. The goal is that you see the first actual changes in behavior, letting go of the old ones.

Honor the strengths | The first step is to work *with* your existing culture, not against it. Where traditional cultural transformation programs often focus on replacing old behavior with new ones, we favor a *strengths-based approach* that concentrates *first* on optimizing, increasing and intensifying the strongest aspect of the organization. These aspects should not be restricted to the cultural aspects. For example, if your business strategy is clear and well defined, ask yourself how you can make it even better by aligning it with the results of your assessment. Similarly, launching a new risk-allowing, entrepreneurial approach in a risk-avoidant culture needs to be done in a slow, risk-aware way.

Choose your bright spots | Think about *where to start* your cultural change initiatives and *who* to involve. Some departments are more important and/or more influential than others. If your organization aims to be more customer-intimate, it makes sense to start cultural change initiatives in the front office with your service departments, not with your accounting department. Deciding where to start your change initiative should not only be based on the strategic importance of a department, but also on the 'informal influence' of the department, or of the leaders in that department. Ask yourself: who are the people who can influence others not because of their formal authority or position but because of their credibility and relationship network?[81] Identify the 'culture carriers' within those critical departments. How can you enlist small groups of them as sources of positive influence and energy? How can their insights and capabilities be spread across the organization? And how can you use these cultural carriers to counteract negative influencers?

Change (part of) the context first, then spread the message | In their bestseller *Switch*, brothers Chip and Dan Heath have convincingly described why it is so hard to make lasting changes in companies and communities, as well as in our personal lives: our minds are ruled by two different systems — the rational mind and the emotional mind — that compete for control. The rational mind wants a great beach body; the emotional mind wants that Oreo cookie. The rational mind wants change, the emotional mind loves the comfort of the existing routine. Emotions make us act to get our short-term satisfaction, while rationality often focuses on long-term satisfaction. Guess who wins this game most of the time? The brothers Heath suggested ways to manage both the rational and the emotional mind but they also found that 'shaping the path' – influencing the organizational context – is a third and powerful way to help create lasting change.[82]

Think about how to change the context to facilitate cultural change. For example, start with a makeover of the workplace: the physical arrangements of things, the layout of the offices, the use of color, the signs at the entrance, and so on. Create a more inviting and warm environment if you want to promote a more intimate relationship with your customers. Put performance graphs on the walls of the coffee corner if you'd like to create a more performance-oriented culture.

Changing (part of) the context is a powerful sign that shows you are *committed* to change. Make sure you make changes visible, and quickly. Start with small things that have a big impact. The parking lot might be muddy and unpaved – get it fixed. The reception area might be dirty and dark – sort it out. Only after this kind of repair should you begin to talk about your project of 'enlightening the customer'.

Act your way into new thinking | Culture is much more a matter of *doing* than saying. Perceptions of the effectiveness of change initiatives are influenced more by what people see happening than by what they hear from managers as intention. When launching cultural change programs, companies often start with listing a whole set of key values, creating a behavioral code and printing glossy cards for everyone to use. Keep it simple. Pick some key behaviors – ones that are tangible, actionable, repeatable, observable and measurable – and start with those. Act your way into new thinking. Launch initiatives that affect how the work is done (work practices), but also pay attention to people-related behaviors (more symbolic actions), such as how people relate to each other, or how information is shared between employees and managers.

Make new behavior the standard | Culture is a cornerstone of your competitive advantage. It's imperative to sustain and anchor the new behaviors in your management infrastructure. This new behavior needs to become the new norm. Habits and routines are automatic and repeated behaviors that relate to 'the way we do things around here'.[83] Typically, behavioral habits looks like this:

Asking for a different behavior is asking for a different outcome. Changing *routines* is the hard way; changing *the trigger* is often the better Choice. Getting into your sportshoes being at home, smelling the dinner, having the joyful kids around you is hard. First going to the local park, run, then go home makes it easier. Changing the trigger (home to park) helps you to overcome the hurdle of being disciplined.

Anchor the culture in your management infrastructure | A cultural shift will not happen by asking people to change behaviors alone. It also requires changes in the most important management processes:

- Do you screen and select new employees, in particular leaders, who will integrate well into the culture?

- Are new hires taught about the culture?

- Is there a new type of dialogue started between the different stakeholders: can certain topics be raised and discussed that were impossible to talk about before?

- Is culture-compliant behavior part of your performance reviews?

- Are heroes of the new culture recognized as role models?

- What can you do to change how your team works to better reflect the new culture?

- Are the right people in the councils and on the committees?

- Do your customers see and feel your desired culture?

Use informal interventions to reinforce the required behavior | Use informal levers of change in addition to formal elements (e.g. performance management, HR management, reporting structures capability systems). For example, do you as a manager take time to engage in networking events? Are you present in the cultural committees you created?

AETNA'S INFORMAL APPROACH TO CHANGE

At Aetna, one of the largest American health insurance companies, CEO John Rowe explicitly sought out informal interactions with employees. These included social visits, ad hoc meetings, impromptu telephone discussions, and email exchanges. He and President Ron Williams focused on getting cross-sections of people to reflect on how they were feeling and on identifying their sources of anxiety and concern. Separate non-hierarchical forums among peers and colleagues were also held across the company to discuss Aetna's values – what they were, what they should be, why many of them were no longer being 'lived', what needed to happen to resurrect them, and what leadership behaviors would ensure the right employee behaviors.

One early and important networking effort by Rowe was to identify a core group of 'key influencers' – potential leaders who could offer invaluable perspectives on the cultural situation, regardless of their level in the hierarchy. Rowe began interacting with a cadre of about 25 influencers and within a few months expanded the group to include close to 100. These discussions not only gave him insights about the staff but created a rapport between him and a respected group that disseminated his message both formally and informally.[84]

Empower the ambassadors | A cultural change needs *makers*, not breakers. Every company has people who are promoters of the culture project. Leaders and non-leaders who earn respect from what they say and how they act. Recognize these people and encourage them to align their work and management styles so they can keep demonstrating what it looks like to live the culture.

Use story-telling to ritualize the performance of key habits and routines | New habits are unlikely to become embedded in organizations without diligent and concerted efforts to socialize them. One tried-and-tested socialization effort is to use stories that get told over and over again to illustrate to newcomers the importance of certain behaviors and the depth of commitment displayed by that various company personnel members. Companies like FedEx, Nordstrom and Microsoft spend time collecting those stories because they serve the valuable purpose of illustrating the kinds of behavior the company encourages and reveres.[85]

Organize parties and ceremonies | Many managers see parties as a waste of money and time. We believe, however, in the art of partying. We believe that the more 'cultural parties' you organize a year, the more successful you become. Here's what we mean: parties are not just opportunities to bring people together to drink and dance. They are moments in which you can highlight the main strategic messages of the company, acknowledge ambassadors and role models, and organize a platform to share best practices. If communication and learning is coupled with celebration, you can create a powerful cocktail for cultural progress and business success.

Stimulate, don't tolerate | Culture is the responsibility of the top leadership team, *not HR*. It is not an option to not align with the desired culture. Encourage and inspire your people as much as you can, with positive approaches and passion; by offering all the required resources and giving constructive feedback. Aside from this, however, create clarity on where the boundaries are, on what is unacceptable and non-negotiable. Create consensus on the consequences of not complying with the new way of doing things. These Non-Negotiable Rules (NNR's) might result in some people changing roles, or worse, needing to leave. We will discuss these NNRs later on in the chapter on the connection battery.

Become a performance-oriented culture

Changing an organization that suffers from a conformance-oriented culture occurs when you create a *result-oriented* culture, in which individuals and the organization focus on outputs rather than on inputs. It's no longer about all the efforts you've taken to get a result; it's about the result itself.

There are several things you can do to bring about a performance-oriented culture in your organization. The first thing is to make performance and results high on the discussion agenda. Be transparent about performance — both good and bad. Boost confidence by being appreciative of what has been accomplished, but also stimulate the desire to stretch results. Be clear about expectations too: *define* the outputs and end results. Force people to think whether their actions and initiatives have delivered clear benefits for the customer. If not, stop the initiative. It's important to distinguish between what *needs* to be done and what is actually feasible. Discuss the constraints — what prohibits your employees from delivering the intended outcome. By doing this you also clarify what you need to change to get better performance. Finally, create commitment at all levels to remove — not add — complexity from your processes and systems. A healthy culture tries to enable the future, not to control the past.

Ask people what performance can be expected when there is a real emergency. In the military, the installation of new radio systems in military vehicles typically took years to go through design, development, production, testing and installation. However, in crisis situations, some replacement projects suddenly get finished within weeks. Why is it suddenly possible to get to a result quickly during a critical situation? Every company has expediting procedures, allowing things to happen that normally are not possible.

Find the parts of your conformance procedures that are killing your performance. Look for intelligent ways to separate 'dangerous', complex exceptions from simple, common rules that can be applied in 99 percent of all cases. Conformance-oriented cultures are often dominated by a fear for mistakes that originates from a catastrophic past failure. However, a complex conformance procedure doesn't lead to better protection by adding multiple inspections that are generally okay; research has demonstrated that after a while, the first inspector often skips the inspection under time pressure, assuming that the supervisor will check the results anyway.

Under the same conditions, the supervisor may very well believe he can occasionally skip inspecting the outputs of his worker. The bottom line is that whereas the process has built-in double inspections, the reality is that products frequently leave the building without having undergone quality control. Control and inspections are of course essential to assure quality, but when it comes to conformance, more is not necessarily better. Dare to question the relevance of all steps and be creative about alternative approaches.

Create a culture of courage

Changing a toxic culture is a difficult task, but an essential aspect of a successful change implementation. Leaders play a crucial role as they are often the source of the problem. The top team has to set the right tone and be a role model. Toxicity in the top team will spread to the rest of the company. It is highly contagious and it rubs off onto everyone. As a top team member be sure to stay away from the toxic cliques. Resist the temptation to haul with the wolves. Do not get involved in gossiping about others and do not condone it. Toxic organizations need to stop complaining in the corridors, and come with solutions to the boardroom table.

However, this takes courage. Fixing a toxic culture is about having the *guts* to challenge how decisions are made. It is about creating an environment of safety, transparency and fairness, where people feel they can talk about anything and expose the elephant in the room. Only courage will allow you to dare to look at who is doing what and where.

Courage demands transparency in the decision-making process: what are the rules to follow, who's in charge for what, and when is management-by-exception appropriate? Dare to include different perspectives: the customer, the supplier, the shareholder, the employee. Question criteria, procedures, habits and obvious attitudes. But remember: for every piece of feedback on what is not working well, suggest at least three alternatives to fix it — nobody likes people who only complain. Solicit thoughts and suggestions from employees at all levels. Don't allow a toxic culture to kill creativity.

ZAPPOS' UPLIFTING CULTURE

Online shoe retailer Zappos is known for its extraordinary customer service, which has included delivering flowers to a customer whose mom passed away and talking to a customer for over eight hours.

CEO Tony Hsieh says: "Our number one priority is company culture. Our whole belief is that if you get the culture right, most of the other stuff, like delivering great customer service, will happen naturally on its own."

Zappos has what we would call an uplifting culture. "Decisions need to come from the front lines — people who are closest to customers. Zappos lets customer service reps decide what's best for the customers instead of having specific policies for each case. That trust can go a long way with the customer service reps.

Don't let HR and Legal make the decisions. Tell them they're great for some things, but ultimately, it's the manager's decision. Limit their power in an organization. They can make things more bureaucratic if they aren't contained."

Hsieh says it's important that managers and supervisors get to know employees on a personal basis. He says they've tried this at Zappos, and the results have been better communication between employees, relationships are better, people are willing to do favors for each other, and higher levels of trust are established.[86]

Establish a culture of 'we'

Creating common goals and working together towards them sounds like a no-brainer. Still, we often see teams that are in fact nothing more than the sum of individual competent professionals, each with their own objectives, trying to reach their personal bonuses (and stardom). In a collaborative and supportive environment, everyone understands that the group (and end result) matters most, not who did what and who gets the credit. Literally encourage 'we' sentences instead of 'I' sentences.

By emphasizing what teamwork and collaboration bring to the company, you will encourage people to think more with a group mentality and to be more supportive of others.

The first step in creating a group mentality is to set a common language. The bigger departments become over time, the more they develop their own language. Create a common point of view. It's not about: What do *I* or *my team* think about this, but rather what *we* think about it. Let people experience the problems and roles of others. Ask them to explain things for their colleagues. Communication needs to go both ways: receiving and retransmitting.

Secondly, organizations need to make people collaborate, connect, and work together. Balance the me/we paradigm. Most people love to be part of a team! In assigning tasks and creating job roles, address how the group is contributing to the higher goals and how everyone is contributing to it individually. Show how a specific role impacts the role of others and the success of the organization. Praise your team as a group, but also provide feedback to each individual in one-on-one meetings. Encourage people to help each other. Create a common identity (team name, color), a common location, a common language, and share the burdens ("we all went through this together"). Reward, or at least publicly acknowledge, those who provide support.

Create a culture of possibilities

An opportunity-seeking culture focuses on the future, not on the past. To make this shift, you can *reduce hierarchy, increase autonomy* and *encourage diversity.*[87]

Reducing hierarchy allows for more honest and open feedback and discussions among employees and managers. Organizations need to find a balance between discussing their weaknesses and threats and the opportunities and outcomes this feedback can bring. Put these topics on the agenda and ask people to discuss them. Start small; do it politely. Don't be a bull in a china shop — it will be counter-productive. Along the way, see who is on your side.

Another way to stimulate an opportunity-seeking culture is to *increase autonomy* by providing employees with time for innovation and creativity. Google's philosophy of '20 percent time' is an interesting illustration of this. Google encourages employees to spend 20 percent of their time working on what they think will most benefit Google.[88] Successful innovation needs a huge amount of idea generation, even if some of these ideas seem rather unrealistic at the start. Some of the famous '20 percent products' include Google News, Gmail and AdSense.

One way to *encourage diversity* is to embrace insights from outsiders. Of course your situation is unique, but that is no excuse to shut yourself off from the rest of the world. An opportunity-seeking culture is eager to learn from others, not to copy and paste, but to be inspired. Consultants' opinions and benchmarking information can be a great source of idea generation. This will connect you with outside trends and ideas that may not have caught your attention yet. Looking at success stories from others will push you to challenge long-held beliefs of what is possible and what is not.

OPPORTUNITY-SEEKING CULTURE AT DAVITA HEALTHCARE PARTNERS

An example of a company with an opportunity-seeking culture is DaVita HealthCare Partners, an American kidney care organization. To keep all employees focused on the external environment, DaVita abandoned its organizational chart. Structure focuses too much attention on the hierarchy and not enough on understanding the local marketplace and broader environment. This external focus is supported by a hard-and-fast rule that moves information up the hierarchy quickly: "Whenever there is a director and three or more team members in a room, there's a town hall meeting." In these meetings, any question can be asked about any subject. If the director doesn't have an answer, the question goes into his or her email and has to be answered within 48 hours. All that information gets funneled to top management for consideration.

Thrashers[89] and underperformers, with inward-looking and politicized management, find this level and intensity of communication inherently difficult. They are too busy vying for turf, resources, and position to dispassionately consider the implications of outside signals. The external focus of agile companies enables them to face up to brutal facts and separate the wheat from the chaff.[90]

Firms with an opportunity-seeking culture instill an entrepreneurial culture with a 'can-do climate'. Diversity stimulates organizational creativity so that employees are vigilant and able to come up with appropriate answers to changing needs and circumstances.[91] Employees see opportunities instead of barriers, and look beyond the ways things are done to the way things could be done.

LIVING VALUES AT CHÂTEAUFORM'

Châteauform', a European organization that offers seminar venues for large international companies, is a great example of a company with strong values. The company is one of the most service-oriented companies in its industry and offers much more flexibility than any hotel chain or other seminar center. It is a customer intimacy organization *pur sang*.

Jacques Horovitz, the founder of Châteauform', explains the role that values play in managing the organization: "[To become a customer-intimate company] I had to give the maximum of autonomy to my teams, so they could react, adapt, innovate, and listen to customer needs. That is why I created a company managed by values, rather than by rules.

Managing by values means building an organization where every member of the team agrees with and believes in the same values as other members of the team. Managing by rules means creating safeguards, regulations to minimize deviance from a predefined behavior. The difference in autonomy is quite large. Rules prevent autonomy. When values are shared, trust is paramount. It allows autonomy. I like to show my teams the following graph to visualize this. Suppose you have two circles of the same size. The core represents how the company is managed. The outside circumference represents the 'limits' (e.g. no cheating, no stealing,....). In a company managed by values, the 'distance' between values and limits is quite large, which means a large degree of autonomy. In a company managed by rules, this distance shrinks, reducing autonomy."[92]

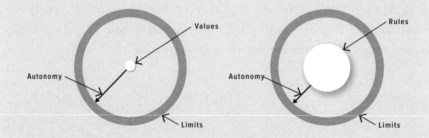

Châteauform' has identified a set of seven values vital to its organization (represented in the graphic below). How does the company live the values? How does it demonstrate every day that these values guide the behavior of the employees? For Horovitz, "managing by values means, first of all, to have common values. Second, they must be shared or espoused: people must identify with them. In order for people to believe, these values have to be demonstrated by management practices, they have to be reinforced by the leadership, by the rituals and symbols, and by the reward system."[93]

Horovitz shares some examples of how the company demonstrates its commitment to the values. "Take, for example, 'love for the customer'. Each site is a customer satisfaction center and not a profit center (management practice). Contrary to conventional site management, I don't ask the people who run the sites to look at their sales (centralized) or costs but to make the customer happy. In terms of leadership, for instance, the executive committee, including myself, spends one week a year replacing a team on site. One of the rites and symbols we have created is the 'seven shields' [see the illustration below], with each shield representing a value. An annual ceremony rewards the sites that have best exemplified this value. Finally, in terms of rewards and recognition, every site receives an extra bonus based on the customer satisfaction."[94]

For each of the values, Horovitz and the Châteauform' team have identified concrete management practices, leadership styles, rites and symbols, and specific actions on rewards and recognition.

CULTURE: IT ALL STARTS WITH OUR 7 VALUES				
VALUES	DEMONSTRATED BY MANAGEMENT PRACTICES	REINFORCED BY LEADERSHIP	REINFORCED BY RITUALS AND SYMBOLS	REINFORCED BY REWARDS AND RECOGNITION
LOVE FOR THE CUSTOMER	Customer satisfaction centers	Show time for the Steering Committee	Celebration of the knights, shields & poems	100% of bonus on customer satisfaction
FAMILY SPIRIT	3-week induction cooptation	Flying school; everybody involved in an opening	« Family House »; born in Châteauform'	Bonus of headquarters based on satisfaction of the sites vis-à-vis HQ
LEARN, ALWAYS LEARN	Week « in another way » for all Training budget	Live my life	All Teachers OSCAR Astonishment report	Coach
LOYALTY, HONESTY	Transparency	Golden eye	Sweet or Sour measured on site	Free shares for all
DARE, ALWAYS DARE	No boss for sites LNI	Godmother /Godfather	Exchanges,annual fair of best ideas	Extra shares for mobility
CONTRIBUTION RATHER THAN ATTRIBUTION	Mobility Godmothers & Godfathers	No special treatment Am I disturbing you? Week « in another way » for the Steering Committee	Say why before what or how No titles	Low salaries get increase first
RIGOR AND PERFORMANCE	Everything is measured and formalized Budgets in 2 days; Booklet	Say how much and when and why; Card game of our « home » leadership	Customer # 1 in all agendas Booklet on the Culture	No individual bonuses if the company does not make its overall budget

Key messages of this chapter

The culture battery is crucial in amplifying energy throughout the organization. It's also one of the toughest to manage, partially because most managers think of culture as something difficult to understand, difficult to define, and difficult to manage. As a result they underestimate the power of culture as a source of social energy or fail to see the danger of a dysfunctional and unhealthy culture.

In this chapter, we've provided you with five characteristics of an unhealthy culture as well as what it takes to have a fully charged battery (see Figure 29).

An empty culture battery FROM...	A fully charged culture battery TO...
A fluffy culture with lifeless values	A culturally competent organization with living values
A conformance-oriented culture	A performance-oriented culture
A toxic culture	An uplifting and courageous culture
A defensive culture of 'me'	A collaborative culture of 'we'
A risk-avoidant culture	An opportunity-seeking culture

Figure 29 • Summary: From an empty to a fully charged culture battery

How do you create a healthy culture that amplifies social energy through cohesion and drive? We provided the following recipes to tackle a dysfunctional culture:

- You don't change your company culture overnight. *It takes time* to work through physical artefacts and daily behaviors to eventually change the basic assumptions that shape the culture of your organization. Be patient.

- *Measure it.* What is the current culture? How does this manifest in your organization? And what should it be in the future?

- When transforming your culture, start by *working on your cultural strengths.* Define where and with whom you will start your cultural initiatives, and then identify a few critical behaviors that help to change an unhealthy culture in a healthy one.

- *Reduce the distance between people*, between leaders and employees, between workers and co-workers, between insiders and outsiders. The healthy culture generates social energy.

- Finally, *anchor the new behavior in your management infrastructure.* Recruit and educate employees and leaders who reflect the desired values.

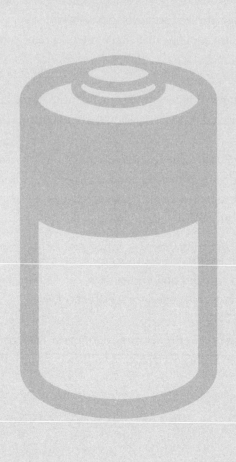

Chapter
6

CLEAR ACTION PLANNING & IMPLEMENTATION

———

The physical energy

Key questions

How do you select the right ideas when there is so much that needs to be done?

How do you make sure change becomes integrated as a daily practice?

Do you really need a methodology to find the solution to our problems?

Everybody is already so busy. How do you create time for implementing change?

How do you make sure we get it right the first time?

HOW WELL IS *YOUR* ACTION PLANNING
AND IMPLEMENTATION BATTERY CHARGED?

Tick whether you agree or disagree with each of the following statements.

		AGREE	DISAGREE
1	We launch change initiatives based on a strong project mandate that clarifies scope, boundaries and expected results.		
2	Our individual change initiatives miss a strong 'why': they don't address day-to-day operational problems or customer needs.		
3	We define unrealistic time horizons for the implementation of individual change projects.		
4	Resources assigned to our projects include budgets, IT support, and dedicated time for team members.		
5	In our organization, we deal with problems through analysis of reliable data and direct observation of our practices.		
6	We use prototyping and experimentation as a way to assess the value and risks of alternative solutions.		
7	We periodically (weekly/monthly) assess variance towards expected progress and results to learn and adjust.		
8	We fail to embed the results of change projects in standard operating procedures.		

Give yourself one point each time you agreed with the following statements:

1   4   5   6   7

Give yourself one point each time you disagreed with the following statements:

2   3   8

What is your total score on eight?

INTERPRETING YOUR RESULT

Score	Implications
0-2	Your action planning battery is an energy drainer. Your organization is unable to translate strategic projects into concrete benefits for the customer. You miss the project and process management skills to deliver quality projects on time and within budget.
3-4	Your action planning battery is weak. You may have clearly defined the scope of your projects, but you need to prepare your projects adequately, manage the change well, and create commitment and ownership within your team members to maintain success. Unfortunately, you don't score well on most of these items.
5-6	Your action planning battery generates energy for the change project. You're able to finish projects well and to embed them in the organization. There are some areas for improvement though. Do you use prototyping when you come up with a solution for a problem? Do you screen projects regularly? Do you embed the results of your change projects in standard operating procedures?
7-8	Your action planning battery is well charged. Your organization systematically delivers projects that create benefits for the customer or generate capabilities towards a more strategy-focused organization.

Spark for reflection: FoxMeyer's failure of ERP implementation[95]

FoxMeyer was a large drug wholesaler in the US in the mid-1990s. Drug wholesalers distribute pharmaceutical products to chain stores, independent drug stores and hospitals and may offer certain information-based services to their customers. The drug distribution industry is highly competitive, and there is a strong pressure to cut costs and increase efficiency.

Due to the intense competition, FoxMeyer needed an IT solution that would help it to make complex supply chain decisions and meet increased cost pressures. In 1992, the company decided to hire Arthur Andersen (now Accenture) to implement an Enterprise Resource Planning (ERP) software package. The implementation cost was budgeted in 1994 at $65 million. The final bill was more than $100 million, and the performance of the application was unacceptable. After taking on a $34 million charge to cover uncollectable shipping and inventory costs in 1996, the company was forced to file for bankruptcy.

The project had met with big problems from the start, including project implementation challenges. One of the major problems was the over-ambitious scope of the project. Both FoxMeyer's CEO and CIO were strong advocates of the project, but they bet the company on the successful implementation of this project. Consultants also concluded that the timeframe for the entire implementation – 18 months – was far from realistic.

The project was risky because FoxMeyer lacked skilled and knowledgeable personnel. It outsourced the entire project to a consultant. There was no training for the end-users, which led to a hostile reaction from employees, who sabotaged the project. Other factors included insufficient testing, due to the rushed schedule, and a lack of appropriate management control.

The role of action planning and implementation in change

"Just do it" — sounds pretty simple; perhaps too simple to be true. Even the most inspirational goals require the definition of clear steps grounded in the current reality of the organization. Without these, ambitions are often considered wishful thinking, ideas projected by dreamers living in an ivory tower, disconnected from the fire fighters that deal with the everyday problems. That doesn't mean that they don't agree that action is needed — on the contrary. What is essential for them, however, is to understand how to manage change in an effective and efficient way while dealing with overwhelming to-do lists.

As a result, *action planning and implementation* is essential to transit from old to new through:

- identification of critical activities — things that will really make a difference

- definition of clear mandates that assure appropriate allocation of resources — both time and budgets

- use of a fit-for-purpose-methodology that combines data with experimentation and avoids building the plane while flying it

- integration of solutions in day-to-day activities

The best organizations will develop specific capabilities that allow them to excel in the various corner stones of strategic project management and process improvement that lay the foundation for success in this battery.

Characteristics of an empty action planning and implementation battery

In many companies, change is characterized as a set of interventions that chase local success stories, rather than the mobilization of energized self-managing teams that experience change and improvement as trivial to contribute to the success of the overall business. Change is isolated and anecdotal, rather than connected and systemic. How can you recognize that your battery is not fully charged?

 ## Energy is the level of decibels produced: more is better

All organizations define actions to move forward; most organizations don't lack meetings to define lists of action items. At first glance, this could be seen as an energized organization that tries to deal with the current situation. But if these ideas are not screened for relevance and impact, the bucket lists quickly become overwhelming. What initially starts as a suggestion or a quick fix grows to become a time-consuming, never-ending journey. After a while, prioritization is often reduced to management by shouting loudly. This typically occurs in organizations that lack definitions to distinguish between *emergency problems* that ask for a quick and dirty 'just do it' approach, and *other non-critical projects*.

 ## Energy as a lightning strike: suddenly you have it

Have you ever walked out of your boss' office with the feeling that you just inherited something promising, but at the same time had no clue whether this thing had the size of the earth or of a ping pong ball? Or, that you were expected to take care of 'it', without understanding what 'it' means, let alone have an idea of the context, budgets, available resources and responsibilities? Perhaps you were expected to start on it by the end of the week, having received instructions for frequent reporting as a clear sign of 'support'. Yet you wondered why you were never invited to the meeting that brought about this action you had to take...

 ## Herculean energy

Many organizations welcome heroes who are able to move mountains, but turn out to work only on *their own* mountain. They practice 'Work harder, not smarter'. Projects are run by experts who easily see a quick fix solution to problems, but refuse to be pinned down on duration and cost estimates. Discussions are opinion based, interventions are artwork — everyone uses their own preferred approach. Solutions are often add-ons to existing complex procedures. Progress reporting varies from oral presentations to overly complex reports. Both approaches are all but clear and transparent and often summarized down to 'just trust me'. Newcomers take a long time to fit in, facing learning curves of several months.

Big Bang energy

Organizations often prefer implementing big and small changes all at once so that they can contain the amount of trouble as they go through the changes. Requirements of the desired changes are well documented but seem to change continuously. As the scope of the project increases, they continue to push the deadline out. In the end, projects always seem to become bigger and bigger, until you realize you can't postpone the big bang any longer. Even though some projects have taken twice as long and double the budget anticipated, time pressure still often prevents from testing proposed solutions. When the big day arrives, you turn the key with shaking hands. Despite the long preparations, the big bang explosion always seems to create solutions that are in part impossible to control. New solutions also bring collateral damage: while the new system offers bells and whistles, key customizations available in the old system seem to be missing. Implementations are followed by long periods of rework and heavy maintenance.

Decaying energy: sunrise followed by sunset

Over the years, various prestigious projects and improvement initiatives have been kicked off. However, they have rarely been able to demonstrate clear success and if they did, results of success stories were not sustained. As soon as the attention for the initiative faded away, results started to slowly decay. In some cases, your organization might have been better off without the intervention. No surprise, then, that the new approach was never fully deployed within the organization.

Do any of these scenarios sound familiar? If so, your action planning and implementation battery may be close to empty (see Figure 30). The constant 'busy-ness' in your organization is in stark contrast to your less than spectacular business results.

Overview of dischargers

Figure 30 • Why your action planning and implementation battery is empty

The implementation battery and change effectiveness: What does our research say?

When comparing the results of the top 20 percent of performers with the bottom 20 percent of performers in our database, some interesting insights emerge.

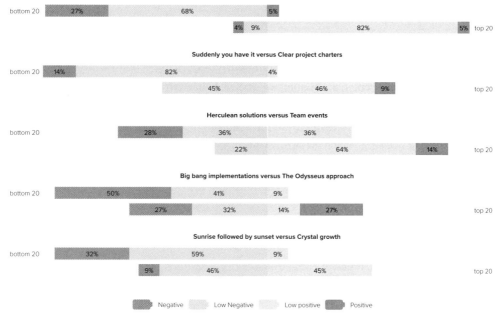

More is better versus Insist on why, who, when

bottom 20 — 27% | 68% | 5%

4% | 9% | 82% | 5% — top 20

Suddenly you have it versus Clear project charters

bottom 20 — 14% | 82% | 4%

45% | 46% | 9% — top 20

Herculean solutions versus Team events

bottom 20 — 28% | 36% | 36%

22% | 64% | 14% — top 20

Big bang implementations versus The Odysseus approach

bottom 20 — 50% | 41% | 9%

27% | 32% | 14% | 27% — top 20

Sunrise followed by sunset versus Crystal growth

bottom 20 — 32% | 59% | 9%

9% | 46% | 45% — top 20

Negative | Low Negative | Low positive | Positive

Figure 31 • How successful and unsuccessful transformers score
on the action planning and implementation battery

Companies that struggle with change also struggle with the action planning and implementation battery. The number of bottom performers with negative scores on this battery is significant. Only a handful of bottom performers show (low) positive results.

Top performers generally score *much higher* on this battery than their bottom peers. Top performers focus more on relevant initiatives and they rely more on team efforts than on heroism to tackle problems. However, on the remaining three criteria, many top performers struggle too – this explains why the action planning battery, together with the infrastructure battery, has the lowest overall scores. Although we all seem to be 'busy-busy-busy' nowadays, it is important for management to pay more attention to this battery.

How to charge your action planning and implementation battery?

Assuring reliable product and service delivery on a daily basis requires sound process management. Managing and continuously improving repetitive tasks, however, is very different from managing projects that introduce new products or processes that enable breakthrough performance through strategic change. As a result, many organizations fail to define a holistic approach that assures the integration of essential skills of both worlds. They launch projects that lack an energetic start, fail to mobilize all stakeholders to fully deploy change throughout the organization, or don't succeed in maintaining the dynamics of their initiatives, anchoring the change into a new way of doing business.

Through a synthesis of best practices of project *and* process management, we have developed a framework that enables organizations to tackle key points for improvement with regard to action planning and implementation (see Figure 32).

Figure 32 • Framework to tackle key points for improvement

Start with the end in mind

Projects that want to inspire should start with *why*[96]. Fully charged organizations start with the end in mind. They define a clear rationale for initiatives that intend to make a difference and translate this into desired outcomes. In reality, when change projects are announced, managers very often emphasize *what* – we are going to introduce a new ERP system, we are going to restructure our organization – rarely stopping to ask questions like: what are the positive effects we expect from the new system or restructuring effort? Who will benefit from these effects? Who are the customers and stakeholders? When do we need these effects to become visible? If projects fail to take into account these questions, they may not be relevant, or their impact may not justify the effort.

When nobody reflects on the desired effects *from the start*, projects often end up as mere reporting activities (this is *what* we have done over the last month), until someone decides that enough work has been done on this item and suggests shifting the attention to *what's next*. Fully charged organizations, however, know which cards to bet on. Their projects and processes are *result oriented*, not content oriented. These projects and processes are ambitious (their impact will make a difference) and attractive (they are perceived as highly relevant in the context of the organization).

Assessing the *effect* of whatever needs to be achieved is central to connecting initiatives to the organization's strategy and to gaining change support from a diverse group of stakeholders. The seeds of success for this first step of the implementation framework lie in a sound connection between the action planning and implementation battery and the management infrastructure as well as the strategy battery.

Prioritizing vital initiatives is further facilitated through the definition of a logical chain of events that clarifies *why first things come first*. Milestones and key deliverables of projects are defined within manageable time frames of one to three months. This allows key players within the organization to achieve a critical mass of cross-functional team players who intensively work together towards the achievement of common goals.

DEFINING THE STRATEGIC RELEVANCE
OF INITIATIVES

A laboratory that calibrates test equipment was getting ready for an accreditation audit. As part of the preparation process, "Hugo", the quality manager, had identified a long list of action items that 'urgently' needed to be addressed. This added to an already long list of initiatives that had been identified as important by top management, including the installation of a new ERP system within the next year. Key personnel were overloaded, working in parallel on major and minor issues without understanding their importance or inter-dependency. Managers were stressed, as the overall implementation progress was slow.

To address this, managers of all levels gathered to create an overview of all actions and initiatives and to group them into strategic themes. Actions without a clear connection to the strategy map were deleted, or in some cases (e.g. nearly finished actions) implemented based on quick and dirty solutions (one person, one day of work). For the most important themes (five of the ten themes in this case), the need for change was articulated from a business, customer, or employee perspective. This also implied defining a project scope for each theme and identifying key milestones and expected benefits, allowing all actions to be prioritized by sequence and expected impact on a monthly basis.

The approach highlighted the critical actions of the audit that also had a considerable impact on the ERP project, clarifying their business importance beyond the scope of the accreditation audit. As other actions were either eliminated or implemented through an accelerated process, prioritization of the more strategic actions enabled a collaborative approach with a purpose on the true business drivers of the laboratory.

Create clear project charters

A good start is half of the work. Many organizations can benefit from investing in the creation of a clear mandate. Top management should take the lead on defining the why, who and when, as illustrated in the case study above. However, middle- or low-level project champions should have the flexibility to influence how and what. A clear mandate signed by both parties is a testament of mutual understanding and commitment.

Every project needs an energized champion

A clear mandate also identifies the appropriate champion and allows this leader to explore the change initiative in order to define the optimal change approach and select the preferred change team members. In other words, champions need to be able to refine the initial change mandate; i.e. clarify the scope and constraints of the project, negotiate expectations for time, budgets and resources, and define a strategy for managing stakeholder expectations. Providing champions with time to reflect on these issues makes the project mandate SMART: specific, measurable, acceptable, realistic and timely. Our research indicates that organizations with mandates that align *ambitions* with *required resources* are far more successful at completing their projects on time.

Make a project charter

In energized organizations, projects are made official through the use of project charters. SMART charters seal the mutual agreement between the *project champion* and the *project sponsor*. The champion takes ownership for the results that need to be achieved, the sponsor represents top management and commits to providing moral support (e.g. in dealing with resistance to change) and practical support (e.g. budgets, time and resources) to the project. Clear project charters are essential for the announcement of the initiative (connection-with-employees battery) and the arrangement of resources (infrastructure battery).

All this should not imply a lot of paperwork — one A3 page should do. Creating a project charter does require reflection and discussion though. If you feel the 'time and effort' involved in creating a sound charter is not worth it, you might want to ask yourself whether it is worth starting the initiative at all. Failing to answer why, to gain a clear understanding of the scope, and to reach a mutual understanding on low- and high-level leadership commitments, is the perfect recipe for resistance to change. This often results in budget and schedule overruns that exceed the initial efforts it would have taken to create a two-page project charter.

SMART PROJECT CHARTERS

A3 thinking[97], one of the cornerstones of the Toyota Production System, has been adopted by many sectors, including manufacturing, engineering design, and healthcare, to support their lean transformation projects. A3 Reports reduce reporting to its essence (two simple pages presented on a single A3-sized piece of paper). Toyota identified three main structures that provide a common language and a shared mental framework for proposal development, problem-solving and variance reporting.

The following reflects the topics that we see as the critical components of a project charter. Good charters are essential to kick off projects. They bind together sponsor and champion: they are in the same boat. Project charters need to be signed and shared in a public announcement of this partnership. They are important instruments for providing clarity for team members and keeping them focused on common goals. This in turn provides a strong foundation for trust and team-building.

| Start with Why | Project Name |
| Problem or opportunity statement | Sponsor & Project Manager |

Start with Why Problem or opportunity statement	**Project Name** Sponsor & Project Manager
End State Outputs: Performance Indicators: Outcome:	**Team Composition**
	Equipment & Materials **Budget**
Stakeholders	**Timeline**
Strategic Alignment	**Scope and Constraints** **Communication**
	Risks

Bring the right people together

Whereas low-energy organizations depend on heroes who excel in crisis management, smart organizations mobilize the intelligence and energy of a well-trained team.

For this to happen, you first need to get everyone together, working as a team. Getting the right people together is a significant practical challenge in many organizations today. Overly full agendas often don't provide many opportunities to meet as a group. This means that critical people may be missing important meetings, a major obstacle for both team-building and fast decision-making.

Organizations can benefit significantly from bringing teams together for a predetermined time period (e.g. three to five successive days for Kaizen Event Improvement Projects[98], or sprints of one to four weeks in SCRUM software development[99]). This allows the team to focus on the project without interruption and free from their other roles or responsibilities. This also significantly reduces reporting efforts – instead of having to report after, say, six half-day meetings, only one summary report after three days will be needed to capture the main insights and progress of the team. Imagine you could use all the time you spend on reporting and answering emails in between meetings on working on your project with your team...

Find your team a pleasant spot to work from

When you bring your team together, it is important to provide them with a dedicated location or meeting room, a brain center from which they can operate. Successful change focuses on what really matters through the collaboration of people that really matter. This implies employees with different backgrounds working together as a team at the real place (*Gemba*), to work on the real thing (*Genbutsu*) with the real data (*Genjitsu*)[100], following the key principles of the Toyota Production System[101]. The team needs to leave the room to collect data on the shop floor, to talk to customers, etc. But they need to be able to return to their brain center, where they can visibly display the information they gathered and build a shared view of the project and the progress they are making.

Bringing your team together in this way has another important effect: you will start to see relationships growing. Social scientists call this the *law of propinquity*[102]: the amount of information that is shared between individuals decreases exponentially with the distance between these individuals. Despite the proliferation of internet connectivity and social media, social network theories demonstrate that networks still emerge primarily because of *personal contact*. If you want individuals to connect with each other, bringing them together for at least three days is a prerequisite for any team building effort. Be aware though: significant conflicts can surface in this time. This is often great news, though: teams have to go through a 'storming' phase[103]. This brings behavioral tensions to the surface and allows the team to agree on their own standards for collaboration. This is particularly important for cross-functional teams where members are often strongly imprinted by functional or hierarchical patterns. This is even more the case with virtual teams, which often start as a melting pot of different international cultures and habits.

Global companies such as Boeing and Danaher as well as the many car manufacturers and IT companies that switched to agile[104] and SCRUM have experienced the direct benefits of bringing teams together to focus on the issues at hand.

Learn from the Odysseus approach

When you start having frequent team events, you need to avoid these becoming purposeless 'family gatherings' or endless brainstorming sessions. You can do this by bringing *bright energy* to the table. According to RuneScape, a popular medieval fantasy game that virtually connects millions of players around the world, 'bright energy' can be used to create or transmute objects. That is exactly what project teams need to do: invent something new, or significantly transform something that already exists.

We believe this can be achieved if teams use an intelligent approach: an approach that penetrates to the source of problems and that is creative in proposing novel yet stable solutions. We call this the Odysseus approach, in a tribute to the Greek legend renowned for his intellectual brilliance, guile, and versatility, which led to the end of the Trojan War. There are three main ingredients for an Odysseus approach.

Develop solutions based on sound data analysis

First, you need a structured approach that supports teamwork and knowledge generation. If you are working on something that exists, data and fact-finding are essential. No data, no analysis. No analysis, no understanding of how ideas or suggestions can really contribute to solving existing problems. We have seen cases in which, on starting to collect data for a proposed project, it was discovered that there was no problem to solve: just a few unfortunate coincidences that triggered the wrong people to share their worries — end of the discussion. We have seen another group discover that they inherited a problem caused mostly by a different department. The implication? The scope of the project had to be enlarged to include this department, or the project would result in frustration as members were held accountable for areas in which they had no authority. A *structured approach* that helps the team to look at facts and figures is required to identify the root cause of problems. Plans that are based on assumptions will not result in reliable products or accurate estimates of timing and budgets.

Develop solutions based on creativity and experimentation

Second, dare to think out of the box, particularly when you need to develop something new. Be ambitious, make your team start to reflect beyond the quick fix and start to innovate, not renovate. But be realistic at the same time: a business is not a wild adventure. Customer involvement, prototyping and experimentation, value and risk assessment are the key ingredients of an intelligent approach that continuously assesses creative ideas. Run experiments that lead to deep insights into things that matter. We see a lot of organizations that run their projects according to student law: they work on the details while postponing the bigger questions to the end, when they realize there is no more time or budget to dig into these. Ask your team members to evaluate alternatives to understand conflicts and constraints. Looking at the bigger picture from various perspectives will set you up for stable solutions. An intelligent approach creates room for creative reflection.

A plan for a solution is not a solution

Last but not least, you need to come to a solution…. not a plan for a solution. We have seen so many companies fall into this trap: they pull a team of specialists together to analyze the situation, they invest in developing novel solutions, and then they leave the plan to… someone else. Imagine if, after decades of war, Odysseus had presented his idea of the Trojan horse to his fellow Greek leaders saying, "Hey, you know what? I think this might work, but don't count on me to lead the troops in the horse!". We believe there is an added value in making the team that is responsible for analysis and design also accountable for the implementation of their own creation. The Odysseus approach eventually needs to lead to self-managing teams. A step that based on our research seems to be the most difficult one to achieve.

A structured approach that stimulates fact-finding, creativity, teamwork and ownership: we admit that this is far from simple to achieve. It is rather easy to fall into extremes. Some organizations achieve impressive results using the Six Sigma DMAIC (Define, Measure, Analyze, Improve, Control) approach while others have experienced that same approach applied by external specialists to create project monsters while delivering rather trivial solutions. Relying more on creativity may sound attractive to the latter. But without the guidance of a structured approach, this rarely creates buy-in from team members and therefore does not lead to self-managing teams either.

ANALYSIS LEADS TO SUCCESS

An ICT repairs service for the Belgian Armed Forces uses a paper-based process to order parts for IT equipment. Order lead times vary from a few days to several weeks. Several workers argue that this is an outdated way of working and argue to implement a new IT system that automates the procurement process. The cost of the project is significant, and budgets can only be allocated the following year. Many companies tend to propose risky, expensive, long-term based technical solutions that copy fashionable practices from other environments, before gaining a true understanding of the problem at hand and carefully evaluating the alternatives. In a similar way, managers tend to copy practices from previous experiences, without understand the need or appropriateness of this practice in their new context.

High-energy organizations, on the other hand, address the root causes of problems through sound analysis of data. They look for high-impact actions that result in the desired strategic effect, but that also have short implementation lead times. They focus on actions they can implement themselves, not on identifying actions for others to take. In the case of the ICT repairs company, analysis of the lead times of the procurement process revealed that long lead times were mainly driven by errors and missing information in the initial request from the repair workers. Half a day of training of the repairs workers and a weekly coordination meeting of one hour between the purchasing department and the repairs unit reduced the lead times to a maximum of five days: at no cost or risk. Within a few months the repairs unit introduced a visual management system for ordering spare parts that reduced the number of purchasing requests by 50 percent and increased the availability of spare parts from 40 percent to more than 95 percent while at the same time decreasing budgets spent on spare parts.

Enable crystal growth

It ain't over till the fat lady sings. In many organizations, management leaves the opera without listening to the final aria. That is, they neglect the management of the transition from project to process mode. Even if a project can demonstrate initial success, it is critical to anchor change results through the institutionalization of new practices and further orientation of an empowered team. The ultimate success of a project is not evaluated by the achievement of a target at a single moment in time, but rather by the commitment and ownership demonstrated by a team to maintain success and, ideally, to stretch their targets over and over again.

Integrate the new solutions into existing processes and systems

Organizations with fully charged *action planning and implementation batteries* carefully integrate new changes in the process documentation of the organization, and make sure to align future training and recruitment needs with updated job descriptions. This is essential to assure the stability of the newly developed capabilities and particularly important for organizations that face high employee turnover.

The best organizations, however, will go way beyond taking protective measures against performance and knowledge loss. Their ultimate goal is to assure the migration towards self-managing teams that continuously refine according to their context, while identifying obstacles that inhibit the next breakthrough results. Through self-analysis, the documentation of best practices, and the promotion of knowledge sharing, these pockets of change act as crystals that lay the foundation for repeated success. Growing these crystals and systematically connecting them through (social) network structures, is what eventually assures the full implementation of change throughout the organization.

Use visual management instead of thick reports

Self-managing teams typically use visual management to support local reflection and information sharing. While traditional reporting is limited to the essential minimum, it remains critical to embed performance measures and dashboards in the regular reporting systems of the organization as well to assure long-term accountability and ownership. All too often, the results of change and improvement projects ebb away when, near the end of the project, performance reviews fail to be integrated in the regular reporting cycles.

5S AT TOYOTA

5S is an approach developed by Toyota to create a clean, structured and standardized professional environment in five steps: Sort, Select, Shine, Standardize, Strictly adhere. It is arguably currently the most popular improvement instrument to be applied by organizations of various sectors. Whereas the initial performance improvement results from 5S initiatives may not seem of strategic relevance, the shift in behavior that is required by employees as well as low, middle and top management to sustain 5S results make it a valuable instrument to evaluate alignment and support mechanisms throughout the organization. Many organizations, however, struggle to implement the last S ('strictly adhere to the standards of the new environment') as they fail to connect the initiative with the leadership of the organization.

Building on the best practices for 5S identified in the automotive industry, a telecommunications company introduced an approach to support the last step of 5S initiatives through the definition of roles for several management levels. Employees would rotate daily on monitoring adherence to a five-minute rule to keep the work space clean (simple activities everyone can do every day in five minutes or less); supervisors would do a bi-weekly assessment to evaluate actions related to each step (things to evacuate [Sort], to rearrange [Select], to clean [Shine], to standardize) and middle management would plan time to work on specific recommendations from supervisors on a trimester basis. Last but not least, top managers would assist middle managers in a 5S audit every six months. The presence of executive team members turned out to have a strong impact on the buy-in from the bottom groups. Several recommendations from the bottom allowed the organization to more clearly demonstrate the importance of specific customer segments and to define the strategic advantage of specific products and services, while highlighting the costs behind other product and customer segments. This allowed the organization to double their revenue over a period of two years, while turning a losing business in a profitable one.

Key messages of this chapter

Charging the action planning and implementation battery is often more challenging than most organizations assume, as it requires building change capabilities that enable you to (re)build the plane while flying it. Figure 33 summarizes the contrasting factors between an empty and a fully charged battery for action planning and implementation.

Ultimately, this battery generates the energy to convert products and processes, in order to optimize their value while eliminating waste and reducing risks. This requires a thorough understanding of the cause and effect relationships that define the dynamics of organizational processes and systems. The results of good action planning and implementation are effective and efficient changes to the current way of running the business.

This battery also assures that the energy of everyone involved in project or process is used for the right purpose, working on things that matter from a customer, business or stakeholder perspective. It brings the right people together in time and place so that they can reach consent (not necessarily consensus) through the use of a structured approach that encourages analysis, experimentation and the evaluation of alternatives. This implies getting your hands dirty — bringing potential solutions to the shop floor and the (pilot) customer.

In theory, many of these approaches can be summarized to the sound application of the Deming cycle — Plan, Do, Check, Act. In practice however, many organizations use a PDCA cycle with exponentially decreasing attention paid to each step: PDcᴀ. The secret of fully charged organizations is that they have stretched the Deming cycle to a PDCACA–PDCACA approach: big improvement steps that are altered with continuous refinements, until deep understanding and reflection create transparency for a next big step.

A fully charged action planning and implementation battery protects you against projects that never end. Sound analysis is critical, but "a good plan vigorously executed now, may be better than a perfect plan tomorrow". This quote from General Patton aligns best with lean kaizen events and agile sprints that practice time boxing (what valuable action can be implemented within the available time period?) instead of scope boxing (how much time do I need to cover the implementation of the full scope?). This provides for many organizations a welcome alternative to create balance between *reflect* and *do*, and *build* and *run* the business.

An empty action planning battery	A charged action planning battery
FROM...	TO...
More is better	Insist on why, who, when
You have it	Clear project charters
Herculean solutions	Team events
Big Bang implementations	The Odysseus approach
Sunrise followed by sunset	Crystal growth

Figure 33 · Empty versus charged batteries for action planning and implementation

Figure 33 summarizes the key elements to get the action planning and implementation battery fully charged. How do you assure action planning and implementation delivers the physical energy to efficiently transform actions into benefits and capabilities? Our main recommendations include:

- Start with why. Encouraging your workers to take action is not enough — assure the relevance of your initiatives while keeping the end in mind.

- Develop an A3 project charter. This creates a strong handshake between the champion who is accountable for the results, and the sponsor, who assures the availability of time and resources.

- Organize team events. Provide your team with a place where they can jointly focus on the project for a couple of days without interruption. Promote teamwork, not heroism.

- Invest in a flexible methodology. Stable solutions are the result of data analysis, creativity and experimentation, but also of coaching and ownership.

- Embed the results in an environment of self-managing teams. Sustainable initiatives assess their own performance to identify the next challenge.

Chapter

7

A STRONG CONNECTION WITH EMPLOYEES

———

The psychological energy

Key questions

Why does it pay off to build strong connections with your people?

How can you keep people enthusiastic about change and reinforce their commitment?

How can you communicate clearly so that your people really understand what you mean?

How can you handle resistance?

People are tired of change. How do you handle this?

HOW WELL IS *YOUR* CONNECTION BATTERY CHARGED?

Tick whether you agree or disagree with each of the following statements.

		AGREE	DISAGREE
1	In our organization, everyone feels the change, but nobody really knows where it leads to.		
2	Our organization sees employees merely as means to improve performance, not as persons behind the function.		
3	We actively engage employees in change initiatives that impact them.		
4	Our employees experience a daily reality that contradicts with the main messages sent by managers.		
5	Our change approach includes education and training in project and process management for employees.		
6	Leaders spend a significant amount of time coaching employees on the floor.		
7	We communicate frequently about change and openly share information related to change initiatives.		
8	In our organization, people feel appreciated for their change efforts.		

Give yourself one point each time you agreed with the following statements:

3   5   6   7   8

Give yourself one point each time you disagreed with the following statements:

1   2   4

What is your total score on eight?

INTERPRETING YOUR RESULT

Score	Implications
0-2	Your connection battery is empty as you neglect the psychological aspects of change. Your employees need to be supported in the overall change program, but your organization neglects some of the basic processes in committing your employees to the change. As a result, we believe your employees will resist your change initiatives, rather than embracing them.
3-4	Your connection battery is weak. It's great that you see your employees as more than just 'resources', but what do you do to engage and support them in their change journey? We are afraid the answer is: not enough.
5-6	Your connection battery generates psychological energy; there is a sufficient level of trust between managers and employees and your people are encouraged to embrace the change. Pay sufficient attention to support your people in their individual change journey and don't forget to praise and recognize them for their change efforts.
7-8	Your connection battery is a strength to leverage in the change program. Your organization has paid a lot of attention to building a committed workforce. You communicate well, you support with training, and you recognize and reward well.

Spark for reflection:
ING changes change management[105]

In early 2008, the Dutch retail-banking unit of ING Group merged its two previously separate banking units in the Netherlands: ING Bank and Postbank. The two units had been sister companies for a long time, but the top team at ING Group believed it was time to integrate them. This was an uncommon merger: the merger of two units within the same group with similar operating models and the same overarching cultural traits. The top team realized that the complexity of this process should not be underestimated. Decisions that in more conventional mergers would be assessed more objectively were at risk of being taken for granted.

The top team of the new (merged) unit worked out an ambitious plan for the future and built a strong program where emphasis was placed on executional certainty. That meant transparency around each specific program in the program portfolio as well as around the overall effort. The company had implemented a rule-based traffic-lights system to categorize a roadmap's progress against completion of milestones.

The rigor in the program was complemented by an equally strong effort to build an enabled and engaged organization. The senior management of the new bank knew the value of crystal-clear communication and crafted an overarching story for the logic of the merger. They emphasized that change would not happen overnight: it would be a three-year journey, during which the bank would invest a lot in helping employees adapt to the new situation.

Managers invested a lot of time in translating the new values of the company and the new behaviors into what an employee would experience every day. Managers got structured training toolkits to help their employees craft their own change-behavior plans. A 'ready, willing and able' poll was introduced to learn more about employees readiness and willingness for change. At the same time, ING created buzz with creative internal marketing campaigns. Some of the programs involved pictures of behaviors that employees were invited to judge as 'hot' or 'not' — that is, 'in' or 'out' of compliance with the expected behaviors. Each month, website users voted for that month's best picture. The company also repeated the key messages in magazines, online interviews, video clips and many more communication channels.

The role of connecting with employees in change management

Regardless of the size of your organization and the number of employees effected by your initiative, ultimately, changing organizations implies *changing people*.[106] This type of individual change is deeply personal and happens one person at a time. Each individual has to let go of old behaviors to learn new ones. This transition can be an unpleasant, sometimes painful experience for the individual. However, as individual resistance against change grows, it often becomes a painful experience for the organization as well. If ultimately the individual doesn't come to fully commit to the change and experiencing the benefits of the change, change is very often going to behave like a sponge ball: it plops back into its original state as soon as any external pressure is off it.

Organizations implementing change regularly underestimate the extent, timescale and complexity of the efforts needed by their leaders and managers to overcome resistance and to build commitment. Anxious, uncertain, overwhelmed, confused or ignored, people don't feel good and will have little commitment to the proposed change. In fact, the only change they will be in favor of is a change in leadership.

Characteristics of an empty connection battery

The tension of silent energy: The calm before the storm

Everyone 'feels' something needs to be done, and you can tell from the number of meetings of managers that something big is about to happen, especially if there is a tendency not to share news. Suddenly the storm breaks. Bad news is shared: globalization, increased competition, financial drawbacks. A major restructuring is inevitable. The underlying message: seek shelter or get drenched.

The rain hits everyone at the same time: "You all received our two-page leaflet earlier today. This afternoon there will be an official press release. In the following days, more details will be shared with the representatives of key stakeholders." Communication about the future of the company is infrequent and all top-down. As such, the future remains uncertain to everyone else for a long time.

🔋 Directive energy generation: *Befehl ist Befehl*

Everyone in your organization recognizes the lack of people orientation. Every message communicated starts from *the company's perspective*: why it is difficult to make more profit, why we should work more on quality to beat the competition, why it is necessary to centralize to become more lean and mean. There is hardly ever a perspective that starts from the people's view. As a result, people feel misunderstood and are demotivated.

Companies don't put any effort into trying to understand, let alone handle, the short-term consequences of the change for the employees:

- 🔋 Humans are seen as resources for performance. They are money-making machines.

- 🔋 People management is actually function management. An individual is the function he or she has and the tasks and agreed upon outcomes. No one really cares about the person behind the function.

- 🔋 Change messages are fact based, delivered by distant spokespersons.

If the company does not know how to handle the short-term emotional needs of its people, they feel misunderstood, (ab)used and disconnected.

Organizations sometimes try to compensate for this by developing very detailed plans: "It's all in the manual, so if you carefully read through the instructions everything will be crystal clear." In fact, you just have to follow the guideline: 'Just do it'. Unfortunately, too many details in plans and a '*manu-militari*' approach for execution leave people disengaged and make them puppets of a system that tries to control everything.

It is amazing to see how much time the senior executives themselves need to go through the various stages of individual change, from denial over resistance and exploration, to commitment (Figure 34, The famous Kübler-Ross Change Curve, is a model consisting of the various levels or stages of emotions which are experienced by a person going through a phase of change). Once top management has seen the light, however, they often expect their employees to graciously accept the change based on simple, rational announcements. Obviously, that's not how it works.

Executives and senior managers are the first to understand that change is needed. That is often a difficult process for them. They will go through the same phases of coping with change and loss as we all do, but the impact on their motivation and energy is lower as they have more control and authority, and are closer to the sources of information. When the senior managers understand something is wrong and start thinking about recipes for change, the middle management is still in the phase of denial. They don't understand why their bosses are suddenly anxious and nervous. Only after some time does middle management also start to see the need for change. The same process occurs between middle management and the rest of the organization. There is a staggered shift between the groups in these phases of coping with change. And the more change is imposed on people, the stronger the negative impact on their energy and motivation.

What happens next? Senior level has come to the phase of acceptance. They know why and how to move ahead. They are convinced of the path to follow. Roadshows are organized. Corporate communication is set up. Change agents are lined up. The majority of the organization, however, still feels demotivated and confused, as they haven't had time to 'grieve' for their losses. Senior management does not understand why the company does not move. They blame their people for being unwilling, resistant and unfit for the new world.

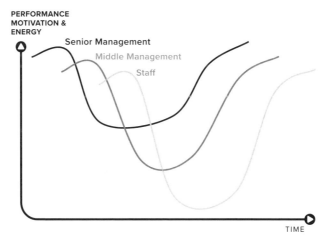

Figure 34 • Kübler-Ross' shift of change experienced by different hierarchical level

---

 Energy of selling and telling

All too often, employees experience a daily reality that does not align with the headlines of the messages sent by their managers. Executives hold their wishes and desired situation as real. They act from their ivory towers and don't realize what is really happening on the floor. They face a distorted reality.

If that's the case, there will be mistrust between the people at the top and those underneath them. Actions are therefore more important than words. Even if managers have good intentions, people's perceptions are driven by what actions are put in place. In many organizations, however, talk is cheap. Nothing triggers employee cynicism more than when supervisors and managers don't practice what they preach:

- They talk about entrepreneurship, but kill every idea even before it has been tested.

- They promote open communication, but more often than not, the doors are closed, the agenda is full and the discussions are (too) short.

- They talk customer orientation, but did not visit any of their customers for the last six months because there were higher-priority items on the list.

When there is disconnect between the message and the reality, cynicism will fester and grow. Initiatives stall and frustration increases.

Fading energy: silent resistance

Decisions need to be made fast and top managers assume that if nobody raises an issue, everyone supports the change. You could argue that in principle this is not a bad thing, but in practice this way of going faster actually slows an organization down when implementing the change. There are plenty of popular ways to assure acceptance by silence. A meeting on Friday afternoon, a briefing in a big room with representatives of all departments (who dares to speak up?), a complex thick report sent to your employees who are already overloaded by work or emails. There are many ways to avoid true involvement.

The problem with this approach is that you don't get to understand the true sources of resistance. People who go silent on feedback often go silent on execution. In the worst case, this can lead to them only doing what they are told, intentionally strict adherence to the instructions — even the errors — and escalating every problem to superiors. Some employees may even decide to simply neglect the change and hypothesize that it applies to others. Not being able to handle these 'rebels' can be a major burden and obstacle for keeping employees that struggle with the change motivated. We mentioned them briefly in chapter 5 on the culture battery: BOHICA people have a motto of 'Bend Over Here It Comes Again'. They will not resist; they will give no feedback. Once you turn your back, they will turn to their old habits again.

One shot energy: fire and forget

Many studies show that a high percentage of employees confirm that they get no or very little recognition for their efforts. Confront company managers with these figures and most will become defensive. They have the conviction that their employees are recognized and praised. But when looking in more detail, the high-performers and the big achievers are in the spotlight. Often these achievements are linked with directly or indirectly bringing in money. The more modest achievers are left out.

Some recognition *might* occur after reaching certain objectives, but it lasts only as long as the project. There is little support for self-development or encouragement for new initiatives.

Overview of dischargers

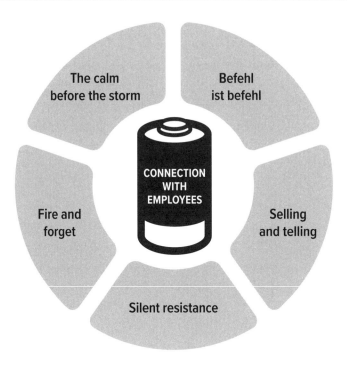

Figure 35 • Why your action planning and implementation battery is empty

If your organization shows several of the characteristics mentioned above, your connection battery lacks energy to support individual change. You fail to provide sufficient psychological energy for your organization. Even if you believe you have a sound plan that makes perfect sense, nobody is ready to follow your lead.

The connection battery and change effectiveness: What does our research say?

Successful transformers use their connection battery differently than unsuccessful transformers. Figure 36 shows that companies with a high change effectiveness score significantly better on four of the five elements of our connection battery.

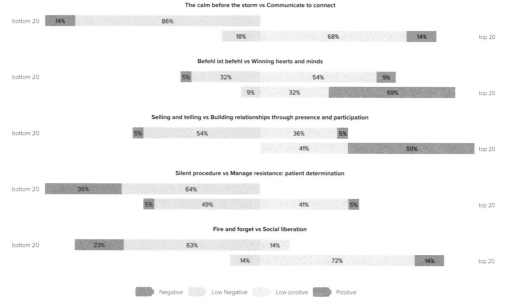

Figure 36 • Connection scores for successful and unsuccessful transformers

There is a significant difference between successful and unsuccessful transformers in *communication*. Successful transformers pay more attention to empathic storytelling. Their senior managers also support individual transitions with their presence and participation. As in the ING case study in the introduction of this chapter, they coach more, give more time to digest the change, appreciate employees for their change efforts, and create an environment where people are stimulated to embrace change.

Unsuccessful transformers score low on most of these elements. The 'winning hearts and minds' dimension is the biggest exception. But demonstrating compassion and support, or even welcoming participation, is unfortunately not enough when initiatives start off cold and lack determination and reinforcement near the end.

How to charge the connection battery?

In theory it is rather easy to connect to the whole world. Just by reaching out to friends of your friends, you can get introduced to the seven billion people on our planet in less than seven steps. Which does not mean you *want* to actively connect to everyone. When it comes to true friends, the people that we completely trust and actively want to share our life with, most of us will report far less impressive numbers.

In a similar way, you can rather easily share the news of a new change initiative with all your employees. A simple 'copy all' would do for that. Unfortunately this is insufficient to develop strong connections that can drive change. We see a lot of organizations that fail to connect the change in behavior required by their employees to the change that they have in mind for their organization. To overcome this obstacle, we developed a model that synthesizes several insights from the dominant theories on individual and social behavioral change. They can be easily memorized as '*smaller steps enable the steepest success*' (see Figure 37).

Although these insights don't necessarily need to be tacked in a sequential way, we have brought them together in *five essential steps* that gradually strengthen the tie between the individual and the organization. These steps align well with what most people will experience when they go through their own process of how to cope with change. You will notice that whereas the first steps have a stronger focus on messages that support individual change, the last steps rely more on mechanisms that promote success to drive social change.

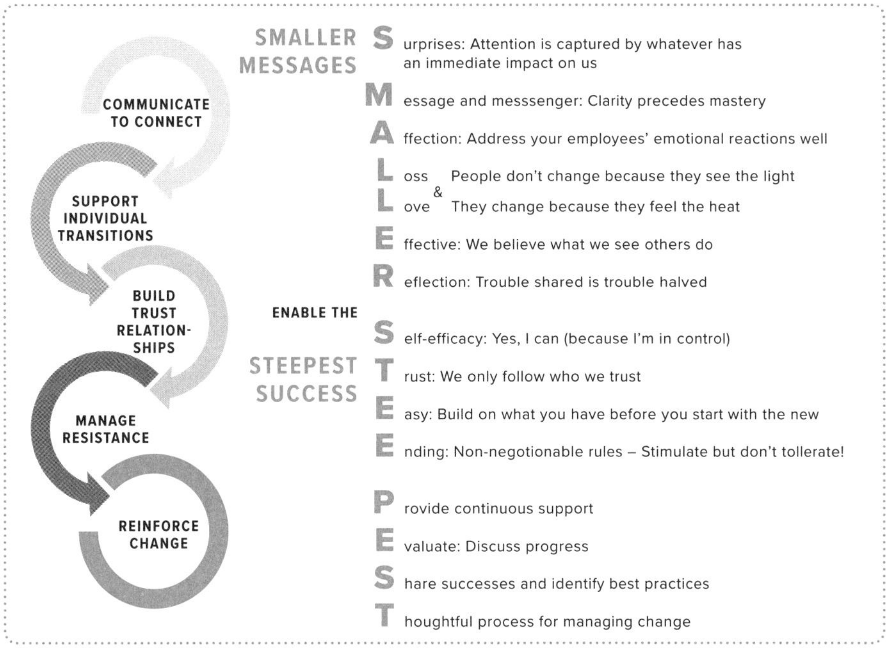
COMMUNICATE TO CONNECT
SUPPORT INDIVIDUAL TRANSITIONS
BUILD TRUST RELATION-SHIPS
MANAGE RESISTANCE
REINFORCE CHANGE
SMALLER MESSAGES
ENABLE THE
STEEPEST SUCCESS
S urprises: Attention is captured by whatever has an immediate impact on us
M essage and messsenger: Clarity precedes mastery
A ffection: Address your employees' emotional reactions well
L oss People don't change because they see the light
&
L ove They change because they feel the heat
E ffective: We believe what we see others do
R eflection: Trouble shared is trouble halved
S elf-efficacy: Yes, I can (because I'm in control)
T rust: We only follow who we trust
E asy: Build on what you have before you start with the new
E nding: Non-negotionable rules – Stimulate but don't tollerate!
P rovide continuous support
E valuate: Discuss progress
S hare successes and identify best practices
T houghtful process for managing change

Figure 37 • Smaller steps enable the steepest success – Strengthening the tie between the individual and the organization

Communicate to connect

Surprises: attention is captured by whatever has an immediate impact on us

A crisis or a burning platform can be an important driver for top leaders to charge the top team battery. In a similar way, the rest of the organization also needs a wake up call that captures their full attention, before they will even consider revising their intention to change. All too often, change leaders use the wrong wake-up call. When talking about the challenges to overcome, managers try to create a sense of urgency by showing the organization's pain. Declining margins, loss of market share, increased competition... Unfortunately, people are not engaged or motivated to integrate the change based on the 'pain' of their employer. It often needs more 'personalization' for people to feel the urge to change.

Attention is captured by whatever has an immediate impact on us. When you communicate, make sure you use examples of 'Why we need to change' that are linked to people in your audience. Use real cases that resonate. Let's say your organization has to become more customer centric and entrepreneurial. From an organizational point of 'pain' you could argue that this is needed 'to sustain the company's market position'. Most employees will not, however, be motivated for behavioral change by this argument only. Especially not when they can do their job in a comfortable situation, with good salaries, bonus systems and long years of experience.

But suppose that Eric, the product manager, is in the audience. Eric has this great talent of being an excellent team leader and inspiring innovator. Moreover, working with people and leading a team is a *conditio sine qua non* for Eric in order to feel appreciated and to feel proud of the job he is doing. What if you used statements like this: "We need to become more entrepreneurial in the coming years. Why? Because we want to sustain the company's market position, and because we want to ensure that people like Eric [pointing at Eric in a friendly way], who are experts in their field, still have the chance to work together with teams to stay motivated and be ahead of technology and trends, so that they can remain the leader and the expert they have always been."

A mere mentioning of some of the talents and important values of people can make a difference. In large audiences, we recommend you pick out some participants, or use personalized statements that apply to most people in the audience. Just make sure you do not restrict yourself to the organizational perspective alone.

Message and messenger: clarity precedes mastery

To assess the seriousness of the announcement, people often look to the name(s) of the messenger(s). Most of us are heavily influenced by the originator of the message and expect in general that big changes come from big chiefs. To assess the feasibility of the next steps, however, people like to read the response of their direct superiors as well. We tend to be very sensitive to misalignments between messages that come from different levels, which we generally take as a clear encouragement to 'wait and see'.

Make sure the messages from your leaders are aligned throughout the company. *One message, one voice.* Make sure you know what people have heard and understood. Managers often think that communication is only about information sharing — this couldn't be further from the truth. All human beings filter received information or they simply forget. Your people will capture only a fragment of the information sent. The message here is: *force clarity!* Make sure everyone walks out of the room with the same, clear messages. Don't be afraid to ask some of your employees to summarize what they have heard. You will be surprised by the answers. Even if all seems clear at the end of the meeting, keep your finger on the pulse, as your connection might fade over time due to less focus and the noise of the day.

TIP: LEARN TO DOWNCHUNK

Many managers prefer to speak in 'up-chunked' language — generic language, with lots of buzz words that sound intelligent and right, but have little call to action. The advantage of up-chunked language is that it does not require you to think and that it rarely leads to conflict.

Using 'down-chunked' language requires you to make choices and become concrete and factual. You can do this by using words on bodily functions and senses like 'see', 'hear', 'do', 'touch', which makes things more clear for the listener.

- Example of *up-chunked* language: "You need to communicate more on our corporate strategy and get them all aligned as soon as possible". There is little chance of creating conflict with this statement, but it has no call to action.

- The *down-chunked* version: "I will organize a half-day meeting every Friday from now on and have you prepare your version of what you understood from our corporate strategy. We will then create one version, acceptable to all of you, by the end of June." There is more chance of conflict here (why Friday?, why a half day?, I don't have time to prepare, June is too soon), but expectations are clearer and there is a call to action.

Attend any meeting and you are bound to hear up-chunked language most of the time.

When you communicate about change, don't leave your people in the dark. Be transparent about what you've done, what you're doing, and what you will do. It gives people more comfort, knowing what is going to happen, and if you deliver on your promises, you build credibility as a change leader. Be honest, too. Acknowledge ugly truths of daily problems and challenges that everyone is noticing. Hiding the truth, trying to minimalize, or even worse, ignoring the pain is counterproductive. It creates distance instead of connection. Underpromise, and overdeliver.

Affection: address your employees' emotional reactions well

To show affection for everyone who is impacted by the change, it is a good idea to leave time for employees to personalize the message themselves. True connection comes from deep interactions and respects the emotional triggers that are initiated by change.

In contrast, when people are *urged* to change, they generally start to point a finger or they pick up the gloves and start to fight ("If I am going to be hit, you will be hit too!"). You may be familiar with the popular quote: "No one likes change but babies in diapers". Yet even babies expect *you* to do the dirty work.

How you deal with the reactions of your people is crucial. It's important not to dismiss them because "these are only emotional reactions". Some of the ideas that arise from this initial emotional response may be valuable for future steps, others may need to be repositioned, giving you clarity on what can or cannot be expected ahead. Be sure also to articulate what will *not* change. This type of stability management is essential to address destructive fear that is driven by speculation and tends to start in the coffee corner following the initial announcement. These rumors may find their way to social media too, where they can do even more harm.

Support individual transitions

Bad communication is one of the main reasons people resist change. Although a good start, it is not enough to show people the need for change and to point to a brighter future for the organization. You have to support each person to reflect on *their* future and path ahead. You need to win the hearts and minds of everyone. Here are our recommendations to do this well.

Loss and love: people don't change because they see the light. They change because they feel the heat

All human beings want to avoid pain and achieve pleasure. Because pain is perceived by the brain as a threat, we will feel an intense reaction. We all have moments in which we become afraid, or angry or sad about things that we cannot control. We will generally do what we can to avoid this state or to get rid of it. We want to survive, and for as long as possible. This is an important message for managing individual change.

People do not like losing anything that is currently important to support their needs; they want to hold on to what they have. Change often involves letting go, whether completely or partly. Change is painful for most of us. It creates uncertainty, then fear; it may lead to sadness when things are not evolving as we expected, or anger if we lose control over our lives or when a sense of injustice builds up.

In those moments, what people need to overcome their emotional barriers is not long speeches with 'convincing' arguments. They need support to deal with their pain. As a leader, you are not always in a position to take away your people's pain. But there are some ways within your circle of influence that can alleviate the pain for your employee. It's the small things that make the difference; small tokens of appreciation ('love') for the human being behind the function.

How can you incorporate understanding, compassion and emotional presence in practice?

- Discover what people are passionate about. Get to know what they love to do, at work or outside of it. Look how you can incorporate these passions or interests into your story of change.

- Be a psychologist. Talk to the human being behind the function and personalize the message. Familiarize yourself with their results of a personality profiling test (Insights, MBTI, DISC, HBDI, COSI, etc.). Dare to tackle their emotions: get their fear, frustration, passion, beliefs on the table. Help your people have a better view of the situation. Let them do self-assessments of the situation, 'simply' listen.

Interact. Strong relationships are built on the combination of frequent engagement, time spent together and deep interaction. Spend time talking about things other than business-related projects. Get to know them better. You might also discover what emotional barriers are making it difficult for them to embrace the change.

Effective: we believe what we see others do

People are more open to doing what they have seen is effective elsewhere. They are more open to change if others are doing it too. Bearing this in mind, it can be helpful to use practical illustrations, even if these come from other departments or organizations, to stimulate reflection on your proposed change program. This can help employees assess the technical and organizational issues behind the change. Even more importantly, it also helps them to assess their own capabilities within regard to the proposed change. This will allow them to determine the level of personal success or failure that they link to the projected change. Conclusions about this easily translate into emotional behavior. Whether this turns into tears of joy or tears of anger is less important: what matters is that people are no longer denying the change.

We also believe what we can *experience* ourselves. Make change a *sensory* experience, rather than just talking about it. Research suggests that our limbic system (emotions) is stronger than our cortex system (rationality) when it comes to driving behavior for change. John Kotter, Harvard professor and change guru, argues that see-feel-change is often more effective than think-analyze-change.[107] Provide illustrations, pictures and, if possible, allow your people to speak to employees that have been through the desired change. That will be more efficient than boring PowerPoint slides.

Reflection: trouble shared is trouble halved

Humans are social beings, community creatures. We want to share our feelings, fears and ideas. We need to feel that we are all in this together and we love support and feedback from our colleagues. However, sharing is a dynamic process. We build, rebuild and change the informal networks in our personal and professional lives. Managers who succeed in seeing and using these networks, bringing people within them together to reflect and share, will create strong support groups for behavioral change. Good relationships are essential to keep employees motivated.

Self-efficacy: yes, I can (because I am in control)!

Change often means employees have to adopt new skills. Employees resist change not only because they fail to see the need for change, but also because they fail to move. Movement is unlikely until employees plainly see a promising path to competence.[108] As a manager, how do you pave that path for your employees?

The best way to figure out what the change brings for your people is for them to try it. People generally put more trust in changes they have tried themselves, possibly on a smaller scale. They also more actively support change that hosts their own ideas. As a result, it is important to leave room for co-creation to avoid the common 'not invented here' syndrome, whereby people reject suitable external solutions to problems in favor of solutions they invented themselves. Experimentation, of course, introduces risk. What if this key pilot project fails? What will the response of our sponsor, change manager or champion be if I am not able to deliver what they expect? Reassuring answers to these questions are crucial to assure experimentation in a 'safe' environment under the guidance of trustworthy leaders and coaches. If employees succeed in the experiments, this leads to high levels of self-efficacy with regard to the change.

Self-efficacy is the confidence we have in our ability to achieve intended results. It's an important driver of *individual readiness to change*. There are several ways to increase the self-efficacy of your people, but the most important is to start small. Use micro-bites to finish the big meal. Give a lot of feedback, review past successes, make the success visible, and provide good coaching.

Trust: we only follow those we trust

Creating self-efficacy among your employees is key to getting them committed to change. For an organization to move into transformation, employees also need to have an acceptable level of trust, or rather: *no distrust.*

Talking about trust in a professional environment, we mostly refer to the trust that people put into their leaders. With an acceptable level of trust, employees are willing to take risks, even when this scares them. It's important to know *how you can build trust.* Below is a 'formula' from David Maister, former Harvard professor and expert on business management practices, that presents what they believe to be the key dimensions of trust.[109] This model was developed to help teach professionals how to build deep relationships with their customers. We've adapted their model to help change leaders build better relationships with their people.

$$T = \left(\frac{C + R + I}{S}\right) + H$$

T = Trustworthiness

This is the ability to be relied on as authentic, honest and truthful. It's the trust your people have in you as a change leader.

C = Credibility

People love to feel secure. People will assess your credibility based on what you say and how you present yourself. Credibility is achieved when you're accurate, believable, and honest. It's okay too, to show them that you are highly capable — consider sharing testimonials from other teams or professionals.

R = Reliability

Say what you do, do what you say. Behave in consistent ways. If you make promises, deliver on them, quietly, and on time. Always communicate changes in agendas, action plans, timing and expectations. Reliability is heavily discredited when people are confronted with unexpected news that put them in a difficult situation. As a leader, ask for feedback and also accept spontaneous feedback as a gift that allows you to consider your actions and behavior.

I = Intimacy

Listen, properly. Ask questions. First seek to understand before seeking to be understood. Understand what matters to people and try to integrate that into your leadership style as much as possible. Be interested in the details of the other person's life. When your team member tells you that his youngest daughter is taking her piano exam this week, enquire after her when you next run into him. (Watch out: get the details right or you will sabotage your efforts to be attentive and interested.) Intimacy is also daring to be vulnerable. Share personal stuff in an honest way. People need to be able to read you, both physically (your body language) and psychologically. Though hiding your shortcomings might appear to make you look stronger initially, it undermines your trustworthiness in the long run.

S = **Self-orientation**

Make sure you do not have a hidden agenda. Talking genuinely about your credentials is fine. Bragging is not. Neither is always trying to be right, always wanting to have the last word, or taking credit for achievements that were a team effort. You get the picture: don't make it all about you. Make time for the things that are valuable for your people.

H = **History awareness**

The journey called life brings us myriad insights, experiences, successes and failures, which all shape our beliefs, values, norms and assumptions, and affect the way we look at the world, at other people. Our life experiences are filtered in the brain according to internal representation systems. For example, you might only trust someone if you receive the right signals according to your personal belief system. The better you understand another's background and history — and the more you share yours — the better you will be able to connect and find common areas within each other's belief systems, which increases feelings of trust.

Create stability and manage resistance

Once the fundamentals of the change have been figured out, and experiments or pilot studies have demonstrated the feasibility and acceptability of solutions, many organizations claim victory. In reality the battle is just beginning. You have built the car — now you need to build the assembly line that will make your whole organization successful.

Aristotle taught us: "We are what we repeatedly do. Excellence then, is not an act, but a habit." Unfortunately, it is difficult to change habits and easy to fall back into the old ones. Still, there has been extensive research on making new habits stick and below is a summary of our recommendations for implementing patient but determined 'resistance management'.

Easy: build on what you have before you start with the new

You can increase the odds of inspiring real and lasting behavioral change if you harness the power of *stability management*. We believe that stability management is as important as change management to charge your connection battery, your battery of *psychological change*. In reality, 'quick' change mostly ends up going very slowly. Trying to rush change after change tends to turn out badly. Not only do people get tired of change, but they also feel that every day feels like a challenge now. They start resisting the new approaches, trying to protect the stability of their working lives.

We are strong believers in 'organizational silence': moments in between (intense) change projects when the organization has time to institutionalize the new behaviors, systems and structures.

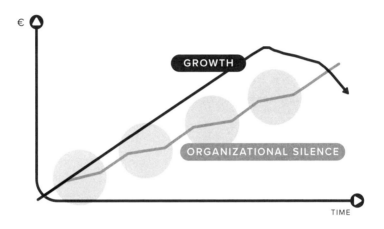

Figure 38 • The importance of organizational silence

Figure 38 illustrates these ideal organizational 'pauses'. Instead of rushing the change (which will lead to stress, burnout and, quite likely, failure), we integrate moments of 'silence', when the organization goes back to mostly 'business as usual'. In the long run, this approach will lead to a healthier culture, more engaged employees, and more sustainable results. It's like holding a glass of water with a stretched arm — easy to do for 30 seconds, but a hell of a job if you have to do it for an hour. Yet organizations consistently insist on relentlessly pursuing change and end up struggling with implementation due to the endless number of initiatives that need to be implemented one after the other. The organization forces its people to keep their arms stretched all time, until the effect on their physical and psychological health becomes unbearable.

How to put all this in practice? In explaining your change project, tell your people *what stays the same* in addition to what is changing. It's a natural mistake: you want change to happen in the organization, so you talk about change. However, studies have shown that people are more motivated to continue an effort or reach an objective when you are able to create the feeling of 'progress' rather than 'starting from scratch'.[110] You create an impression of the latter when you talk only about what will change. People begin to feel that they have to start all over again and throw away everything they've done. Getting this right is not so difficult — use the table in Figure 39 in your change discussion, focusing on particular topics (in this instance, more customer centricity in the organization). Much to the delight of your employees, the list on the left will generally be longer than the one on the right, enhancing the feeling that the change is "a value-add to our business as usual". Doing this will also help you as a manager to reflect on the business as a whole, forcing you to clarify and list all aspects of the topic at hand.

NEW APPROACH TO CUSTOMER CENTRICITY	
What stays the same?	What will be different?

Figure 39 • Stability management: Talk about what will stay the same as well as what will be different

It is important to remember that (most of) your employees will prefer to stick to the skills they have been using for years — yes, even if they know these skills are no longer relevant or valuable. Make sure you invest enough time into supporting your employees to become competent in the new situation. Allow them to decide when they feel competent — not you! People like to have some form of control over what is happening to them. When you do not connect your change efforts to what your people have already been doing, they will quickly lose interest and fall back on previous habits. You have to create clear links to what people *do* know and *can* do.

Ending: NNRs, the Non-Negotiable Rules

Change is all about people. If *they* don't change their behavior, nothing significant changes. This transition from 'ending' to a 'new beginning'– letting go of the old behavior and moving into the new – happens one person at a time, day after day. You can't just snap your fingers and hope the switch happens.

Employees need to be supported to adopt good behavior, but they also need clear signs for bad behavior. They need to understand the criteria and consequences for acting badly. We call these criteria NNRs, Non-Negotiable Rules, a set of criteria that you agree on in advance as being clear boundaries between appropriate and inappropriate behavior. Think about traffic rules: going over the speed limit might feel justified if you need to urgently get to the hospital for your sick mother, but a judge will fall back on an NNR, because *the law is the law*.

Change cannot be successful without clear NNRs. However, we often see managers applying these when things go belly-up, without ever having achieved a consensus on the rules and their consequences if broken. This approach will only create resistance and a feeling of injustice. So how do you introduce NNRs? And what do you do if a high performer – let's call her Linda, a competent and well-respected 45-year-old country manager – breaks a NNR?

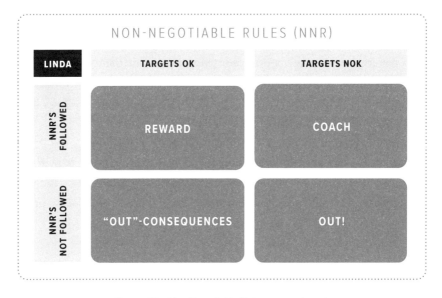

Figure 40 • Non-Negotiable Rules versus targets

Figure 40 shows the various options and outcomes that leaders have put forward. In our case, Linda is in the lower-left quadrant: performing well, but not playing within the boundaries of the NNRs. We all agree that turning a blind eye because Linda is, after all, performing, will have negative consequences. It won't be long before her colleagues follow her example. So what's the solution here?

First, after you've talked about the change project, introduce the NNRs in a meeting and explain which criteria are non-negotiable and why. For example:

> From 1 October, we will not accept any reporting done in the old system. Only reports generated with the new system will be valid and accepted. Reason is that we don't want two systems with information sitting in both of them.

> Every pitch in front of the client will need to have a presentation of our new digital platform. Reason is that we want to promote working digitally with are customers as well.

> Every Monday morning from 8:30 to 9:30, we will have a project meeting. No excuses other than emergency personal crises will be accepted. The reason is that it is crucial that we see each other at least once a week, and this is the only moment when it is possible.

Second, communicate these NNRs to your team and discuss them. Allow your people to ask questions and give feedback, even to adapt within reason (for example, meeting on Friday may work better for everyone). Make sure you have buy-in from your team members.

Third, set up a meeting shortly afterwards — the NNR meeting needs to be fresh in their minds — to check the NNRs have been understood in detail. Set up individual or team meetings, depending on what is more appropriate. If you decide on one-on-one meetings, ask these kinds of questions:

> *What do we agree upon as a consequence/outcome if you have reached the agreed upon targets and followed the NNRs?* (Employees should have a clear idea of the rewards of this path.)

What do we agree upon as a consequence if after sufficient feedbacks/comment/warning, you still have not followed the NNRs? The answer may surprise you! For example, people tend to give themselves more severe consequences for not reaching a committed goal than what you would give them.

We recommend writing these NNRs down and making sure all parties have a copy. You may want employees to sign the document – though be aware that some employees may find this petty, which can undermine the process.

Above all, make sure you act consistently on these NNRs and their co-created consequences. If you refrain from following up, you will lose all credibility.

Leaders should be sensitive to people's resistance to change efforts, but not tolerate a refusal to change. Stimulate, but don't tolerate. In the end, clear endings occasionally imply ending relationships. Members who, after repeated coaching and guidance, don't manage to change their behaviors may need to be excluded from the team, and perhaps be placed elsewhere. When someone refuses to play, it makes no sense to keep them on the field.

Reinforce change

Like culture, engagement is not something you just 'fix'. It is a long-term process that can only be successful if the whole organization is involved. You need to work on it every day, bit by bit, measuring your impact and results along the way. Here are some guidelines to getting there.

Provide continuous support

Profound change means that employees need enough time to learn new skills and adopt the new behaviors. To prevent your people from becoming tired and feeling lost, you will need to offer support and coaching – not just from top managers, but also from local change champions.[111] Your local change champions must ensure that the change is drilling down to every part of the organization. They act as role models for the new behaviors and ensure that individuals apply the change in their area. Local change champions are crucial to make the link between the strategic change objectives and the work done on the floor. Top managers tend not to spend enough time building a network of local change sponsors and supporting them in their coaching activities.

Committed local champions are essential for translating the organizational purpose into something that is tangible and personal for adapters-to-be. They identify where the change projects gain or lose traction, and ultimately drive change success. Do you know who the local change champions are in each key area of your organization? Do you know who people turn to for advice, or which colleagues they consider friends in times of distress?

Evaluate: discuss progress

Continuous feedback is important, and it must happen in both directions. Ensure that employees have the opportunity to receive feedback from their management team, coaches and co-workers on a frequent basis. Remember: we do what others do. But we need to know what others are doing, and how they perceive us and what we are doing. Feedback can (and should) be both positive and negative. "You did this well" as well as "you can do this better". Constant feedback allows everyone to make improvements in real time. Many companies offer feedback sessions annually or bi-annually, which may allow poor habits to become entrenched and motivating effects of positive feedback to wear off. Taking time at least once a month for a quick review of performance, to set expectations and offer encouraging words, will keep employee motivation high. Direct feedback is the best way to keep things on track. Remember also that it is more important to be helpful than to be nice.

In return, make sure that your employees have the opportunity to provide feedback *to you*. Reinforcement of desired behavior is effective when your employees are able to give input into what works and what doesn't work. So collect systematic feedback from your employees. Set up regular feedback sessions, or launch surveys where they can ventilate concerns and provide suggestions.

Share successes and identify best practices

It's as important to recognize and praise employees when things go well as it is to support and coach them when things go wrong. Money may attract people to your door, but something else has to keep them from going out the back door. People need to feel appreciated, and *recognition programs* help meet that need. Talking to many executives, and especially their subordinates, it's mind-boggling how few managers do this. The excuses are predictable: "I don't have the time." "People get paid to do their job, so why appreciate something that is normal?" "I find it too soft." "Real performers don't need it." Research has shown that acknowledgement is a key reason people feel motivated and engaged[112]. Even a tap on the shoulder and a "thanks, well done" go a long way.

Celebrating successes, especially early wins for the project, are often cited as key elements of successful change. In our chapter on the culture battery, we pointed to the importance of parties and ceremonies. It's important that you organize parties not just for the entire company, but also that you cascade 'partying' down into smaller parts of the organization, such as departments or even project teams. Parties celebrate successes, create a vibe and make your people proud.

Celebrating successes also means that you have identified best practices that can be shared with the rest of the organization. Some companies organize contests to actively search for those best practices. Contests can translate into instant engagement in an office. For example, send out small cameras to every location and or department with a request for employees to pick a company value and show what it means to them. Tell them that the most inspirational video will win. Give modest prizes and post winners on the company intranet, and your entire company might be more connected and engaged than before.

A thoughtful process for managing change

Getting your employees engaged is not particularly complicated. What is required for this to work, however, is the application of a thoughtful process for managing the *people* side of your change project. It's important to link this with the rational side of project and process management that we described in the previous chapter.

For many organizations, getting your employees engaged is seen as the last step in a change process, as the top half of Figure 41 illustrates. As you will have gathered, we recommend that you integrate the connection processes in the project and process initiatives. If you involve your people early in the business improvement initiatives, employee involvement will be greatly enhanced. We will explore this further in Chapter 9.

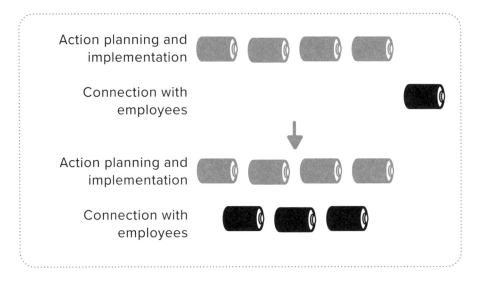

Figure 41 · Integrating action planning and connection initiatives

Key messages of this chapter

This chapter dealt with the challenges of connecting the change with your employees. People's *individual commitment to change*, which is necessary for change success, can prove difficult to build and sustain. People are at the core of successful organizational change, but they also represent a challenge to the change journey. All too often, employees are relegated to the role of impediments on the path to goals, rather than as the keys to achieving these goals. Managing change therefore implies turning an empty connection battery into a fully charged one.

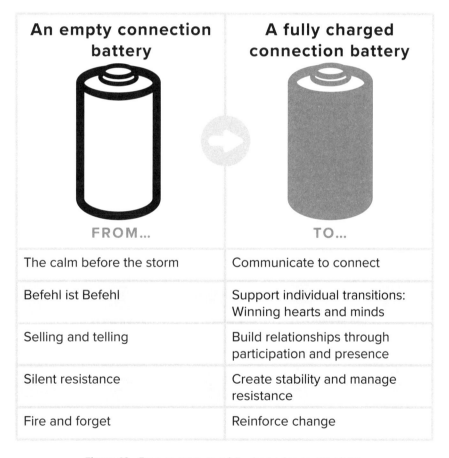

An empty connection battery	A fully charged connection battery
FROM...	TO...
The calm before the storm	Communicate to connect
Befehl ist Befehl	Support individual transitions: Winning hearts and minds
Selling and telling	Build relationships through participation and presence
Silent resistance	Create stability and manage resistance
Fire and forget	Reinforce change

Figure 42 • From an empty to a fully charged connection battery

Figure 42 illustrates both the characteristics of an empty connection battery as well as our recommendations to get this battery fully charged. What is key to the generation of the kind of *psychological energy* that increases security and commitment of employees?

- Communicate to connect. Communication is not just about transmitting information, it's about finding out what people think and feel about the change.

- Win the hearts and minds of each employee by supporting them in their individual transitions.

- Build relationships of trust through presence and participation. Encourage your people to explore. This lays the foundation for self-efficacy.

- Manage resistance by making it easy for your people to change but also by setting clear Non-Negotiable Rules (NNRs).

- Reinforce change by providing support and continuous feedback and by sharing and celebrating successes.

Chapter

8

PUTTING IT ALL TOGETHER

———

Getting an overall energy
snapshot of your organization

Key questions

What can you do
if you have varying
energy levels across
your batteries?

What is the role of
the change history
and context on your
change program?

What are the
typical energy
drivers and energy
drainers of change
programs?

What are
their effects
on change
effectiveness?

What are the common
change pathologies
that companies face?

In the previous chapters, we clarified the difference between positive and negative energy levels per battery. The chapters allowed you to assess the energy level for each battery and provided you with recommendations on how to charge them. But most change programs involve the charging of multiple change batteries. How do you put all this information together? And what are the crucial elements of an energy analysis?

An energy analysis consists of the following major steps:

- Analysis of your energy gainers and energy drainers

- Analysis of the change batteries — identification of change pathologies

- Analysis of the change history and context

Analyze your energy gainers and drainers

The first step of a rigorous energy analysis is to identify your energy gainers and energy drainers. Before you start reflecting on implementing various change interventions, it is wise to assess the presence of short circuits that can significantly reduce your organizational energy level, and of elements that generate positive energy and thus significantly increase your energy levels.

Based on our research, we identified *10 energy drainers* and *10 energy gainers* of key consequence for your organizations' change program (see Figure 43 and Figure 44). The energy drainers explain why most of the companies in our study with a low change effectiveness — the bottom performers — are losing energy. These are the areas in which bottom performers score particularly low relative to the other companies in our sample. If you have identified a number of these energy drainers in your organization, then change can become problematic. The first column of energy drainers consists of the most dangerous statements. If your organization reflects a number of these, it is at risk of becoming a political battlefield. Change is going to be a struggle. Your change program will need to address some of these items from the start for it to have any chance of success.

MOST SIGNIFICANT ENERGY DRAINERS

1 In our organization, top managers' selfish needs are more important than collective goals.

6 Our top team has failed to allocate significant budgets to fund our change initiatives.

2 The members of our top team don't trust each other.

7 Our organization fails to systematically collect information on how well we meet the (changing) needs of our customers.

3 The top team has no clear mandate and lacks support from major stakeholders to transform the organization.

8 When errors occur, employees and managers blame their colleagues or find excuses in the company's systems.

4 When new initiatives are proposed, 'no' is the norm, 'yes' is the exception.

9 Most people believe that change happens too quickly and causes too much disruption.

5 Our organization sees employees merely as a means to improve performance, not as persons behind the function.

10 Our change approach lacks education and training in project and process management for employees.

Figure 43 · Top 10 list of energy drainers

The energy gainers are characteristics from top performers in our sample that bring a lot of positive change energy to the table. If you ticked several of these boxes, your organization has developed important sources of energy to switch from a reactive to a proactive change mode. If you ticked many items in the second column, you may be a change champion. For many organizations, these are the elusive Holy Grail. Tackling these elements may not be obvious but if you do find a way to implement them, they can truly boost your change success. However, you will generally need to manage your energy drainers first to really take advantage of or improve on the energy gainers.

MOST SIGNIFICANT ENERGY GAINERS

1 Our change vision is inspiring: it generates energy within the organization.

6 We use prototyping and experimentation as a way to assess the value and risks of alternative solutions.

2 Our strategy clearly outlines who not to serve and what not to provide.

7 We manage to complete our initiatives by limiting the number of projects that we try to implement concurrently.

3 We lead important change initiatives ourselves, not through external specialists.

8 We systematically identify best practices and opportunities to simplify our change approach.

4 Our individual change initiatives start with a strong why: they address day-to-day operational problems or customer needs.

9 In our organization, change communication is both top-down and bottom-up.

5 Our organization has defined clear value propositions for our core customer segments.

10 We periodically (weekly/monthly) assess variance towards expected progress and results to learn and adjust.

Figure 44 · Top 10 list of energy gainers

Analyze your change pathology

While our research demonstrates that every battery is strongly correlated with change success, the probability of long-term sustained success further increases if several batteries are addressed at once. In an environment where change has become more persistent and pervasive, it's important to develop capabilities that allow you to charge *all* your change batteries.

An effective change program addresses the root causes of the organization's problems. The batteries of change are a useful instrument to get a better view on your change challenges. The overall goal of a successful change program is to get positive energy from all your batteries. Then you've built capabilities that allow you to deal with fast-changing circumstances. Our research revealed that 35 percent of the companies in our sample were energized and healthy.

Most organizations don't reach the ideal state. They suffer from energy losses in one or more of the change batteries. We found several patterns of energy loss. This section presents the most typical change pathologies that we encountered in both our research and consulting practices. Although there are several theoretical combinations of change pathologies possible, our research revealed that most companies fit in one of the following categories: chronically-ill organizations (30 percent), mechanistic organizations (4 percent), delirious organizations, (17 percent) and finally, paralyzed organizations (6 percent). Only 8 percent of the companies could not be classified in one of those pathologies.

We also investigated the link between *change pathology* and *change effectiveness* (see Figure 45). As expected, the fully energized organizations are also the most effective. The chronically ill organizations struggle most with change. 74 percent of them have a negative change effectiveness score. 18 percent of the chronically ill organizations even completely fail to achieve the objectives they've set. The other three change pathologies – the delirious organization, the mechanistic organization and the paralyzed organization – score relatively well on change effectiveness. They achieve 'low positive' effectiveness scores. They have achieved moderate success with their change programs, but none of them is fully satisfied with their change journey. One third of the delirious organizations and the paralyzed organizations struggle with change.

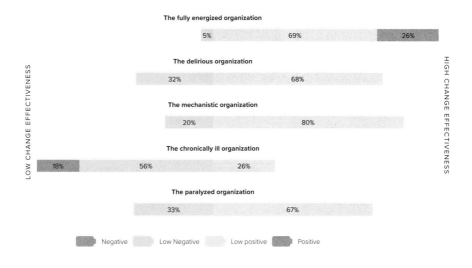

Figure 45 • Pathologies and change effectiveness

Let's discuss each of those pathologies in greater detail and examine how some organizations got back on track.

The delirious organization

The delirious organization has emotional batteries that generate positive energy, but its rational batteries are energy drainers. A delirious organization has an ambitious top team, with a healthy culture, and committed employees. Such companies have a strong purpose and pay attention to creating a collegial and supportive environment for their employees. Employees are committed to help change the course of the organization. The problem with a delirious organization is with its rational change batteries. A delirious organization lacks clarity and structure to achieve its business targets. Overly entrepreneurial organizations fall in this category: these are companies that chase opportunity after opportunity and operate in a continuous ad-hoc mode. They don't lack the drive and ambition and their people are committed, but they bounce or drift from one project to the other without a clear destination in mind.

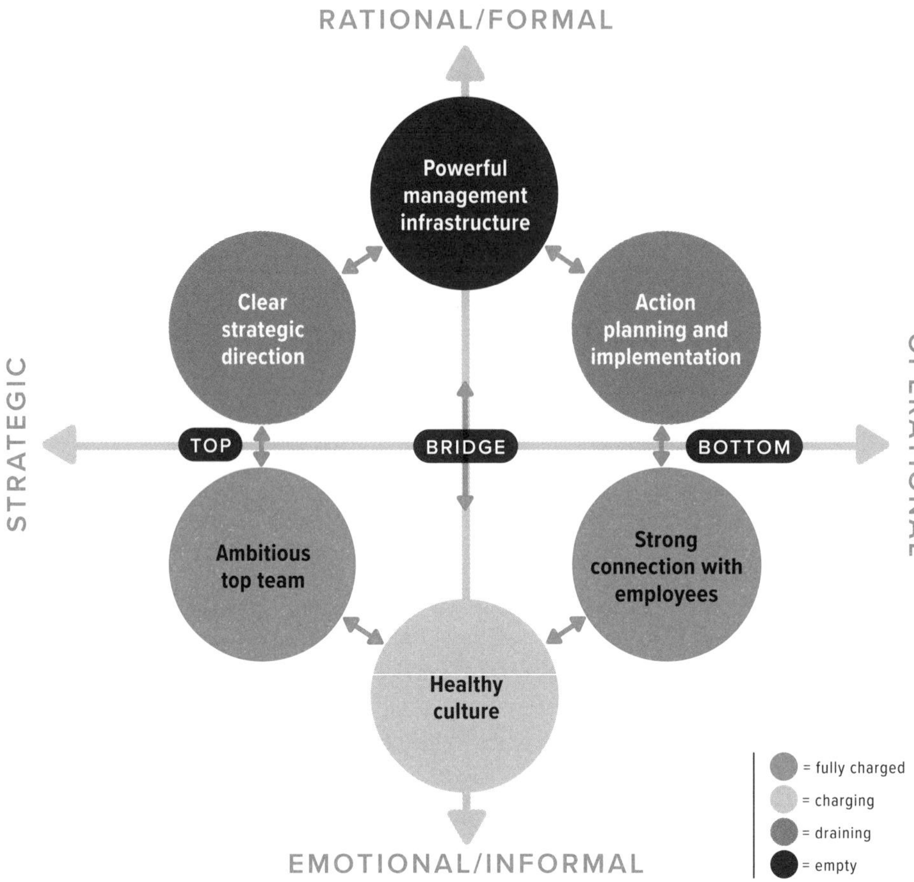

Figure 46 • The delirious organization

HOW ZENITH DENMARK CHARGED ITS RATIONAL CHANGE BATTERIES[113]

Zenith Denmark is an animal health firm that is part of a big international health corporation. Johan Svenson was appointed Managing Director at the end of 2011 and found a company with a cohesive top team and a healthy culture. The company had gone through a merger but had paid significant attention to the people side of that merger, resulting in 50 happy and committed employees.

But in his first budget meeting with the corporate management, Svenson had to announce that his organization hadn't met the imposed financial targets. He discussed possible strategies to increase revenues with his superiors at headquarters, but didn't get much concrete input. Those corporate managers were solely interested in the financials, and gave autonomy to the business managers to decide how to achieve them. Svenson realized that his executives had set strategic goals, but that the Zenith Denmark was lacking a clear business strategy to realize these goals. He knew that Zenith was known for its service orientation in the market and wondered whether he could build a strategy on that foundation.

Svenson organized a two-day strategy workshop at Vlerick Business School in April 2012, where the six-person top management team discussed the company's ambitions and the strategy to realize those ambitions. They chose to make the company the most 'customer intimate' in the market, a logical choice as the company had already started to take actions in line with that strategic model. They specified clear choices and identified action plans for the three business lines: companion animals, swine and poultry, and ruminant.

Now that the top was aligned, Johan Svenson reflected on how they pass the message on to the rest of the organization. Simply communicating the new strategy would not be enough to create the buy-in he needed for successful execution. In October 2012, Svenson organized another two-day seminar for all employees. The company closed over this time — a first in its history. The employees discussed the internal and external challenges of the organization and Svenson began to feel that enough people were ready to move to the next step.

Svenson and his management team chose six employees to discuss the strategy in greater detail and build a strategy map [see below]. As outlined in the chapter on the management infrastructure battery, a strategy map is a graphical presentation of how a company addresses its major strategic goals. Zenith's strategy map revealed how the various strategic objectives were connected and how customer intimacy was translated into financial, customer, process and people objectives. It was the road map of how Zenith Denmark was going to tackle its strategic challenges.

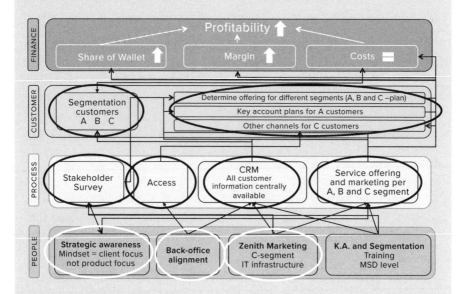

To implement these strategic challenges, six cross-functional teams were created, headed by a member of the executive team and a team leader. These teams would be the main vehicles to roll out the action plans. In addition, each business line would have to set up its own initiatives to roll out a customer intimacy strategy. Svenson realized that the concept of 'customer intimacy' was too abstract to be meaningful to employees. The organization therefore talked about 'Love Affairs' instead [see illustration below]. He challenged the people: "Would you do that in a relationship?" "Would your customer get warm from this initiative?" People joked about these 'Love Affairs,' but Svenson had succeeded in bringing this topic to their attention. And in line with the new theme, he designed labels for each team. Each team had to launch an initiative that helped to address one strategic objective.

On the Strategy Day that was organized in April 2013, all six teams presented their projects. At the end of the day, the group voted for the best project. The members of the winning team got an exclusive evening at a top restaurant. Needless to say that, for the next competitions, teams were more motivated to present a good project. Indeed, the overall quality of the projects increased significantly. Zenith Denmark now organizes these competitions every six months. With this combination of approaches, the company ensures that it moves towards more customer intimacy, slowly but steadily.

This example illustrates how to charge your rational change batteries while maintaining or even improving energy in the emotional batteries. Zenith Denmark defined its strategy, first in the executive team, and then repeated the exercise with the middle managers and the rest of the organization. The strategy map was instrumental in translating the strategy into a portfolio of projects, and progress was tracked for each of these strategic objectives. Cross-functional teams implemented those strategic projects, so that attention was paid to help building the business and not just running the business. Note that the installation of a team competition also helped to generate positive energy in the culture battery. There was more drive and performance orientation, and the cross-functional teams contributed to an even more collaborative spirit within the company.

This approach helped Zenith Denmark to gain extra market share and manage its costs. Overall profitability increased significantly and, in 2015, Johan Svenson was promoted and became a divisional manager at Zenith Animal Health Group.

The mechanistic organization

The mechanistic organization is the opposite of the delirious organization. Mechanistic organizations have positive rational change batteries but negative emotional ones. This is an overly analytical and super-rational organization. The top team has worked out clear strategies to optimize financial performance and has set up a powerful management infrastructure to follow up on the change. Employees work on projects to realize the expected benefits of the change. Change is planned and programmatic.[114] In itself, there's nothing wrong with well-functioning rational batteries of change. In mechanistic organizations, however, the obsessive focus on finalizing project after project and reaching financial milestones shifts the attention away from the more intangible aspects of a successful organization, such as culture, aspiration, and good relationships between employees.

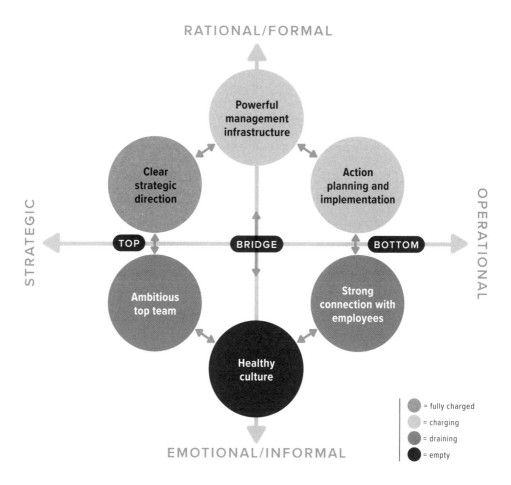

RATIONAL/FORMAL

STRATEGIC

OPERATIONAL

EMOTIONAL/INFORMAL

Powerful
management
infrastructure

Clear
strategic
direction

Action
planning and
implementation

TOP

BRIDGE

BOTTOM

Ambitious
top team

Strong
connection with
employees

Healthy
culture

= fully charged
= charging
= draining
= empty

Figure 47 • The mechanistic organization

In a mechanistic organization, there is no inspiring aspiration, just short-term financial targets to achieve. The culture battery is running empty as well: mechanistic organizations are cold and often infused with a toxic culture. Some are very performance-oriented, but the fanatic search for order and perfection also creates a culture that is over-critical and that leaves little room for error. This type of organization lacks social support mechanisms to give employees a feeling of security or safety that supports learning. Such a demanding, results-driven organization that lacks social support is fertile ground for burnouts. People may perform well for a limited time, but the mechanistic organization's individualistic, depersonalized, and authority-driven nature limits the effectiveness of the change program in the long term.[115] Although one could argue that many listed companies exhibit characteristics of a mechanistic organization, only 4 percent of the companies in our sample were qualified as such.

How can you leverage the strength of the rational change batteries and at the same time get those emotional batteries charged?

TACKLING THE PEOPLE CHALLENGES IN THE MERGER BETWEEN NORWICH UNION AND CGU[116]

February 2000 saw the result of a giant British insurance merger: CGNU, now called Aviva. The new unit would combine the general insurance and life insurance business of two British insurance companies: Norwich Union and CGU, the latter being itself the result of a previous merger. The general insurance business, called Norwich Union Insurance (NUI) was unprofitable, and the CEO of the unit, Patrick Snowball, an ex-military man, focused on restoring the profitability of that unit. Snowball admitted that in the first two years of the merger, the focus was almost exclusively on profitability. People were relocated to save costs, processes were rationalized and optimized and little attention was paid to the emotional side of the business. When the executive team presented its new strategy in November 2001 at the Five Lakes Hotel to the senior staff, the audience's reaction was silence, followed by disbelief and anger.

The Five Lakes Conference was a wake-up call for the executive team, Patrick Snowball included. They thought that the improved financial results would create a positive vibe throughout the organization. But that was not the case. At the conference, the results of the first Internal Morale Survey were shared with the senior staff. The directors had expected poor results but were shocked by what they read. Employee satisfaction was at an all-time low. Staff turnover rates had increased by almost 30 percent and commitment levels were slumping. And in the Broker Survey findings, NUI came fifth out of five.

In response, the team decided to set up a task force of 15 people to increase the morale of employees. They started with reaching out to the top 100 directors and spent one and a half days in a leadership session, discussing what leadership meant to them, what they aspired to, what they wanted and what they wanted eliminated.

Commitment from the top would prove essential to make the change happen and this meant making sure the ideas were on the executive team's radar and embedded in metrics. In January 2002, the top team decided that profit would be no longer the sole metric to focus on, and they set targets for key financial, service and morale indicators. Snowball called this 'the three pillars', and the targets were cascaded into the different businesses and departments. This was an audacious move reflecting the fact that both customer and employee satisfaction scores had turned extremely low in 2001.

Norwich Union Insurance also spent many efforts reconnecting managers and staff. Natural champions and supporters were identified; they were to be the path breakers to promote new behaviors in line with the new strategy. The task force also introduced the Service Morale Profit (SMP) Daily Huddles. These daily standup meetings had to direct employees to the business goals, but also ensured better communication and more commitment. Managers had connected with their directors, but not with their employees. Face-to-face communication was much more effective than the one-way communication approach of the previous years. Managers also spent more time listening to the issues and grievances of their staff and customers. The middle managers realized that their role was about more than being an administrator.

A video room was introduced for all staff to air their views. Both managers and employees used this room to let off steam and openly share what they hated. Senior managers allowed this — they realized that people had been treated badly and let them have their say. The company also created a communications newsletter to spread the word further. Managers were appointed in different leadership project teams with the goal of involving people in the change and looking for supporters. The company expended huge effort rolling out local leadership programs to convince local managers of the need for this new approach.

NUI also created a 'Removing Blockages' database, whereby the local leaders could point to the blockages that prohibited them offering a great service. These were issues that were raised during the daily huddles but could not be resolved locally.

The company also introduced new information flows, called 'Horizontals', quarterly meetings for senior and middle managers. The goal was to bring people from different departments together to focus on new thinking and share common issues. The company also invested in a network of full-time business coaches and organized leadership surveys and employee satisfaction surveys to keep track of the evolution of its service and morale. Patrick Snowball summarized as follows: "It's keeping a single direction but reinventing and reiterating on a constant basis. The main message has to be simple to explain to people, but done in multiple local ways… and you have to 'hammer it', repeat it at every meeting." In other words, numerous interventions, individually modest in size, but all consistent and in line with the overall message.[117]

This example shows how, after an obsessive focus on the rational batteries, Norwich Union Insurance shifted gear and paid equal attention to the emotional side of change. It incorporated initiatives at the top and at the local level, and worked on transforming the company culture. During that period, financial performance continued to improve, but other performance measures were moving in the right direction too. Staff turnover dropped from 30 percent in 2001 to 12 percent in 2004.

The chronically ill organization

In our database 30 percent of the companies fit the category of the chronically ill organization. This is an organization with huge change problems. This organization loses energy in both its rational and emotional batteries. Changing a chronically ill organization is a tremendous task as it involves both tackling severe business challenges and simultaneously addressing cultural and people issues. At the same time, you have a divided top and a disconnected group of employees who are resisting rather than supporting change.

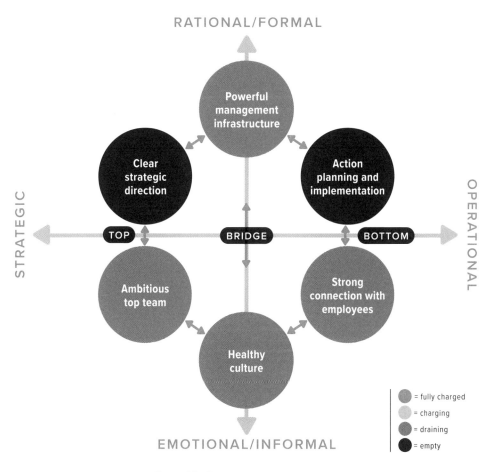

Figure 48 · The chronically ill organization

BECOMING THE MOST TRANSPARENT AND TRUSTWORTHY INSURANCE COMPANY[118]

We referred in chapter 2 to Interpolis as a company with an inspiring aspiration. But the story of Interpolis goes beyond the formulation of a huge ambition. It's a great example of a company that has been able to generate a lot of positive energy with a compelling change program, tackling both the rational and emotional batteries of change.

In the 1990s, this Dutch insurer had become a big organization focusing on managing insurance policies rather than serving customers' needs. The financial results were bad and the company was in dire straits. Jan Vullings and Piet van Schijndel were sent to help the company reduce costs and increase profitability and customer and employee satisfaction. They reduced the workforce from 2,400 to 1,800. But the pair knew that reducing costs wouldn't fundamentally change the company's competitive position.

In 1995, Interpolis started a radical transformation program called 'Solid & Certain'. Vullings and van Schijndel formulated an ambitious plan to make insurance 'crystal clear' and to be the first company to simplify insurance through simple communication and relevant solutions. Interpolis would stick to its promises — "a promise is a promise" — and would be open and honest. The company would create new and simple insurance products and change its processes to be fast, easy and painless.

All this started on a small scale: five Interpolis employees in the back office tried out the concept within one of the 700 local Rabobanks, the key distribution partner for Interpolis. At that moment, there was no business case, only a deeply rooted belief that this new approach could work in practice. In 1997, the first new, integrated insurance product, the 'All-in-One Policy' was launched in the market. The company also developed a clear marketing strategy whereby attention was paid to building a consistent brand. Crystal clear solutions were the core theme in every marketing message.

Customers reacted positively to the new initiatives and Interpolis expanded the scope of its change program. It reviewed its most important back office processes, such as claims declaration, communication, and claims payment and settlement. The company used structured improvement projects to redesign its processes. What was striking in this approach was that the company emphasized *trust* to the customer in all it did. If the customer filed a claim, Interpolis would pay the next day. "You can leave your receipts at home — we believe you," was their motto. Of course, the company controlled a small sample of its customers and when the claim operator felt that something was wrong, the company investigated the claims in greater detail. If fraud was proven, the customer ended up on a black list and was kicked out.

This way of working required a fundamental change in culture and dealing with employees. Interpolis tackled this cultural transformation in an integrated way and changed HR practices, IT and communication systems, and the working environment. The 'New Way of Working', as the cultural change program was called, aspired to create an open culture where all employees could bring up ideas to improve work practices to delight the customer. In 1996, Vullings and van Schijndel used the new head office to reenergize the organization and seek new ways to increase customer centricity.

Becoming the most trustworthy insurer implied that you put trust in your employees. The executive team at Interpolis communicated extensively and involved the staff members in all operational decisions. Interpolis was one of the first Dutch companies to introduce the 'Flexible Office Concept'. No more fixed work stations. Everybody selected a place to work that best fit the activity or task to be performed — senior executives too. Work time was made flexible, investments were made into essential information technology in order to stimulate communication, and workers were encouraged to work from home. In this way, the managers gave autonomy and responsibility to employees when it came to arranging their own work schedule. To top things off, the insurer formulated a 'New Employee Profile', where attention was paid to recruiting employees with the right competences *and* attitudes.

Additionally, Interpolis built a truly great office space. With a focus on great building design and simple business systems that supported autonomy, flexibility and freedom, individuals became the focal point of attention rather than buildings or hierarchies.

As a result, Interpolis grew spectacularly: premium income increased and Interpolis took market share away from its most important competitors. Profit margins increased, and the company also grew its employee base. In 2004, Interpolis employed 5,173 people, far more than the original 2,400 of the early 1990s. The growth continued, even after Vullings and van Schijndel retired. In 2005, Interpolis became a subsidiary of the Dutch Achmea Group.

The paralyzed organization

The paralyzed organization has a strong head, but weak legs. Six percent of the companies in our sample belong to this category. The batteries on the left side of the model are well charged, but unfortunately the batteries on the right (i.e. the action planning and implementation battery and the connection with employees battery) are not. The paralyzed organization fails to translate its change vision and strategy into tangible actions supported by employees. Such an organization has an ambitious top team and great strategic capabilities. They scan the environment and develop strategies to cope with the moves of competitors and disruptors. The energized top team develops vision after vision, strategy after strategy, plan after plan.

But the organization desperately struggles with execution. Strategies fail to get implemented because the top team is too far removed from daily operational activities. Implementation is considered less important, somewhat boring, and is assigned to middle- or lower-level managers. The top team gets into a careless delegation mode: they consider implementation a detail and thus lack an appreciation for practical considerations and emotional concerns. They spend months reflecting on the ambition and direction of the organization, but once they have seen the light, they expect outsiders to get on board after a simple briefing.

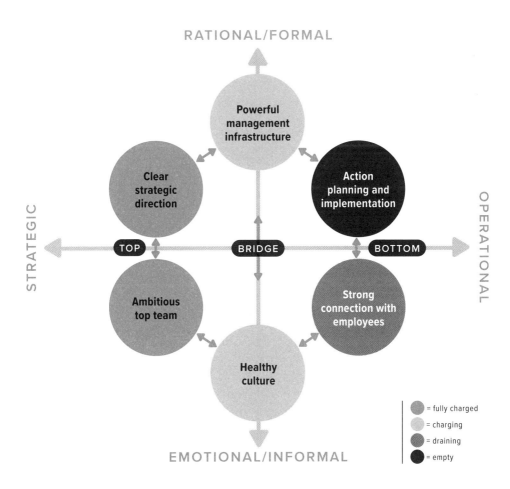

RATIONAL/FORMAL

STRATEGIC

OPERATIONAL

Powerful management infrastructure

Clear strategic direction

Action planning and implementation

TOP ─ BRIDGE ─ BOTTOM

Ambitious top team

Strong connection with employees

Healthy culture

EMOTIONAL/INFORMAL

= fully charged
= charging
= draining
= empty

Figure 49 • The paralyzed organization

Analyze your change context and history

Assessing the energy levels of your batteries is essential to make a sound diagnosis of your change capabilities. But deciding on the type and sequence of specific interventions also requires an accurate understanding of the *context* and *history* of the organization. This is similar to a medical doctor who knows about the disease (pathology) of a patient through diagnosis, but needs to find out more details about the context and history of the patient to decide on the precise treatment and medication. Perhaps you have developed an allergy against a medication that the doctor should be aware of (history), perhaps he should know that you will be traveling next week (context).

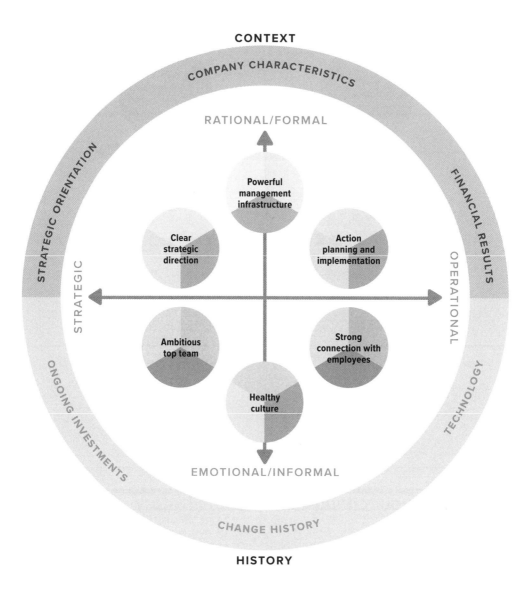

Figure 50 • The role of context and history in defining your change approach

Your *financial results* play a crucial role. When you are facing bankruptcy, it is often easier to create positive energy for change within your top team by establishing a clear sense of urgency among your team members. Interventions to charge the top team battery may require a lot more effort if there is no clear emergency.

You can't ignore important *company characteristics* either: setting up a change program for a large company operating from different sites is different from transforming a small- or medium-sized enterprise. Your position in the organization, your personal credibility and your personal network are important to consider as well. A middle manager who wants to initiate change may find it more difficult to connect with top executives and their personal network than an executive who is already part of the top team.

The overall *strategic orientation* of the organization matters too. Although the generic change capabilities will be similar for a product leader compared to a company focusing on cost leadership (operational excellence), the specific change interventions often demand different skill sets, and as a result, you will need different expertise to support you.

Historical elements can also largely influence the design of your change program. In any company there is a legacy that imposes path dependency: a road construction company is not going to switch to becoming a railroads construction company overnight. In theory, you can change anything; in practice, big magic takes more time and different people. The availability of a specific *technology* can make it easier or more difficult to support a particular treatment. It can be a blessing or a pain to support specific batteries.

Furthermore, you have to consider the change projects you are already working on. Major investments of ongoing or planned initiatives can make or break your change program. They can be important obstacles for change, or become important levers for change. Athletes who face the same injury may decide on a different treatment depending on the games they still have to play.

Finally, you have to understand the *change history* of the organization. Things that worked or failed before, generally have a huge impact on the dominant mindset and beliefs of the organization — what 'can be done' and what 'cannot be done' around here. Understanding the history of change success and failure will also allow you to identify former change heroes and foes and to assess the current credibility of the leaders involved. Assessing the profile of these leaders will generate important insights with regard to the type of interventions that leaders have used to drive their organization in the past and the type of support or resistance that you can expect from key players in the organization depending on the credibility of the leader. Patients will more easily accept unpleasant messages or treatments from doctors who can present a clear track record of success.

We realize this may seem a lot to consider, but we are sure that all these elements have an impact on the focus, pace, sequence and initial steps of your change program. We strongly believe everything should be made as simple as possible, but not simpler (Albert Einstein). What we offer is a guide that will help you achieve success by design, not by chance.

Key messages of this chapter

Any successful change starts with a good analysis of the energy status of your company:

▌ Analyze your energy gainers and drainers. These are the elements that can make or break your change program. Don't allow energy drainers to impact your change program. The more you succeed on working on energy gainers, the more your change will help you to become a top performer in change.

▌ Then identify your change pathology. Which batteries are losing energy? This chapter identified several typical change diseases. Each one required a different treatment. Make sure that your change program addresses the right issues.

▌ Finally, be aware of how your change context and history influence your change approach.

The next step of a change program is to identify the key interventions to get your batteries charged and to get your organization energized again. Which interventions to launch and in which order to launch them, are the next chapter's topics.

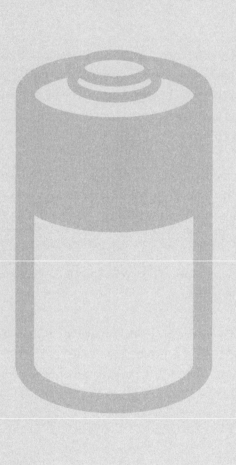

Chapter

9

ENERGY DESIGN PRINCIPLES

———

From analysis to intervention

Key questions

What are the major change initiatives to launch?

How should you proceed when launching interventions that cover multiple batteries?

What are the most important energy design principles to create a healthy energy profile?

So far, we have provided you with a more complete analysis of your organization's overall energy level. You have identified your energy drainers and the root causes of why change is difficult. You also understand where and how your change history and context can impact your change program. Several batteries generate negative energy, so you need more than a short-term painkiller.

Now it's time to launch initiatives to turn a bad situation around. We have shared many illustrations of potential interventions in each chapter. Which initiatives to launch depends on which batteries generate negative energy. Building change capabilities is ultimately about charging those batteries that are negatively loaded. But many organizations need to work on several change batteries simultaneously. If you know which interventions to introduce, where do you start and how do you proceed?

Balance

One of the core messages of this book is that successful change requires connecting the rational side with the emotional side of change. Only then can change be integrative. Some of the pathologies that we've described in the previous chapter suffered from an imbalance between the rational and the emotional batteries of change. As a result, some of the typical change interventions aim to restore balance between the rational and emotional batteries at each level of the organization.

You may have noticed that our battery model spans *three organizational levels*: the top, the bottom, and a third level that is the bridge between the top and the bottom. Figure 51 shows that each organizational level is linked to a pair of batteries, a rational one and an emotional one. The next sections show why it's important to manage both the rational and emotional batteries of change at each level.

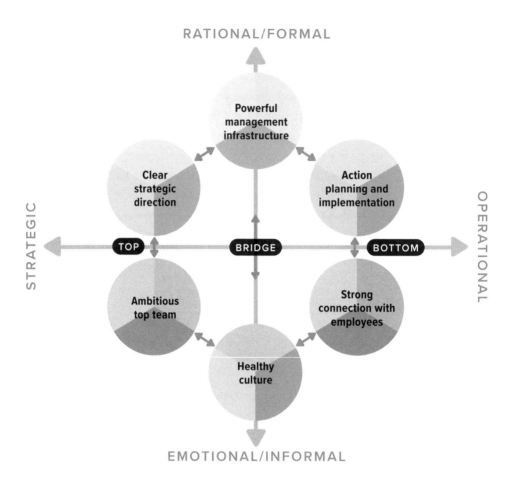

RATIONAL/FORMAL

STRATEGIC

OPERATIONAL

EMOTIONAL/INFORMAL

Powerful management infrastructure

Clear strategic direction

Action planning and implementation

TOP   BRIDGE   BOTTOM

Ambitious top team

Strong connection with employees

Healthy culture

Figure 51 • Managing balance of energy across the change batteries

Setting the tone at the top

Change starts with an ambitious team at the top that plays to win and that has defined a clear vision and strategy to build a competitive advantage. Creating balance at the top implies working on strategy analysis and formulation while growing a dynamic leadership team and increasing interaction with key internal and external stakeholders.

Successful change at the top requires that both your top team and your strategy battery are charged. If one of the batteries remains empty, your change program will suffer. Not long ago, we were approached by a leading local professional services firm that asked for help for a leadership development program. We soon discovered that this company was *chronically ill*. When we presented our batteries model to two members of the executive team, they realized that they missed a clear strategy, but also that the introduction of a new strategy would meet a lot of resistance from both top and middle managers. The company's performance was slowly going down, but there was no real sense of urgency yet to change the course of the organization.

We organized a strategy session and a leadership coaching session for the 150 most senior managers. This was also the kick-off of a larger change project. The company spent about half a million euros on developing a new strategy and launching leadership sessions. The sessions revealed that most middle managers welcomed the idea of a clearer and more focused strategy, and most agreed with the new strategic direction. But the leadership coaching sessions also pointed out that some of the top managers clearly did not support the change in strategy. Despite our recommendations, this was not taken up by the executive team. The company now had a strategy, but one that was not fully supported by the top nor cascaded down to the lower levels of the company. The strategy was just a nice brain exercise captured in a flashy PowerPoint presentation. Each department continued with its priorities, the silo wars continued, and middle managers became more frustrated than ever before.

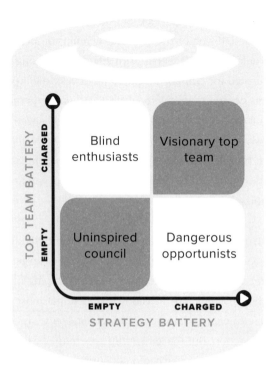

Figure 52 • Setting the right tone at the top

This story is a good example of a team of dangerous opportunists. The organization has a clear strategy but there is no commitment, no 'band of brothers and sisters' to support it. Only when you have a visionary top team, can your change journey move in the right direction – then you have a top team that is committed to a clear destination. Strategy requires making choices. But in a team of egos, choices result in winners and losers. When those choices are not supported by every executive, individual team members start to be loose cannons. They will use every bump in the road to revisit the discussion and to prove they are right.

If you have an ambitious and cohesive top team but the strategy remains unclear, you typically have a gang of blind enthusiasts who jumps from opportunity to opportunity. Needless to say, this lack of direction hurts your change effectiveness. If both the strategy and the top team battery are empty, then the top of your organization largely promotes *status quo* rather than change. They may spend a lot of time interfering in operational issues or fine-tuning organizational structures and reporting systems, but there is a substantial danger that they lack passion and orientation to guide transformational change.

How do you ensure that your top team and strategy battery are charged? The main recommendation is that when you organize strategy sessions with your top team, you also build in time to discuss the *functioning of your top team*. Making those issues discussable without finger-pointing is an important step that often creates a new dynamic in the top team. When top executives disagree on important matters and they're not used to or capable of having fundamental strategy discussions, relationships between executives can sour. A good strategy discussion can bring these frictions to the table. It points to issues that you can no longer neglect. When executives find it difficult to agree on these issues, you may need to introduce conflict management techniques to reconcile top team members. One manager told us: "The strategy workshop cost us a lot of energy but has generated a lot of energy as well." Clarity and a willingness to build a true team can boost a top team's energy. Clarity with regard to the strategic direction can strengthen the ambition and cohesion of the top team and vice versa.

Strengthen the core

The bridge batteries — the management infrastructure battery and the culture battery — are extremely important batteries in our change model. They ensure that strategies get translated into concrete goals and action plans, that they are adequately monitored, and that important lessons and insights are shared across the organization. At the same time, these batteries ensure that the passion and energy of the top team spread throughout the rest of the organization, creating highly motivated self-directing teams. The bridge batteries — they make the bridge from the left batteries to the right and vice versa   ensure that the organization is able and willing to change in the proposed direction.

Both *change capabilities* and *change competence* are important ingredients of successful change. We associate change capabilities with an organization's knowledge and skills (ability), and resources (capacity) to change. Companies with a powerful management infrastructure are better able to build such change capabilities. When we say that an organization has developed change competences, we mean that capable individuals also demonstrate a clear willingness to change. They are committed to change their behavior, such that, collectively, the organization uses its capabilities for change as effectively as possible.[119] Creating a healthy culture is a prerequisite for creating a safe environment for change that sees change as a collective opportunity – and not an individual threat – and thus for creating an organization that is eager to change. This is captured in Figure 53.

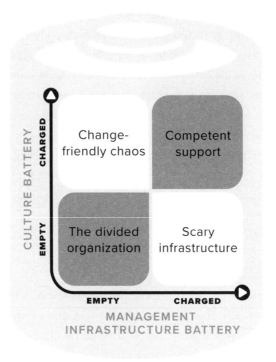

Figure 53 · Strengthen the core

Building 'competent support' takes time. Companies that fail to address time to 'build the business' while creating a healthy culture significantly limit the chances of their change effectiveness. We refer to the chapters on a powerful management infrastructure and a healthy culture for recommendations on how to charge each battery. But again, it is important to work on the batteries simultaneously. You cannot create an infrastructure for a learning organization if there is a conformance-oriented culture or no drive to improve. Similarly, your ambition to continuously improve cannot be sustained if you don't measure whether you have achieved your goals. We recommend reflecting on the cultural implications of working on your management infrastructure. Conversely, when launching cultural initiatives, make sure they are embedded in your management infrastructure. How can you do that?

For example, when you build strategy maps with strategic objectives and initiatives, use cross-functional teams to staff your projects (like in the Zenith Denmark case). When you define key performance indicators and you build a performance management system, ask yourself how this can be used to create a more performance-oriented culture. Include employees in the definition of the metrics and allow them to select additional metrics that further explain the performance of strategic goals. This will reduce the tension between the hierarchies as employees will feel more understood, and start to see the metric system as an opportunity to demonstrate that they want to contribute to the organization. Changes in your management infrastructure will also lead to changes in your culture battery.

The reverse is also true. You can build a healthier culture by leveraging your performance management, communication, or your capacity and prioritization system. Providing resources to entrepreneurial ventures will help to boost your opportunity-seeking culture. Being more open and explaining strategic decisions using your communication systems will help to create a culture of transparency and trust. Probably the most powerful management system to use is the company's reward system. Rewarding is an important symbol of appropriate behavior. Bonuses and prizes are powerful tools to change an organization's culture.

Review meetings are typically instruments of the management infrastructure that middle managers use to track performance on goals and initiatives. Many organizations spend a large portion of these meetings on reporting, or at best, on evaluating progress of initiatives or goals. This strongly reflects a command and control culture that focuses on managing individual projects but fails to strengthen the core. In organizations that are overwhelmed with initiatives, this results in marathon meetings where active participation of most of the participants is reduced to reporting on their initiative. Today this implies everyone hiding behind their laptop or mobile phones to work on emails and other work while faking listening to the presentations of others.

RECALL review sessions provide an alternative structure to help organizations strengthen their management infrastructure. RECALL is a memo technical aid, developed by Geert Letens and Eileen Van Aken, a professor from Virginia Tech regonised for her expertise on performance measurement. This abbreviation stands for Report, Evaluate, Communicate, Adjust, Lessons learned, Leadership. It provides a canvas on which to organize reporting and evaluation activities, but stretches the typical activity-oriented reports to include a clear evaluation of results, approach and people, as already clarified in the chapters discussing the planning and implementation battery. At the middle-management level however, what is important to evaluate is the impact of one initiative on other organizational goals and initiatives to avoid sub-optimization. Moreover, synchronization of activities across multiple initiatives needs to encouraged. The impact an initiative can have on internal or external stakeholders should stimulate enhanced communication. Based on the overview of the status of all activities, adjustments have to be made on priorities for key personnel, budgets and other critical resources. This may include adjusting scope, timings, budgets and expectations for initiatives as well. Important lessons that emerge from the four first initiatives need to be captured and shared with the organization through formal and informal networks. Encouraging results and desired behaviors deserve to be rewarded and recognized by the organization's leadership. This includes reflections on individuals that could benefit from training and coaching as well.

While RECALL sessions provide a way to connect individual performance expectations with the goals and ambitions of the organization, they also provide powerful instruments to shift the culture of the organization. The improved collaboration between low-level managers and middle managers reduces the power distance that can lead to a toxic culture. The cross-functional and cross-departmental discussions encourage a culture of collaboration and stimulate proactive, performance-oriented behaviors. The goal is to turn RECALL sessions into areas for dialogue between various organizational members that promote systems thinking, team learning and the development of a common language that supports the creation of a culture of we.

STRENGTHENING THE CORE AT NYU LANGONE MEDICAL CENTER

In July 2007 Robert Grossman became the dean and CEO of NYU Langone Medical Center. The institution consisted of both the NYU School of Medicine and NYU hospitals, but faced a fading reputation, an eroding market position and an operating loss of $120 million that year. When Grossman took over, he worked on an inspiring stretch vision to bring the organization back to the top of the medical and academic world. He also developed a strategic road map to clarify how the vision was to be achieved, and how the various teams could contribute.

Starting in 2008, a task force worked out a performance management system with the input from all chairs, and identified relevant metrics to measure excellence and the potential sources of data for measuring progress. The IT department provided the online dashboard that had been used as the basis for individual department review meetings. After a year, Grossman opened access to the dashboard to all the department chairs. The company also formed a high-level task force aiming at sharing data more broadly. The data transparency signaled a commitment to meritocracy and an ambition for performance excellence.

Grossman also started upgrading talent in key positions. He realized that the 33 department chairs played a crucial role in the transformation process. Unfortunately many of these chairpersons were entrenched in the legacy mindsets Grossman was seeking to change. So Grossman recruited new chairpersons according to new profiles: no longer the excellent researchers or clinicians, but people high in emotional intelligence and executive leadership capabilities. He paid attention to balancing national searches and internal promotions. Anticipating the need to navigate around some entrenched incumbents, Grossman and his top team instituted six-year chair terms and established a faculty committee to redraw department boundaries. By 2015, 30 out of 33 department chairs had been replaced, and faculty in all departments were getting used to the higher expectations that reflected a top-performing institution.

Ten years later, NYU Langone's reputation has improved significantly, the faculty group practice has grown fourfold, and the financial loss has turned into an operating margin of 10 percent.[120]

Leading change at the Gemba

Successful change requires that problems need to be solved at the source, or at the *Gemba* ('the real place').[121] That implies managing both incremental improvements and large-scale projects in a structured and transparent way to improve the business or create clear benefits for the customer. At the same time, sustainable change also requires connecting to employees, stimulating their involvement, anticipating potential resistance and developing front-level leadership.

When launching local change initiatives, you need to address both the rational and emotional battery. Overcharging one of the two batteries will lead to energy losses. When you put too much emphasis on action planning and implementation, the emotional side of change will be neglected. This occurs when the organization relies on mercenaries – external consultants or internal specialists – who neglect employee involvement and lead the change with a too directive approach. Be aware that your change projects will stumble over a lot of resistance.

On the other hand, overcharging the connection battery may result in overinvolvement and overexcitement of your employees. If this is not paired with an acceptable structure for action planning and implementation, it can lead to an overflow of ideas and local initiatives that eventually will exhaust all resources. Many organizations have witnessed this problem when they introduced an idea box to collect improvement suggestions from employees. Generally, the idea box fills up for a few months, but then after a while the box remains empty as the organization is not capable of dealing with the overflow of suggestions. This is what happens when your organization is staffed with greenhorns, people with good intentions but lacking the necessary change capabilities.

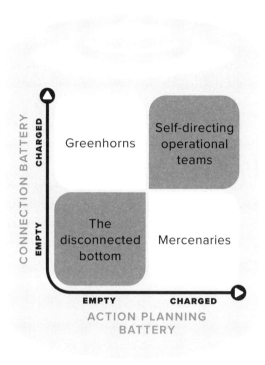

Figure 54 · Leading change at the Gemba

Only when you have self-directing operational teams, will you have a well-equipped and committed army ready to help you to achieve your strategic goals. Without this, your change effectiveness will suffer because your troops are badly equipped for the task, lack the conviction to succeed, or miss the authority to decide and act locally with the overall strategy in mind.

How do you manage both the rational and emotional side in a local change initiative? How do you achieve a well-equipped and committed army of self-directing teams? For this purpose, Letens and Van Aken have developed a model to successfully manage projects while paying attention to the people side of change. This model is derived from TransMeth ('Transformation Methodology') and incorporates both elements of the action planning and the connection battery.[122] It is presented in Figure 55.

The model works as follows: in order to manage local initiatives successfully, change leaders need to capture the attention of the employees involved. This implies emphasizing the need for change and clarifying how the project fits in the big strategic picture of the organization. It's not sufficient, however, to bring only the big strategic story. Local change leaders also need to scale the big story down to a smaller story that reflects the current context and desires of local employees. It needs to connect to things they have seen or witnessed themselves: a problem in their local context, a request from a customer, a move from a competitor that was announced in the media. A burning platform[123] and strategic direction that make sense will move employees into a state of awareness, but nothing more than that. This is the initial task of the local change leader and his sponsor at the middle- or top-level of the organization. This is step 1 in the model that is often completed during the kick-off meeting of a project.

In the next step, leaders guide their people in analyzing the current situation. Your employees need to explore the limitations and undesired characteristics of the 'AS IS' situation and assess the implications of the change on their context. The Trans-Meth model proposes that if you let employees do self-assessments, the 'awareness to change' will turn into a 'desire to change' more quickly.

In step 3, the leader takes charge again of the change, summarizing the insights of the current situation analysis into a meaningful picture that highlights key areas for change and linking the local vision for change to targets and goals. This way the change leader specifies the end result of the initiative and identifies criteria to judge when the end result is achieved.

In step 4, employees start to experiment and develop solutions. Here the employees take the lead again. They work out an acceptable solution for a given problem, evaluate alternatives and develop insights about how to change. This leads to practical knowledge about how to change. TransMeth assumes that the more this knowledge builds on the insights generated by employees, the more likely it is that employees will become stewards of the proposed solutions.

When employees have found an approach that works, the next step involves systematic deployment. It is the change leader who is responsible for ensuring that good solutions get embedded in a company's way of working. This requires the leader to actively support the transition: he needs to sufficient free time for coaching. This step implies a lot of trust in the leader, trust that should have been built throughout the previous steps, demonstrating his/her capacity to be a visionary-listener.

The final step is when employees are incentivized to self-assess the effectiveness of the new solution. Has the new solution led to the desired outcomes, or is there more work to be done? What can be done to bring the local change vision to the next level? It's important not to look just at results, but also to evaluate to what extent employees have followed a particular methodology. Are they able to repeat a success story? Also look at the motivation and the commitment of the employees to adopt the change. Are people *really* committed and enthusiastic about the new approach?

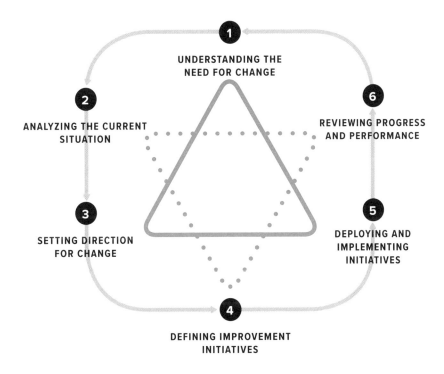

Figure 55 • TransMeth model for leading change at the Gemba

Figure 55 depicts a Star of David in the middle of the TransMeth model. This Star of David indicates who should take the lead in each particular step. In the steps connected by a straight line, it is the local champion who leads the dance. In the steps connected by the dotted lines, the employees are in the driver's seat. Switching responsibilities is a good way to assure both top-down and bottom-up communication and involvement. It helps to pay attention both to the technical project side as to the soft people side of change and to get both your *action planning* and *connection batteries* charged. Creating balance between these batteries helps to link the rational with the emotional side of change. It helps to 'emotionalize' the rational batteries of change and to 'rationalize' the emotional batteries of change.

Flow

The principle of balance ensures that energy is distributed evenly between rational and emotional change initiatives. Balanced interventions mainly take place between people at the same level — among the top team, middle managers, or members of a project team. *Flow initiatives* ensure that energy circulates between these various organizational levels as well. Change then becomes inclusive.

Flow is about building bridges between the top and the bottom of the organization. Flow is needed to align the left part of our batteries model with the right part. If too much attention is paid to initiatives at the top, there's a big chance that change won't be implemented. When on the other hand, change only addresses local issues, a company will never succeed in tackling its true strategic challenges. Research from McKinsey shows that transformations that involve people across the organization in the design process are more likely to be successful. All too often, leaders only look at the usual suspects — that is, the top-management and transformation-leadership teams — to staff change programs and projects. If you involve *key influencers* in the design of your change, your chance of change success increases significantly.[124]

You create flow first by assigning clear change roles and responsibilities for leaders at different levels, and second by launching joint initiatives where people from the various organizational levels meet, discuss and connect. The goal is to reduce the power distance between the levels and to provide more tangible and moral support, through budgets, understanding and advice for leaders that champion the various change initiatives.

Assign clear change roles and responsibilities

Successful change requires that the right people get involved in your change trajectory, from the top to the bottom. But in the rush to get change efforts moving, many executives delegate project teams without giving them the authority to deal with certain key decisions on how to run the change. Executives tell us that they don't have time to follow up on the efforts of all the project teams. "Just find the right people and get them going," is their thinking. Unfortunately that's not how it works.[125]

Delegating change to people who are not willing or capable to change merely creates more frustration. How many right people *do* you have in your organization? And what does it mean to 'get them going'? Laissez-faire leadership, or strict control and stifling supervision? If there is no handshake between leaders at the top and leaders at the bottom of the organization, 'just find the right people and get them going' is often perceived negatively by low-level leaders. It is great to empower people, but at the start of a change program, the credibility of low-level leaders increases when they publicly receive the support of powerful people in the organization. In a similar way, when push comes to shove and low-level leaders face sabotage efforts from some employees, they need to be able to fall back on higher-level leaders. Simply delegating projects doesn't provide enough support for low-level or even middle-level managers to influence important stakeholders.

If you follow the recommendations of change management consultants, you need a change initiator, a supportive top team, change agents, sponsors, coaches, champions, supporters, implementers, facilitators and followers. That's a whole bunch of people. What exactly is the role each should play in the change process? We believe this question needs to be answered clearly to launch an effective change approach. Poor understanding, execution and coordination of the roles change leaders need to play undermine both change design and implementation. Initiatives often stall, for example, when there is a mismatch between a sponsor's words and actions, or if confidence in the change agent is low.[126]

In sport, every successful athlete needs a sponsor, a manager and a coach. In change management, a similar approach applies: at every organizational level we need leaders to pick up specific change responsibilities, so that leaders *at all levels* find it easier to support each other.

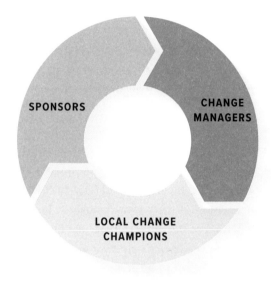

Figure 56 • Three key roles in successful change

Sponsors are ultimately accountable for the success of the overall change program. They ensure that the transformation achieves the desired business objectives and delivers the benefits from the change to their business. They typically are top leaders who have the organizational power to legitimize change initiatives, reward commitment and provide consequences for not changing. They design and monitor the evolution of the transformation to assure the organization's batteries are charging and assure the availability of budgets for the transformation. Above all, they are the primary role models for change. Their words and actions need to reflect the key principles of the desired transformation. Their presence at well-chosen moments of specific initiatives serves as a source of inspiration for the transformation and provides other roles of the change program the credibility to lead.

Change managers typically design and manage annual change programs. Building on the set of principles, guidelines and expectations of the sponsors, they manage the portfolio of ongoing change initiatives. This implies they mobilize change leaders at the local level, providing them the time and resources that they need. Equally important however, they plan for the training and support. They monitor results, needs and insights from the local initiatives to distil and share lessons learned. This role is often picked up by middle managers who, through frequent feedback and interactions with local change leaders and their team members, contribute to development of a healthy culture. They are architects of networks that facilitate collaboration and knowledge sharing and serve as coaches for local change leaders. As such, they set the tone for improvement, integration and open communication.

Champions are the local change leaders. They lead their teams to the expected results within the agreed time and cost. They coach their team members to develop the skills that are needed to sustain local success. Equally important, they also guide them through the various stages of individual change. In other words, they work on *results*, *process* (how to approach a particular initiative through structured problem solving; how to support it with sound process project management) and *people* (communication, empathy, resistance management, involvement and motivation).

In order to be true advocates of various approaches to charge the batteries and to become role models for change, leaders at all levels need to become familiar with the roles and responsibilities above. As in reality many organizations are not familiar with these types of roles, the development of appropriate leadership programs is often essential. Each of the roles makes different contributions throughout the change process. In the next sections we will clarify how the principle of flow stimulates collaboration between the various roles at the top, bridge, and bottom of the organization.

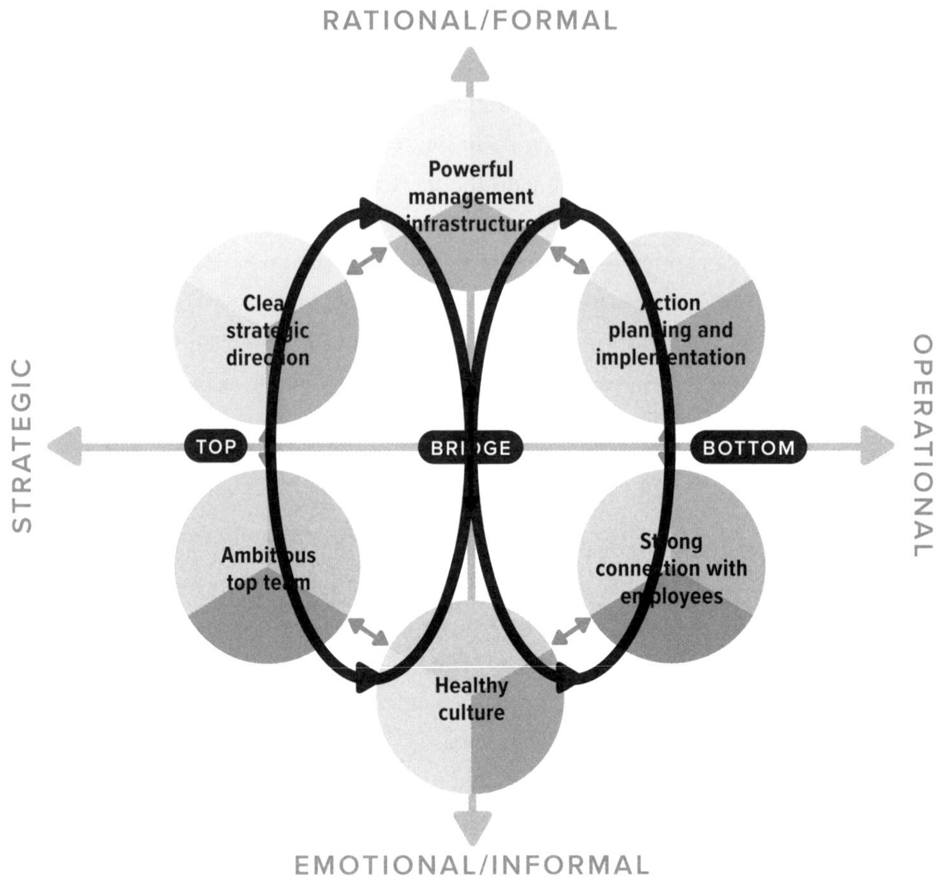

Figure 57 • Creating energy flow in change

Energy flow at the top

Getting your top batteries charged is done mainly by the executive team. Initially, one or two members of the executive team take up the role to sponsor change at the top: they initiate discussions on the need for change and coach the rest of the executive team to the point that all can serve as committed sponsors of the overall change program. As a result, the executive sponsors screen to what extent the executive team fully supports the conclusions and acts as a team. They keep an eye on the dynamics at the top team and ensure a safe and energizing environment that allows for having tough discussions focused on strategy and change. They are the brains of the organization and determine its future, but they are also the lungs with which the organization breathes.

The executive sponsors play a crucial role in facilitating the discussions that set the tone at the top. They orient strategy and change discussions within the top team and are responsible for making sure that this important process doesn't dilute. They summarize the main conclusions of those discussions, and identify the next steps and tasks to be performed. Key tasks include communication to other management levels and the rest of the organization. Very often however, the top team needs further input to make better-informed decisions and to enlarge the collation of change energy flow; i.e. a better connection with the other levels of the organization is essential to accomplish this.

As a result, senior managers play an important role in this process too. Most senior managers will be asked to translate the strategy to their department and to define functional objectives that align with the strategic choices of the organization. This process will largely determine the priorities for resources (time and budgets). Bad alignment of tactical goals with strategic choices will lead to a poor implementation of the strategy. Senior managers will also typically be appointed as change managers, responsible for rolling out projects and executing the change in their department. (In smaller organizations, it's possible that a senior executive takes both the role of sponsor and change manager.) The change managers need to fully understand the change ambition and strategy and should challenge the top team if the ambition and strategy are unrealistic or based on the wrong assumptions. They also need to serve as role models for change in their department and transfer the spirit of the top to their context. If these change managers witness openness and collaboration between the executive sponsors, they will be encouraged to practice the fundamental principles of the transformation at their level as well

Some organizations even involve lower-level champions in the strategy discussions. The idea is that if those influencers or high potentials are involved in the discussions, they will be able to help implement change initiatives better and faster. Mostly, these lower-level managers do not contribute significantly to the strategy decision-making, but it can be a deliberate choice to involve them anyway. Their presence signals openness, trust and involvement. This largely contributes to the transfer of the desired culture and certainly supports the creation of awareness and interest at lower levels of the organization. These elements are important levers to accelerate the implementation of the strategy and the change program and its underlying principles.

Creating energy flow at top through the involvement of sponsors, change agents and selected champions, lays the foundation for the alignment and inspiration of leaders throughout the organization.

Energy flow through the core

Getting your bridge batteries charged is crucial in successful change. The management infrastructure battery and the culture battery amplify the social energy and control the systemic energy in your organization. The bridge batteries help to prioritize and support change efforts. They also assure the development of a human network that characterizes a healthy culture. They keep track of the overall change success from a result, process and people perspective. At the rational level, this implies translating the overall strategy into a portfolio of initiatives, allocating resources, and keeping track of progress. At the emotional level, it's about developing new social networks that reduce gaps between organizational members and promote change as a learning opportunity.

Here the change managers play a central role again. Together with the executive sponsors, they define the portfolio of change initiatives for the next two to three years. Then they run the 'program management office'. Companies that take a systematic approach to prioritizing initiatives and following a structured methodology are more successful than companies tackling projects in an ad hoc way. Change managers are responsible for setting up such a change methodology. This allows them to closely work with local change managers as they review the progress of particular change initiatives. A common methodology stimulates collaboration between the members of local initiatives but also contributes to the development of a common language that encourages collaboration and understanding across initiatives. In addition, change managers seek to understand the informal organization, actively looking for ways to promote connections between different members of the organization. They set up communication and training efforts that seek to influence the desired behavior. They should also identify cultural barriers that are reflected in the discussions among organizational members and set up cultural initiatives that promote respect and understanding. They are sensitive to the history of the organization and how that translates in mindsets that reflect undesired paradigms and actively look for ways to challenge and change limiting mental models. Perhaps most importantly, they identify local change agents who are the best fit to run the individual projects.

In this process, the role of executive sponsors is to ensure that the change managers have sufficient budgets to attract human and financial resources for running the initiatives. Sponsors have an important political role to play during the transformation. One of the most common problems that we encounter in large organizations is what we call 'delegated change'. Rather, sponsors cannot disappear once they've attended the kick-off of the change program or a specific change initiative. One of their key roles is to communicate the strategic choices and the desired culture to promote change. Sponsors should continuously legitimize the need for change within the organization and reinforce the story by spotlighting where success is being achieved. They work with the change managers to set and announce important targets and deadlines.

Equally important, however, is that sponsors and change managers need to agree on systems that reward the right behavior. Executive sponsors should openly engage others and build a coalition that supports the change. Developing a system that recognizes and rewards the behavior the organization wants to see more of, and punishing what is considered inacceptable (NNRs), is one of the more difficult challenges for which sponsors and change agents need to come to a consensus. Working together on the development of a reward system is an important way for sponsors to coach change agents on the implementation of cultural change. In our experience this is one of the most challenging discussions of a transformation effort as it implies the identification of new symbols of success and the recognition of new heroes, such as early adopters, at all levels of the organization. They have to identify successful projects and put them in the spotlight.

Though charging the bridge batteries must involve local change champions, it's clear that their role is even more explicit when leading change at the Gemba. To strengthen the core, they particularly need to function as antennae that share important signals from the bottom of the organization. Ultimately, they often determine what is feasible, from a technical but also from a human perspective. Whereas sponsors and change managers know best what needs to be done to respond to conditions within the market, local change managers know what can be done within the current context of the organization: what the organization is capable of doing, and what employees are willing to do. Good change managers bring problems and risk to the attention of the change agents, but also propose alternative solutions to overcome the identified challenges. They share information on people, progress and results, helping change managers to reflect on both local measures to support the champions, and on measures that need to be taken within the overall change program. Examples of critical information include actions where the organization can get the biggest bang for their buck as well as the equally important links to personal needs from key individuals at the bottom of the organization. Change managers need to signal the need for both physical and emotional support. We refer to the RECALL process explained in the previous chapter as a valuable instrument that facilitates the collaboration between champions and change managers in review meetings.

Stimulating the collaboration and coordination of sponsors, change agents and champions at the core, creates energy flow that assures practical and moral support for local initiatives and largely determines the development of a healthy culture throughout the organization.

Energy flow that supports change at the Gemba
Change at the bottom is about launching individual projects that fit in the overall portfolio of initiatives. Here the local change champions pick up the major role. Local change leaders have to run and finish individual projects with their teams. They are accountable for the complete and timely implementation of the change projects in their areas. The TransMeth model that was introduced earlier in this chapter helped to explain how in successful local projects, responsibilities are switched between the local change leader and the team members. Switching responsibilities is a good way to assure both top-down and bottom-up involvement and communication.

The change managers' role here is to ensure that local change leaders have all the resources to successfully complete the individual change projects. Local champions cannot fulfill their role until their needs and concerns are tackled. That's the function of the change manager, who needs to provide training and emotional support. This implies they act as coaches, and actively participate in local projects at well-chosen moments to share advice on methodology and approach. They recognize the champion and his team for using the appropriate methodology but at the same time encourage creativity and teamwork. They should highlight how each individual project fits in the bigger story and support the local change manager when coordination or support from other change initiatives or departments is needed.

The role of the executive sponsors is to assure the champions and the change agents are committed to the project and to the duties of their roles. They provide projects with credibility through their words and actions: they sign off the project charter and clarify the need for the project at kick-off meetings. They periodically assess the dynamics of the team to evaluate the spirit of the transformation. This implies they intervene when needed to clarify the values of the transformation and to reconfirm the commitment from the top. They show interest in the results of pilot tests and use these to re-inject energy into the team when needed. They understand the value of their presence at the Gemba in times of victory and defeat, and are not scared to privately confront individual resistors when necessary. They also understand the importance of their role to assure sustainability of performance. As such they plan follow-up visits to reconnect with the local champion and his team a few months after the delivery of the project results.

If there is one key word that all roles share, it is *coaching*. Every manager's first job at any level is to coach the development of leaders or organizational members at lower levels. Coaching is therefore the best way to assure energy flow among the various roles of the change program. It implies that sponsors at the top know what it takes to be a change agent, and that both sponsor and change agent understand the reality of being a champion. This is a prerequisite for change that is well understood by the top performers in our study, which include this principle throughout their leadership development programs.

We realize all this takes time. But we also know that energy flow that eventually hits the Gemba, the place where the real value of the organization is created, assures things actually get done. It transforms a culture of 'just do it' to a culture of 'we have done this'.

As already mentioned, in smaller organizations people can take several roles. But it's still important that people understand what roles and responsibilities they have to play when trying to assure flow among the various levels of the organization. Even if it means that they have to wear different hats at different occasions.

Both small and large organizations can further stimulate energy flow by organizing *flow events*. Flow events are two- to three-day meetings where sponsors, change agents and champions and other key players of the organization meet to jointly work on focused topics of the change program. What we recommend is for organizations to have at least one 'breathing in' and one 'breathing out' session per year.

During a *'breathing in' session* the various players of the organization come together to focus on the left half of the battery model: strategic orientation and the identification of strategic goals and initiatives, as well as inspirational activities that clarify purpose and meaning, and reflection on their connection with the key values and culture of the organization. Sponsors and change agents largely determine the agenda during this type of event, which aims to bring fresh air into the organization. These meetings connect the organization with the outside world and energize the change program through a focus on strategy and spirit. It can of course be beneficial for a selected number of key change champions to be involved in this as well.

'Breathing out' sessions put all emphasis on the right half of the model. They are essential to focus on implementation, not idea generation. The focus here is on achieving benefits, both tangible (actual results) and intangible (capabilities). This means the agenda is largely dominated by change agents and champions. Key activities are mostly internally oriented, trying to achieve an overview of all the practical and emotional obstacles that the organization faces before being able to fully deploy sustained change throughout the organization. This is an important exercise to re-prioritize projects and initiatives, but also to identify opportunities for sponsors and change managers to assure security or stimulate commitment from employees. Pilot projects and success stories are provided the opportunity to share results with a larger audience to gain recognition and visibility for their

work, but also to provide employees from other projects with the opportunity for networking and knowledge sharing. 'Breathing out' sessions focus on results and connection.

We believe both approaches are essential to build cohesion and drive among the various roles and to assure focus on performance and improvement. Organizations that put too much emphasis on one type of flow (*in* or *out*) will slowly destabilize the batteries in their organization.

Notice that the purpose of these events goes way beyond the rational benefits of alignment and prioritization. The events are first of all opportunities to develop a common language, to strengthen the ties of the change network and enlarge it, and to stimulate new connections. Fully charged organizations are highly networked organizations that know there is a time to jointly reflect and a time to jointly act.

Key messages of this chapter

While chapter 8 identified the main initiatives to launch to manage your change successfully, this chapter concentrated on *how to design these initiatives*. As we don't believe in a fixed step model, we've provided you with energy design principles to help you set up your portfolio of initiatives.

- The first design principle is to maintain balance between the rational and emotional side of the change journey. Even if your change initiative concentrates on one side, you should be aware of maintaining balance throughout all organizational levels. This chapter explained what balance means when setting the tone at the top, when strengthening the core, and when leading change at the Gemba.

- The second energy design principle ensures flow between the various organizational levels that are involved in any change project. A good change project should affect both the batteries at the right and at the left of the model. Our major recommendation is to assign clear responsibilities and change roles in the change program. Another recommendation is to launch focused events where different people meet, work together, and connect. All this will increase the likelihood of change success significantly.

Chapter

10

BOOSTING CHANGE ENERGY

———

Building your change architecture

Key questions

How do you shift your attention from managing a change program to building change capabilities?

What needs to be done to boost energy in your organization?

What is your energy ambition level?

This final chapter describes three ways in which managers use this batteries model. Some use the model to cure immediate pain. Others have used it to start a more profound change program addressing several change batteries. These organizations improved and were able to deal with their change challenges in a much better way. A third category of companies went one step further and invested in building change capabilities to deal with a fast-changing and complex environment. This last category boosted organizational energy and manages it continuously.

This chapter describes what it takes to boost energy across the organization and presents the case of KBC, a financial institution that had to respond to the threat of digital disruption. The company went through a huge change program that transformed it into a more agile organization focusing on performance, empowerment and accountability.

What is the ambition of your change program?

We've presented our batteries model and a more detailed energy scan to many companies. Although they find the concept of the batteries insightful, powerful and easy to understand, they also quickly realize that getting their organization energized is a much tougher journey than they had expected. In our consulting practices, we've come across three typical reactions to the results of an energy scan.

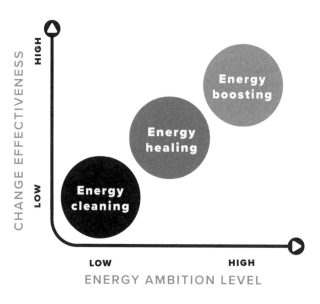

Figure 58 · Three energy ambition levels

The first group of companies is interested in and intrigued by the model. They find it thought-provoking and insightful, and they soon recognize that they have some change challenges to tackle. But they don't want to put too much effort into fully charging all their batteries. Their energy ambition level is to do some '*energy cleaning*'. They look for an immediate solution to their biggest change problems. A typical question is: "Can you summarize your conclusions in three main recommendations?" Companies that want to do energy cleaning only want to fix those batteries that drain energy out of the organization. They welcome help from external consultants, because they don't have the change capabilities and/or the change competences to build a solution themselves. Unfortunately, the effectiveness of those change solutions is low, as their ambition is merely to stop the bleeding. While their intentions may be good, they often quickly return to their old patterns.

The second group of companies realizes that their change problems are not temporary and that there is no quick fix to get back on track. They are aware that their organization needs a coherent set of balance and flow interventions to bring more harmony to the organization. As a result, they launch a big change program to get all six batteries charged. They want to find a cure for their disease: they want '*energy healing*'. Those companies may invest in a change management program, mostly sponsored by a senior executive. But when the situation is back under control, or when the senior executive leaves the organization, interest in the change batteries evaporates. Organizational energy is no longer considered an issue in the company. In some cases – mostly when a new CEO with no interest in the concept of change energy is appointed – we note that the company easily reverts to the old situation as well. The program may be very effective in achieving some valuable change results, but does not generally manage to build lasting change capabilities.

The last group of companies is unfortunately more the exception than the rule. These companies are true 'energy boosters' and work hard to build change capabilities to deal with fast-changing environments. They realize that change is constant. The only answer to survive in a global and turbulent environment is to build capabilities that allow you to renew yourself faster than the competition. This is the only recipe to sustain great performance over a longer period of time. Energy boosters pay as much attention to the way they implement change as they do to the strategy or solution they are trying to implement. Executive sponsors manage the overall change capacity of the organization and they periodically assess the gap between current and desired change capabilities of their organization. Managing change effectively is a core competency in these organizations. They are energy athletes; organizations that thrive on change. To be this kind of organization implies you fully embrace every opportunity to optimize the change energy of your organization and make it a part of how you implement your strategy through a holistic change management approach.

Build a change architecture for energy boosting

Energy boosters have committed executive sponsors with an ambition to embrace change. That commitment translates into building a change infrastructure that boosts energy to all of the six change batteries. Many companies struggle with building a management infrastructure that helps in running the business. Energy boosting requires you to go one step further and build a strong change engine to build your change capabilities.

Figure 59 • The essential components of a change architecture

Change approach principles and goals: the commitment model

It is as important to express a clear will to change the way you build your business as it is to express a clear will to change the way you run your business. Without the former, there will be a focus only on results and not on how the results will be achieved. We believe this matters. Henry Ford once said: "If I had asked people what they wanted, they would have said faster horses." We too are convinced that many managers today want faster results, without understanding what type of organization is needed to obtain these results in a fast changing world. Therefore we believe it is critical that top leaders publicly express their desire to boost organizational energy and to respect energy balance and flow principles with as much conviction as they proclaim to hit — or desire to hit — their financial and other performance targets.

Depending on your current energy profile, context and history, your organization may face a journey of several years before reaching your nirvana. So you certainly want to link bold long-term statements with attractive yet acceptable goals for the development of the change capabilities of your organization for the next year. As the maturity of your organization grows from year to year, your annual objectives can become more ambitious too. But from the start, it should be clear that the ultimate ownership of developing change capabilities and defining the roadmap for change lies at the top. If there are no advocates of energy at the C-level, there is no real commitment to 'change the way you change your business'. As a result, the batteries of change model may become nothing more than a management fad for your organization.

The change masterplan: the delivery model

Whereas the *commitment model* clarifies goals related to change principles and evolving characteristics of the organization from year to year, the *enterprise change masterplan* needs to provide specific planning information with regard to all key interventions. This includes the start and finish dates for quick win projects, timings and budgets for major investments, plans for critical cross-functional projects, scheduling of balance and flow events and major review meetings.

Whereas models such as Kotter's 8-step plan are clear on the optimal fixed sequence of interventions, we know that the reality for many organizations is often different. If the current focus of the organization is on a key investment project that needs to deliver within the next few months, we believe that project deserves the focus of the whole organization, and that withdrawing critical resources from this project for strategic reflection only leads to distraction for everyone. However, while we don't believe in a fixed sequence of interventions, finding balance among all batteries implies that the organization initiate focused initiatives on all levels (top-bridge-bottom) at least once a year. It's not the end of the world if these first initiatives don't achieve a perfect score on approach. For most organizations it will be important to time box their efforts and to learn from their first experience. Balance rules perfection.

Further, the need to control *pace* and *rhythm* of initiatives cannot be emphasized enough. Rhythm provides certainty and therefore acts as a regulating mechanism for the whole organization. If you start introducing a rhythm to review initiatives and goals in the infrastructure of the organization, most local initiatives will start to synchronize with this rhythm, similar to the mysterious sync up of pendulum clocks. Rhythm serves as the heartbeat of your change approach — if you can't hear the heartbeat of your change fetus after eight to twelve weeks, there is a good chance your program is turning into a miscarriage. And similar to the development of a baby, the heartbeat at the start of a new program is generally high, allowing for fast learning cycles. As the organization develops, it also tends to become more capable of controlling its heartbeat, knowing when to accelerate it to increase the pace of change, and when to slow it down, to provide the organization room for recovery.

Some final considerations relate to the duration of initiatives and the effect of seasonality. Many organizations define annual initiatives, linked to annual goals. We encourage organizations to reduce the scope of projects to three or four months. It is generally better to divide bigger objectives into smaller chunks that can more easily be evaluated and adjusted if needed. This makes it easier to demonstrate progress and stimulate collaboration. Most organizations are confronted with significant seasonality effects, either through increased demand or reduced capacity during specific periods of the year. High season or low capacity peaks require all resources to focus on running the business. Working on improvement during this time period is often de facto not happening, or, when it is imposed, often leads to frustration instead of motivation. It is wise to intentionally articulate periods throughout the year to reduce change efforts to a minimum. All things that grow, including change, should respect the difference between winter and summer.

Change leaders: the change leadership model

Great change requires great change leadership. It would be silly to invest in an F1 race car, without reflecting on the desired characteristics of the driver, the team leader and even the pit stop coordinator. Profound change requires getting the right people from the top to the bottom involved in your change trajectory. Unfortunately, we see a lot of organizations in which top leaders have never acted as sponsors, middle managers lack crucial skills required to act as change managers, and low level managers lack training and coaching to be change champions.

As a result, the development of appropriate leadership programs is essential. In order to be able to be advocates of various approaches to charge the batteries and to become role models for change, leaders at all levels need to become familiar with the importance of their change leadership capacities. This implies willingness and learning by doing above all. Developing leadership skills implies leadership coaching. If organizations fail to develop the leadership capabilities that are essential to drive change ownership (willingness, know-how, skills and credibility), people easily revert to their daily habits and old routines. Coaching is one of key components of leadership development at Toyota, where even a coach has a coach to improve coaching and to assure the implementation of their True North values. That may seem like overdoing things at first, but think about it: this is a great way to develop the most critical resource in your organization.

Building change leadership skills takes time. In the short term, many organizations need to seek the help of external specialists to support and develop change leadership skills at all levels. Sponsors typically work with change architects to design the overall transformation, and change managers often work with external change agents to seek support to strengthen the core – the management infrastructure and culture. Last but not least, change champions can benefit from the advice of change facilitators to develop low-level leadership skills.

Figure 60 • Internal and external change management roles

Figure 60 further clarifies how these roles need to support each other to shift the mindsets and behaviors of the whole organization. While technical skills can often be learned from external specialists, coaching between the levels is essential to shift mind and behavior. Recent research from McKinsey reports that successful transformations need to spend time and effort up front to design transformation initiatives that focus on fostering understanding and conviction (sponsor), reinforcing change through formal mechanisms (managers), developing talent and skills (champions), and role modeling (all). While leaders at all levels can pick up any of these focus areas, we have noticed that when employees see the alignment of leaders on various levels, this significantly boosts the credibility of the overall change program.[127]

The human network: the influence model

Ultimately, organizational change implies changing individual behavior. Whereas the connect-to-employees battery already highlighted several ways to guide individuals through change, it should be clear that it is utterly important to *influence the right people first*. Many change books will therefore rightfully emphasize the importance of stakeholder management when defining and implementing a change management approach. Mapping stakeholder groups, their interests and their influence on the success of your change program is indeed a good way to recruit members for your change teams, and to optimize and prioritize communication efforts. Different people may have different perspectives and different interests, and as a result, you need a political lens to reflect on consequences of conflicts and disagreements.

Though 'power' and 'politics' have a negative connotation in many organizations, understanding how to influence people is a critical component of every change program. When used well and for the right cause, it results in less pain and better results for everyone. There are two major concepts to consider from this perspective. The first one relates to the *sources of power*. The first type of power that generally comes to our mind relates to position and expertise, which in many organizations often go hand in hand when expertise is rewarded with promotion. Clearly role-based leaders and advice experts cannot be neglected in change initiatives – in fact, the leadership model presented above encourages organizations to continuously develop the skills of leaders at all levels of the organization. Research has demonstrated, however, that this type of power generally turns out to be particularly valuable to get routine-based activities done.

When it comes to getting things done in the context of a crisis or a major change initiative, basic emotions such as fear and love draw us toward people we feel affection for: people we trust. Developing an understanding of personal friendships in organizations is therefore a second important source of power that should not be underestimated. When people who are central in 'affection networks' are actively involved in change initiatives, this rapidly turns the informal organization into an informed organization.

We are frequently asked by executives how much involvement is required to create change in an organization. Change happens when you can achieve a shift in the dominant coalition in your organization.[128] Involving 10 percent of the central persons in the social network of the organization typically creates a critical mass of change energy that will ignite the rest of the organization.

The second important concept that contributes to influencing stakeholders, relates to *changing the basic characteristics of the organization's social network*. Strong hierarchical structures in organizations typically result in many structural holes in the social network, with the hierarchical leaders acting as powerful gatekeepers between the different groups within the organization. This implies that new ideas and behavior patterns are largely determined by separate group characteristics. This results in strong micro-cultures between departments that often prohibit collaboration on organization-wide problems.

As a result, the change program needs to reflect ways to overcome structural holes and organizational barriers. This includes formal approaches such as creating cross-functional teams and learning groups (where people share experience on topics of mutual interest, such as quality, safety, environmental issues or well-being), but also stimulating informal connections between networks through sport events or sight-seeing trips. Research has demonstrated that smokers typically develop informal networks across the organization, allowing them to more easily connect with change – we are suggesting replicating or finding alternatives to this kind of social network.

Change infrastructure: the support model

All of the previous factors largely depend on information, communication, education and training. The *support model* defines the characteristics of activities that will facilitate the availability and flow of information and knowledge. This includes the creation of a plan for training and education on change, establishing guidelines and templates for information and knowledge management, setting up an intranet website, and defining principles of visual management techniques to support the overall change program. Don't neglect face-to-face meetings and informal conversations in your communication plans either. It is not just the message that counts, but also where, when and by whom. Especially when you want to promote communication from the bottom to the top, you may discover more at an outside lunch, than in your office space.

Whereas the investment in time and resources for building the change infrastructure largely depends on the size of the organization and the ambition of the change program, it is our experience that neglecting to reflect on these topics eventually has a considerable impact on both the success and the timely execution of change programs. As many organizations have experienced with the implementation of a project management office, creating a change management office can result in a bureaucratic monster that consumes rather than produces energy. It is our experience, however, that the problem behind this is not related to the potential benefits that a sound implementation of the supporting model can provide. When the PMO and CMO efforts start to take on a life of their own, this often reflects a culture that focuses on control, and not on change and learning.

Further refinement and continuous improvement

Once you have your change architecture defined, you have to 'build it – try it – fix it'.[129] The basics of how to implement and refine your overall change program are as simple as that: you have to follow the same rules and principles that apply for complex and dynamic project management. You start at a manageable scale, learn from the results, adjust where needed, and then continue to iterate while increasing the scale. This is often far from reality for most organizations. Some have endless discussions to prepare for the ultimate big bang, others mainly live by Nike's motto – just do it – and easily slide away from the intended learning approach to results-driven interventions that aim merely for low hanging fruit. We are not saying it is not worth investing in a sound design of the change architecture — on the contrary. But as illustrated in the previous paragraphs, this design is about laying out the principles of the five fundamental change models. It is not about creating detailed Gantt charts or doing complicated statistical analyses.

What we are aiming for is the creation of a set of principles and models that allow you to select specific projects that can be put to the test, so that you can get some benefits from them, but above all, *learn* from them. This implies that when you start to implement your change program, there is as much emphasis on *evaluation* as there is on *doing*. Most of the organizations we have worked with are particularly weak on evaluation: they take hardly any time to reflect on difference between their change ambition and their actual change behavior. As a result, they don't learn from mistakes or successes. One thing is for sure, however: change without reinforcement is *not* going to bring lasting results. It is not going to result in stronger change capabilities either. Whether your initial focus is top-down or bottom-up, if you don't take the time to periodically asses your change approach, you are not going to create more than noise at the start of your journey, or a temporary big push that lasts for a few months and eventually ends in business as usual.

Here are a few alarm bell signs to look out for after half a year: there is no shift in the commitment of top leaders; the network of people involved in changes is not growing; no employees at the bottom have turned into believers; no short-term benefits have been realized; no difference in time pressure can be noticed; or no customers can testify positively of the changes they are experiencing. If some of these signs are present, you have probably created a big show, and nothing more.

Of course, you are not going to see change in *all* these elements either. Some things will be great, others will remain a struggle for your organization. Some shifts may come from just a few individuals, and may just be visible in one department. Our recommendation is to *look for both strengths and weaknesses*. Far too often we have a primary focus on what went wrong, what causes problems. When it comes to change, it is equally important to identify things that have worked well and need to be repeated. Change is about creating new patterns – this implies repeating positive behavior.

After half a year, your *context* might have changed significantly as well. A new player on the market, a major disaster that upended your brilliant looking forecast, and all of a sudden there is more pressure for results and less time and attention for development. And that is fine. This is essentially what change capabilities should allow you to do: to maintain your course while dealing with new situations.

We clearly recommend that you introduce a pacemaker to assess progress on your change capabilities as well as a brief mid-course evaluation after six months, and a more detailed assessment of your batteries every year. The former will allow you to reinforce the early positive signs of change and to adjust for balance and flow where needed. The latter one will be essential to gradually expand your change ambition, to systematically grow your network of change leaders, and to develop the change maturity of your organization.

Positive energy creates more energy

Successful change and organizational resilience can only be achieved through a periodic assessment and development of the organization's change capabilities to adjust your customized roadmap. The ultimate objective is to address short-term and long-term business needs while developing a critical mass of change leaders at all levels of the organization. External change specialists are often needed to provide short-term support to achieve this. Truly successful change initiatives, however, are characterized by the development of change leadership within the organization. In the end, this is the only way to achieve the full benefits of change and to sustain them.

It all sounds like a lot of work, doesn't it? We would be lying if we said it was not. But we can guarantee that you will be surprised to see how little energy it sometimes takes to get started. And once you create positive energy, the true art of change management is to use that energy to create *more* energy in other batteries. And the more you increase the energy level in a few batteries, the easier it will become to energize the batteries that lag. If you use the balance and flow interventions well, the six batteries of change behave as a dynamic system with several positive reinforcement loops.

The following case study will further inspire you. It testifies of the change capabilities of one of the top performers in our database, which used its capabilities to successfully transform its organization for the digital revolution. We hope this will convince you that perhaps the most challenging paradigm to break for most organizations is to shift from looking at change as a cost to manage pain, towards a perspective that invests in change to thrive in the future.

How KBC gets ready for the digital age

The KBC Group is one of the larger financial institutions in Europe, with 36,000 employees serving its more than 10 million customers. Since its founding in 1998, KBC had shown good financial results. In 2008, however, the company was hit hard by the financial crisis. After six turbulent years, the group had restored profitability to pre-crisis levels by divesting unprofitable units and downsizing the organization.

Determined to ensure that KBC would never get into financial trouble again, CEO Thijs launched a company-wide cultural program – called Pearl – to restore trust and pride among employees, and to turn a hierarchical company (with slow decision processes, heavy structures and a lack of transparency) into a more agile organization focusing on performance, empowerment and accountability.

The company also formulated an explicit strategic goal to create outstanding customer satisfaction through a seamless, multi-channel and customer-centric distribution approach. The company's extensive network of bank branches and insurance agencies would remain crucial contact opportunities for engaging with customers directly, but the company would fully commit to digitization as well.

KBC's response to digitization: Setting the tone at the top

In April 2014, Erik Luts was appointed General Manager Direct Channels. As a member of KBC Belgium's Management Committee, he became responsible for KBC's digitization initiatives in Belgium. Erik's information technology (IT) background had made him very sensitive to IT trends that affected the financial services industry. He knew that digitization would radically transform the industry and that new players would challenge the incumbents' traditional business models. It was crucial to build change capabilities throughout the organization to deal with what many believed would be a continuous change for the financial services industry. At first, his team members on the Management Committee were not convinced of the urgency to change.

A team of some 75 members from a variety of departments and functions was created to investigate KBC's digital readiness and to compose a set of fact books that could help build a case for change with real evidence. The team developed a Customer Behavior fact book, a Competitor Analysis fact book, and an IT fact book to document disruptive trends in the environment and to investigate the implications for KBC. The main conclusion of this exercise was that KBC's leading position in Belgium was indeed under attack from multiple directions. The challenge for the company was to defend its leading position as well as to embrace new opportunities for the future. At the end of the day, the team put forward five digital business models as possible response options and developed feasibility plans for each scenario.

Luts felt desperate at times during discussions with his colleagues, but, after a few months, the Management Committee came on board. The top team felt they had created a 'band of brothers' and felt the urgency to move forward. The top team battery had received a boost of positive energy.

In January 2014, KBC Belgium's Management Committee presented its digital strategy to the Group's Executive Committee for approval. The strategy was named 'Klant 2020' ('Customer 2020'). At the heart of KBC's strategic response was the transformation of the current branch-based business model towards a hybrid omni-channel model for bank-insurance customers. The core model was to build a single concept in which all channels (e.g. branches, agents, advice centers, web, mobile banking) were fully transparent to customers – who choose the channel, not KBC. This meant re-thinking and re-designing services from a customer's point of view. KBC would also set up speedboats (discussed in chapter 3) for the other digital challenges. The new program put the customer's needs – not the product, the service or the distribution channel – radically at the center. The value proposition for all business units of KBC Belgium would now concentrate on being solutions-driven and accessible. KBC would not only offer a new set of commercial applications and products, but would also strengthen and leverage existing core capabilities as well as build new ones for the digital age. The company engaged in a simplification program and invested in hybrid customer journeys, data analytics and online marketing capabilities.

Building a strong core with a sound delivery model

KBC Belgium invested €250 million in the new strategy for the period 2014-20. The Management Committee decided to stop separate digitization projects and limit all other projects to the bare essentials. All digital innovations were grouped under the umbrella of Klant 2020. The program also secured many of the best people of the organization. In only a few weeks, the program had mobilized some 250 business and IT people to staff the project teams. There was a lot of resistance from the middle managers, who lost some of their most valuable employees, but the Management Committee pushed through. KBC Belgium also created an elaborate program management structure to direct and coordinate the execution of the Klant 2020 strategy.

Luts and Johan Lema, the manager responsible for the distribution channels, were the two executive sponsors. They reported back to their colleagues in the Management Committee on a monthly basis. The program included tracks for commercial deliverables in focal businesses as well as tracks catering to the growth of foundational capabilities. Each track was led by a program track manager and a high-level business sponsor (see Figure 61).

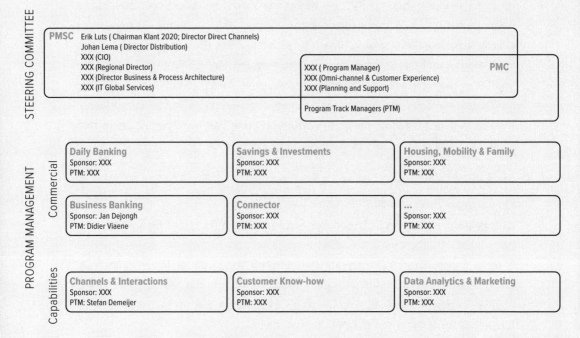

Commercial

Capabilities

PMSC Erik Luts (Chairman Klant 2020; Director Direct Channels)
Johan Lema (Director Distribution)
XXX (CIO)
XXX (Regional Director)
XXX (Director Business & Process Architecture)
XXX (IT Global Services)

XXX (Program Manager)   **PMC**
XXX (Omni-channel & Customer Experience)
XXX (Planning and Support)

Program Track Managers (PTM)

Daily Banking
Sponsor: XXX
PTM: XXX

Savings & Investments
Sponsor: XXX
PTM: XXX

Housing, Mobility & Family
Sponsor: XXX
PTM: XXX

Business Banking
Sponsor: Jan Dejongh
PTM: Didier Viaene

Connector
Sponsor: XXX
PTM: XXX

...
Sponsor: XXX
PTM: XXX

Channels & Interactions
Sponsor: XXX
PTM: Stefan Demeijer

Customer Know-how
Sponsor: XXX
PTM: XXX

Data Analytics & Marketing
Sponsor: XXX
PTM: XXX

Figure 61 • Klant 2020 program structure

KBC's plan was to launch a new wave of projects every six months. The focus domains and the division of the budget between commercial, capability and other investment categories were based on environment analysis, strategy update, technology and sector analyses, and service design exercises. The idea was to have more than 250 projects completed by 2020. These projects had to deliver commercial applications and products, improved IT and data capabilities, and simpler processes for the customer and for the employees. KBC evaluated the program every six months. The Project Management Office collected the facts enabling the Program Management Steering Committee to address questions about the overall performance of the program. Did the project deliver real benefits? Were projects delivered on time and within budget? What about the people skills? What about the commitment of the employees and sponsors?

Building a strong core also implied ensuring sponsorship and mobilizing change leaders at all levels. The company put a lot of effort into mobilizing the senior team and a group of change leaders. It also introduced a new way of working, based on focus, flexibility and agility. This was not so easy for a large, over-structured financial institution. With the introduction of boot camps, minimal viable product developments, and empowered cross-functional teams, the company was able to start the cultural transformation well. The Management Committee was patient and knew that cultural transformation takes time. And it did everything to role model the new behavior. Top managers intervened to make clear to everyone that the digital transformation program was an absolute priority. The argument that something was 'not possible' would no longer be accepted.

Change at the Gemba

KBC Belgium invested a lot in communicating and inspiring the employees. Company-wide conferences — so-called Inspiration Days — were organized several times a year. There were weekly calls with the top team for which everybody could register. The team installed giant message walls in the hallways for people to share comments and suggestions, and screens were put up to display Twitter feeds, thus bringing in 'the voice of the customer'.

KBC reached out to its employees and asked them to share new ideas that would transform KBC into a more digital and customer-centric organization. By working on projects in an agile way, participating in boot camps, and continuously doing cross-project consistency checks, these employees were driving Klant 2020. Each project started with clear performance targets and followed a clear methodology consisting of several phases. The company provided training where necessary. The staff proposed new projects, defended them, and were accountable for both successes and failures. A Klant 2020 project life cycle is presented in Figure 62.

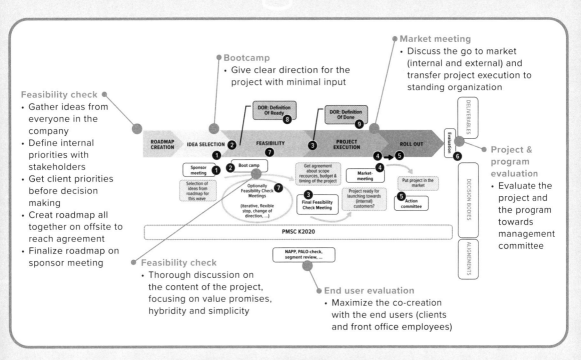

Figure 62 • Klant 2020's project life cycle

Overall, KBC Belgium's Management Committee was happy with the initial results and agreed that the Klant 2020 Program was delivering on its promises. You could feel the Management Committee members' increased alignment around KBC's digital strategy. The program boasted important and highly visible results and the budget was under control.

Still, there were important concerns, such as speed and delivery of the projects. Another major concern was to build a sponsor coalition – a more uniform approach towards coaching projects. Sponsors needed guidance and support. The Management Committee also acknowledged that a lot of work was to be done at the front office of the organization, where people had complained that the pace of change was too fast. Nevertheless, the Management Committee remained determined to continue to progress on the chosen path.

An example of an energy booster

KBC Belgium continues to be a great example of a company that goes for *energy boosting*. There's a clear desire to build change capabilities to be ready for a new disrupted world. This is about more than just getting treated for an energy disease. It is a full commitment to build a new, better and more agile organization. This idea is fully supported by the top team. The company has a well-developed masterplan, a well-structured delivery model and a powerful change architecture. Furthermore, the company pays significant attention to building a leadership network and expanding its human network.

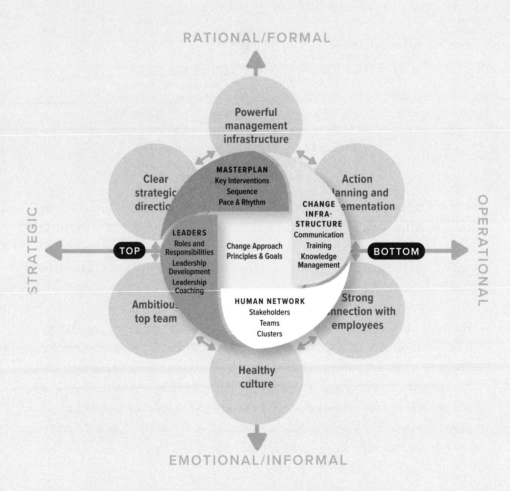

Figure 63 · Energy status of KBC Belgium in 2017

FINAL CONCLUSION

Change management is energy management. Change projects fail because there is a lack of energy to successfully complete change programs and initiatives. In this book we identified six sources of energy that determine change success:

 Intellectual energy provides strategic focus and attention;

 Spiritual energy comes from an ambitious top team and generates purpose and meaning;

 Systemic energy is controlled by an infrastructure that manages performance and improvement;

 Social energy relates to a healthy culture that amplifies energy through cohesion and drive;

 Psychological energy increases security and commitment of employees;

 Physical energy efficiently transforms actions into benefits and capabilities.

Various activities in your organization can generate positive energy to drive change, or negative energy that inhibits change. In extreme cases, negative energy can create short-circuits that completely neutralize all positive actions. The *six batteries of change* are a useful instrument to assess which organizational practices drain energy from your organization, and which ones help you to succeed.

As a change leader, it's your task to infuse the organization with the right energy; to help your organization achieve its strategic objectives and to make this a positive journey for everyone involved. Whether your goal is to get your organization back on track or make it ready for a new era, change programs are difficult programs to implement and require leadership skills from all managers in the organization. The batteries of change provide a framework that clarifies the roles and responsibilities of managers at all levels of the organization: top, middle and bottom. The change challenge is not only to manage the rational batteries of change, but also to infuse a lot of emotional energy into your organization so that both managers and employees become committed to change the company's course.

Organizations fail to implement change because they systematically neglect to charge one or more change batteries. This means launching initiatives to get individual batteries charged. It's equally important though, to have a good view on the energy status of all six batteries of change and to diagnose whether your organization is suffering from a specific change pathology. Healing your organization implies developing change programs that are balanced and that create flow among different management layers. We are convinced that this book provides you with valuable new insights to tackle this healing process.

In the current turbulent environment, building the change capabilities of your organization needs to be ongoing. Boosting the energy levels of your organization is a continuous work in progress. The KBC story illustrates that you're never finished. There are always more batteries that could use some extra charging. To make your organization thrive on change, you have to design a change architecture that systematically connects all sources of energy. This implies *clearly defining change goals and principles, thoughtful planning* and *careful support*, but equally important, *leadership coaching* and the *development of a robust human network*. These five cornerstones serve as bridges between the batteries. They turn the six batteries for change into a dynamic energy system of positive reinforcement loops.

We hope you have been inspired to embark on your change journey and to boost the positive energy throughout your organization. Good luck!

Peter De Prins
Geert Letens
Kurt Verweire

Table of Figures

Notes

1. Williams, R. (2012) "Tour de France 2012: Team Sky Master the Art of Tactics and Teamwork," The *Guardian*, https://www.theguardian.com/sport/blog/2012/jul/20/tour-de-france-2012-team-sky, Website Accessed December 17th, 2016; Gale, R. (2014) "The Aggregation of Marginal Gains: What Can We Learn From the Sport of Cycling?," https://www.linkedin.com/pulse/20140702075656-16203190-the-aggregation-of-marginal-gains-what-can-we-learn-from-the-sport-of-cycling?articleId=8768046596212065254, Website Accessed December 17th, 2016.

2. Kotter, J.P. (2012) "Accelerate! How The Most Innovative Companies Capitalize on Today's Rapid-Fire Strategic Challenges — And Still Make Their Numbers," *Harvard Business Review*, November, 1-13.

3. Stanton Marris (2002) "Energising the Organization: Issue 01 — The Sources of Energy," http://www.stantonmarris.com/wp-content/uploads/2014/07/energising-the-organisation-issue-01-the-sources-of-energy.pdf, Website Accessed April 22nd, 2017.

4. Schwartz, T. and Loehr, J. (2004) *The Power of Full Engagement: Managing Energy, Not Time, Is The Key to High Performance and Personal Renewal*, Reprint Edition, The Free Press, New York, NY.

5. Bruch, H. & Vogel, B. (2011) *Fully Charged: How Great Leaders Boost Their Organization's Energy and Ignite High Performance*, Harvard Business Review Press, Boston, MA.

6. Bruch, H. & Ghoshal, S. (2003) "Unleashing Organizational Energy," *MIT Sloan Management Review*, Fall, Vol. 45 (1), 44-51.

7. Bruch, H. & Vogel, B. (2011) *Fully Charged: How Great Leaders Boost Their Organization's Energy and Ignite High Performance*, Harvard Business Review Press, Boston, MA.

8. This is an exact copy of how we structured these sources of energy loss 3 years ago. Over the years we rearranged some topics based on new insights. The essence here, however, is to show you the act of grouping many sources into 6 clusters.

9. Ibid., p.14.

10. Haidt, J. (2006) *The Happiness Hypothesis: Finding Modern Truth in Ancient Wisdom*, Basic Books, New York, NY.

11. Rodgers, C. (2006) *Informal Coalitions: Mastering the Hidden Dynamics of Organizational Change*, Palgrave MacMillan, Houndmills, Basingstoke.

12. Adapted from Land, M., Hex, N. & Bartlett, C. (2013) "Building and Aligning Energy for Change: A Review of Published and Grey Literature, Initial Concept Testing and Development," *NHS Final Report*, 1-58.

13. Fotheringham, W. (2013) "Tour de France: How Team Sky Climbed to the Top and Stayed There," https://www.theguardian.com/sport/2013/jul/21/tour-de-france-team-sky-froome, Website Accessed December 20th, 2016.

14. Harrell, E. (2015) "How 1% Performance Improvements Led to Olympic Gold," *Harvard Business Review*, October, 1-5.

15. We used the following statement to measure 'overall change success': "The implementation of the change program was successful". We also included three change process effectiveness measures: (1) The change program was implemented within the anticipated time period; (2) The change program achieved the desired performance benefits; and (3) The results of the change program are sustained. The hard performance measures were an average of the following measures: (1) product and service measures; (2) operational and internal processes measures; (3) customer-related measures; (4) financial measures; and (5) market-related measures. The soft performance measures were based on: (1) employee-related measures; and (2) leadership-based measures. We used six-point scales (from 0 to 5) to measure the various change effectiveness scores. Companies with an average score lower than or equal to had a 'negative' change effectiveness. Companies with a score from 2 to 3 were labeled 'somewhat negative.' Companies with a score between 3 and 3.75 had a 'somewhat positive' change effectiveness score. And companies that had average scores that were equal to or exceeded 3.75 were assigned to the 'positive' category. The labels for our questionnaire were as follows: 0 — Strongly disagree; 1 — Disagree; 2 — Tend to disagree; 3 — Tend to agree; 4 — Agree; 5 — Strongly agree.

16. Myatt, M. (2015) "Marissa Mayer: A Case Study in Poor Leadership," Forbes, Article published on November 20th; Alden, J. (2015) "The Last Days of Marissa Mayer?", Forbes, December 14th; Bacon, D. (2016) "Lessons We Can Learn from CEO Marissa Mayer's Leadership at Yahoo", https://www.linkedin.com/pulse/lessons-we-can-learn-from-ceo-marissa-mayers-leadership-doug-bacon, Website Accessed August 29th 2016; Mattone, J. (2016) "Yahoo's Problem? A Massive Lack of Leadership at the Top," Huffington *Post*, March 28th.

17. Myatt, M. (2015) "Marissa Mayer: A Case Study in Poor Leadership," Forbes, Article published on November 20th.

18. Ibid.

19. Myatt, M. (2015) "Marissa Mayer: A Case Study in Poor Leadership," Forbes, Article published on November 20th

20. McManus, P. (2014) "3 Types of Dysfunctional Teams and How To Fix Them," *Fast Company*, https://www.fastcompany.com/3033275/3-types-of-dysfunctional-teams-and-how-to-fix-them, Website Accessed August 26th, 2016.

21. Sull, D. (2009) *The Upside of Turbulence: Seizing Opportunity in an Uncertain World*, HarperCollins Publishers, New York, NY.

22. Casadesus-Masanell, R. (2014) "Setting Aspirations: Mission, Vision, and Values," *Core Curriculum in Strategy Reading*, Harvard Business Publishing, 1-30.

23. Respondents of our research project had to answer around 15 questions per battery. These 15 questions were grouped into 5 elements per battery. We asked at least 4 persons per company to answer our questionnaire. Scores ranged from 0 to 5. When an average score was between 0 and 2, the company obtained a 'negative' score. If the score was between 2

and 3, we assigned a score of 'low negative'. (Not all people even 'tended to agree.') If a company obtained a score between 3 and 3.75, we assigned a score of 'low positive'. And companies with a score of 3.75 and higher got a label 'positive'.

24 David, S., & Congleton, C. (2013). Emotional agility. *Harvard Business Review*, 91(11), 125-128.

25 Ovans, A. (2015) "How Emotional Intelligence Became a Key Leadership Skill." *Harvard Business Review*, April, 2-5.

26 David, S. & Congleton, C. (2013) "Emotional Agility: How Effective Leaders Manage Their Negative Thoughts and Feelings," *Harvard Business Review*, November, 1-5.

27 Katzenbach, J.R. (1997) "The Myth of the Top Management Team", *Harvard Business Review*, November-December, 83-91.

28 "Band of Brothers" is a series of the story of Easy Company of the U.S. Army 101st Airborne Division, and their mission in World War II Europe, from Operation Overlord, through V-J Day - http://www.imdb.com/title/tt0185906/

29 Walsh, D. (2016) "Five Strategies for Leading a High-Impact Team" (Article based on insights from Professor Leigh Thompson), *Kellogg Insight*, Kellogg School of Management, http://insight.kellogg.northwestern.edu/article/five-strategies-for-leading-a-high-impact-team, Website Accessed September 8th, 2016.

30 Lencioni, P. (2002) *The Five Dysfunctions of a Team: A Leadership Fable*, Jossey-Bass, San Francisco, CA.

31 The quote is based on a personal interview with a director of an international animal health firm.

32 Kirk, D. (1992) "World-Class Teams," *McKinsey Quarterly*, December, p. 5.

33 Verweire, K & Van den Berghe, L.A.A. (2006) "ING direct: Rebel in the banking industry", Vlerick Business *School Case Study*, 307-053-1, p.1.

34 Black, J.S. & Gregersen, H. (2008) *It Starts with One: Changing Individuals Changes Organizations*, 2nd Edition, Pearson Education, Upper Saddle River, NJ.

35 Kotter, J.P. & Cohen, D.S. (2012) *The Heart of Change: Real-Life Stories of How People Change Their Organizations*, Harvard Business Review Press, Boston, MA.

36 Verweire, K., Kemperman, J., op 't Hoog, J., & Maas, P. (2016) "Interpolis: Becoming the Most Transparent and Trustworthy Insurance Company," Vlerick Business *School Case Study*, 316-0256-1, 1-16.

37 Montgomery, C.A. (1999) "Newell Company: Corporate Strategy," Harvard Business School Case Study, 9-799-139, 1-22; Harding, D. & Rovit, S. (2004) *Mastering the Merger: Four Critical Decisions that Make or Break the Deal*, Harvard Business School Press, Boston, MA.

38 Day, G.S. & Schoemaker, P.J.H. (2005) "Scanning the Periphery," *Harvard Business Review*, November, 135-48.

39 Leinwand, P., Mainardi, C. (2016) *Strategy That Works: How Winning Companies Close the Strategy-To-Execution Gap*, Harvard Business School Press, Boston, MA.

40 Martin, R.L. (2014) "The Big Lie of Strategic Planning," *Harvard Business Review*, January-February, 1-8.

41 Vermeulen, F. (2012) "So You Think You Have A Strategy," *London Business School Web Exclusive*, http://bsr.london.edu/lbs-article/629/index.html, Accessed March 20th, 2012.

42 Respondents of our research project had to answer around 15 questions per battery. These 15 questions were grouped into 5 elements per battery. We asked at least 4 persons per company to answer our questionnaire. Scores ranged from 0 to 5. When an average score was between 0 and 2, the company obtained a 'negative' score. If the score was between 2 and 3, we assigned a score of 'low negative'. (Not all people even 'tended to agree.') If a company obtained a score between 3 and 3.75, we assigned a score of 'low positive'. And companies with a score of 3.75 and higher got a label 'positive'.

43 Crawford, F. & Mathews, R. (2001) *The Myth of Excellence: Why Great Companies Never Try to Be the Best at Everything*, Crown Business, New York, NY.

44 *Product* refers to the core benefits a customer buys; *price* is about the cost of the goods and services; *access* describes how easily consumers can obtain and use the company's goods and services; *service* is defined as what a company does extra for its customers before, during, and after the sale; *connectivity* is about the quality of the relationship between customer and supplier.

45 Pietersen, W. (2002) *Reinventing Strategy: Using Strategic Learning to Create & Sustain Breakthrough Performance*, John Wiley & Sons Inc., New York, NY.

46 Reeves, M., Haanaes, K. & Sinha, S. (2015) *Your Strategy Needs A Strategy: How to Choose and Execute the Right Approach*, Harvard Business School Press, Boston, MA.

47 Day, G.S. & Schoemaker, P.J.H. (2005) "Scanning the Periphery," *Harvard Business Review*, November, 135-48.

48 Debruyne, M. (2014) *Customer Innovation: Customer-centric Strategy For Enduring Growth*, Kogan Page Ltd., London.

49 O'Reilly III, C.A. & Tushman, M.L. (2016) *Lead And Disrupt: How To Solve The Innovator's Dilemma*, Stanford University Press, Stanford, CA.

50 Baghai, M., Coley, S. & White, D. (1999) *The Alchemy Of Growth: Practical Insights For Building the Enduring Enterprise*, Perseus Publishing & McKinsey & Company, New York, NY.

51 Hinssen, P. (2016) "How To Organize For The Day After Tomorrow – Remote Silo Innovation," http://www.forbes.com/sites/peterhinssen/2016/06/15/how-to-organize-for-the-day-after-tomorrow-remote-silo-innovation/#1f659a3b1617, Website Accessed February 22nd, 2017.

52 Govindarajan, V. & Trimble, C. (2005) *10 Rules for Strategic Innovators: From Idea to Execution*, Harvard Business School Press, Boston, MA.

53 Hinssen, P. (2016) "How To Organize For The Day After Tomorrow – Remote Silo Innovation," http://www.forbes.com/sites/peterhinssen/2016/06/15/how-to-organize-for-the-day-after-tomorrow-remote-silo-innovation/#1f659a3b1617, Website Accessed February 22nd, 2017.

54 Christensen, C.M. (1997) "We've Got Rhythm! Medtronic Corporation's Cardiac Pacemaker Business," Harvard Business School Case Study, 9-698-004, 1-18.

55 Herold, D.M. & Fedor, D.B. (2008) *Change the Way You Lead Change*, Stanford Business Books, Stanford, CA.

56 Black, J.S. & Gregersen, H. (2014) *It Starts with One: Changing Individuals Changes Organizations*, 3rd Edition, Pearson Education, Upper Saddle River, NJ, p. 86.

57 Christensen, C.M. (1997) "We've Got Rhythm! Medtronic Corporation's Cardiac Pacemaker Business," *Harvard Business School Case Study*, 9-698-004, 1-18.

58 Verweire, K. (2014) *Strategy Implementation*, Routledge Publications, Abingdon.

59 Kaplan, R.S. & Norton, D.P. (2004) "How Strategy Maps Frame an Organization's Objectives," *Financial Executive*, March/April, 40-45.

60 Kaplan, R.S. & Norton, D.P. (2004) *Strategy Maps: Converting Intangible Assets into Tangible Outcomes*, Harvard Business School Press, Boston, MA.

61 Pyzdek, T., & Keller, P. A. (2014). *The six sigma handbook* (p. 25). New York: McGraw-Hill Education.

62 Radeka, K. (2012). *The mastery of innovation: a field guide to lean product development*. CRC Press.

63 Liker, J. K. (2004). *The Toyota Way*, Esensi.

64 Nonaka, I. & Takeuchi, H. (1995) *The Knowledge-Creating Company: How Japanese Companies Create the Dynamics of Innovation*, Oxford University Press, New York, NY.

65 Nonaka, I. & Takeuchi, H. (1995) *The Knowledge-Creating Company: How Japanese Companies Create the Dynamics of Innovation*, Oxford University Press, New York, NY.

66 Kniberg, H. & Ivarsson, A. (2012) "Scaling Agile @ Spotify," Crisp Consulting Blog, https://ucvox.files.wordpress.com/2012/11/113617905-scaling-agile-spotify-11.pdf, Accessed March 31st, 2017.

67 Huy, Q. (2015) "Who Killed Nokia? Nokia Did?", Insead Knowledge, Article posted September 22nd, http://knowledge.insead.edu/strategy/who-killed-nokia-nokia-did-4268, Website Accessed August 31st, 2016.

68 Vuori, T.O. & Huy, Q.N. (2015) "Distributed Attention and Shared Emotions in the Innovation Process: How Nokia Lost the Smartphone Battle," *Administrative Science Quarterly*, 1-43.

69 A movie just came out this year (2017).

70 Schein, E.H. (2010) *Organizational Culture and Leadership* (4th Edition), John Wiley & Sons, San Francisco, CA.

71 Ibid.

72 Sackmann, S. A. (2011) "Culture and performance," in N. Ashkanasy, C. Wilderom, & M. Peterson (Eds.), *The handbook of organizational culture and climate*, 2nd Ed., p. 188-224, Sage Publications, Thousand Oaks, CA.

73 Tushman, M.L. & O'Reilly, C.A. (1997) *Winning Through Innovation: A Practical Guide to Leading Organizational Change and Renewal*, Harvard Business School Press, Boston, MA, p. 10.

74 Parr, S. (2014) "Culture Eats Strategy for Lunch," Blog posted July 21st, http://bulldogdrummond.com/blog/culture-eats-strategy-for-lunch, Website Accessed October 24th, 2016.

75 Thompson, A.A. Jr, Strickland, A.J. III & Gamble, J.E. (2008) *Crafting & Executing Strategy: The Quest for Competitive Advantage – Concepts and Cases*, 16th Edition, McGraw-Hill/Irwin, New York, NY.

76 Katzenbach, J., Oelschlegel, C. & Thomas, J. (2016) "10 Principles of Organizational Culture," *strategy+business*, No. 82, Spring, 1-7.

77 Sumantra Ghoshal, London Business School, http://downloads.bbc.co.uk/worldservice/learningenglish/handy/ghoshal.pdf

78 Katzenbach, J., Oelschlegel, C. & Thomas, J. (2016) "10 Principles of Organizational Culture," *strategy+business*, No. 82, Spring, 1-7; Katzenbach, J., Steffen, I. & Kronley, C. (2012) "Cultural Change That Sticks," *Harvard Business Review*, July-August, 1-9; PWC (2014) "A Perspective on Organizational Culture," *Strategy&* Website, http://www.strategyand.pwc.com/media/file/Strategyand-Perspective-on-Organizational-Culture.pdf, Website Accessed October 25th, 2016.

79 Barrett, R. (2006) *Building a Values-Driven Organization: A Whole Systems Approach to Cultural Transformation*, Butterworth-Heinemann, Burlington, MA, p. 38.

80 Cameron, K.S. & Quinn, R.E. (2011) *Diagnosing and Changing Organizational Culture – Based on the Competing Values Framework*, 3rd Edition, Jossey-Bass, San Francisco, CA.

81 Black, J.S. & Gregersen, H.B. (2008) *It Starts With One: Changing Individuals Changes Organizations*, Pearson Education, Inc., Upper Saddle River, New Jersey.

82 Heath, C. & Heath, D. (2010) *Switch: How To Change Things When Change Is Hard*, Random House Inc., New York, NY.

83 Denison, D. & Nieminen, L. (2014) "Habits as Change Levers," *People & Strategy*, Vol. 37 (1), 23-27.

84 Katzenbach, J., Steffen, I. & Kronley, C. (2012) "Cultural Change That Sticks," Harvard Business Review, July-August, 1-9, p. 8.

85 Thompson, A.A., Strickland, A.J. & Gamble, J.E. (2008) *Crafting and Executing Strategy: The Quest for Competitive Advantage: Text and Readings*, 16th Edition, McGraw-Hill, London.

86 Bulygo, Z. (2013) "Tony Hsieh, Zappos, and the Art of Great Company Culture," Kissmetrics Blog https://blog.kissmetrics.com/zappos-art-of-culture/, Website Accessed April 7th, 2017.

87 Beinhocker, E.D. (2006) "The Adaptable Corporation," *McKinsey Quarterly*, Number 2, 76-87.

88 Bock, L. (2015). *Work rules!: Insights from inside Google that will transform how you live and lead*. Hachette UK.

89 Companies whose profitability oscillated between underperformance and outperformance relative to the industry average.

90 Williams, T., Worley, C.G. & Lawler, E.E. (2013) "The Agility Factor," strategy+business, http://www.strategy-business.com/article/00188?gko=6a0ba, Website Accessed November 8th, 2016, p. 5.

91 Deschamps, J.-P. (2008) *Innovation Leaders: How Senior Executives Stimulate, Steer, and Sustain Innovation*, John Wiley & Sons, Chicester, UK.

92 Horovitz, J. (2013) "Managing By Values To Create A Customer-Centric Organization," *Harvard Business Manager*, December, 1-7.

93 Verweire, K. (2014) Strategy Implementation, Routledge, Abingdon, UK, p. 271.

94 Horovitz, J. (2013) "Managing By Values To Create A Customer-Centric Organization," *Harvard Business Manager*, December, 1-7.

95 Scott, J. (1999) "The FoxMeyer Drugs' Bankruptcy: Was it a Failure of ERP?", AMCIS 1999 Proceedings, Vol. 80, 3-222-25.

96 Sinek, S. (2011) *Start With Why: How Great Leaders Inspire Everyone To Take Action*, Penguin, London.

97 Sobek II, D. K., & Smalley, A. (2011). Understanding *A3 thinking: a critical component of Toyota's PDCA management system*. CRC Press.

98 "A Kaizen event is a focused and structured improvement project, using a dedicated cross-functional team to improve a targeted work area, with specific goals, in an accelerated timeframe" Van Aken, E. M., Farris, J. A., Glover, W. J., & Letens, G. (2010). A framework for designing, managing, and improving Kaizen event programs. *International Journal of Productivity and Performance Management*, 59(7), 641-667.

99 A scrum is a team of eight individuals in Rugby. SCRUM software development teams use this analogy to create small teams of strongly integrated members. They focus on the creation of usable deliverables during sprints of one to four weeks. "A sprint is time-boxed development, meaning that the end date for a sprint does not change. The team can reduce delivered functionality during the sprint, but the delivery date cannot change" Rising, L., & Janoff, N. S. (2000). The Scrum software development process for small teams. *IEEE software*, 17(4), 26-32.

100 Masaaki, I. (1997). Gemba kaizen: a commonsense low-cost approach to management.

101 Liker, J. K. (2004). *The Toyota Way*, Esensi.

102 Krackhardt, D., Heckscher, C., & Donnellon, A. (2003). Constraints on the interactive organization as an ideal type. *Networks in the Knowledge Economy*. Oxford University Press, Oxford, 324-335.

103 Tuckman, B. W. (1965). Developmental sequence in small groups. *Psychological bulletin*, 63(6), 384.

104 Agile is a software development methodology that is defined by the Agile Manifesto of Kent Beck et al. Important characteristics include that it is human-centered, with technology and tools receiving a secondary role. It emphasizes close cooperation with customer and fast and iterative empirical learning. Fowler, M., & Highsmith, J. (2001). The agile manifesto. *Software Development*, 9(8), 28-35.

105 Keenan, P., Powell, K., Kurstjens, H., Shanahan, M., Lewis, M. & Bursetti, M. (2012) "How ING Bank Took Change to Heart", *BCG Perspectives*, https://www.bcgperspectives.com/content/articles/change_management_transformation_how_ing_bank_took_change_to_heart/, Website Accessed April 30th, 2017·

106 Hiatt, J.M. & Creasey, T.J. (2012) Change Management: The People Side of Change, Prosci Inc., Loveland, CO.

107 Kotter, J.P. & Cohen, D.S. (2002) *The Heart of Change*, Harvard Business School Publishing, Boston, MA.

108 Black, J.S. & Gregersen, H. (2014) *It Starts with One: Changing Individuals Changes Organizations*, 3rd Edition, Pearson Education, Upper Saddle River, NJ.

109 Maister, D.H., Green, C.H. & Galford, R.M. (2000) *The Trusted Advisor*, The Free Press, New York, NY.

110 Nunes, J. & Dreze, X. (2006) "The Endowed Progress Effect: How Artificial Advancement Increases Effort," *Journal of Consumer Research*, Vol. 32, March, 504-12.

111 Changefirst (2010) *Our Change Management Methodology Overview: How Changefirst Helps You Implement Change*, Changefirst Ltd. Publication, 1-19.

112 Motivation and Employee Engagement in the 21st Century: A Survey of Management Views (2009), Viki Holton, Fiona Dent and Jan Rabbetts

113 Verweire, K. (2015) "Zenith Animal Health Denmark: Creating 'love affairs' with customers," *Unpublished Vlerick Business School case study*, 1-13. The name and country of this company was altered on request of the management team.

114 Beer, M. & Nohria, N. (Eds.) *Breaking the Code of Change*, Harvard Business School Press, Boston, MA.

115 Birkinshaw, J. & Gibson, C. (2004) "Building Ambidexterity Into An Organization," *MIT Sloan Management Review*, Summer, 47-55.

116 Cagna, A.-M. & Galunic, C. (2008) "Leadership, culture Change, and Transformation at AVIVA: Norwich Union Insurance – Case A & Case B," Insead Case studies, 408-034-1 and 408-035-1.

117 Ibid. Case B, p. 12.

118 Verweire, K., Kemperman, J., Op 't Hoog, J. & Maas, P. (2016) "Interpolis: Becoming the Most Transparent and Trustworthy Insurance Company," Vlerick Business School *Case Study*, 316-0256-1, 1-15.

119 Herold, D.M. & Fedor, D.B. (2008) *Change The Way You Lead Change: Leadership Strategies That Really Work*, Stanford Business Books, Stanford, CA.

120 McNulty, E.J., Foote, N. & Wilson, D. (2017) "Management Lessons from One Hospital's Dramatic Turnaround," strategy+business, Article published March 13th, Website Accessed April 11th, 2017.

121 Masaaki, I. (1997). Gemba kaizen: a commonsense low-cost approach to management.

122 Van Aken, E.M., Van Goubergen, D. & Letens, G. (2003) "Integrated Enterprise Transformation: Case Application in Engineering Project Work in the Belgian Armed Forces," *Engineering Management Journal*, Vol. 15 (2), 3-16.

123 Kotter, J. P. (2008). *A sense of urgency*. Harvard Business Press.

124 Basford, T., Schaninger, B. & Viruleg, E. (2015) "The Science of Organizational Transformations," *McKinsey Research Report*, 1-8.

125 Ackerman Anderson, L. & Anderson, D. (2010) *The Change Leader's Roadmap: How to Navigate Your Organization's Transformation*, 2nd Edition, Pfeiffer, San Francisco, CA.

126 ChangeFirst (2010) "Our Change Management Methodology Overview," *ChangeFirst White Paper*, ChangeFirst Ltd.

127 Basford, T., Schaninger, B. & Viruleg, E. (2015) "The Science of Organizational Transformations," *McKinsey Research Report*, 1-8.

128 A 'dominant coalition' is defined as the organizational objectives and strategies, personal characteristics, and internal relationships of that minimum group of cooperating employees who oversee the organization as a whole and control its basic policy making.

129 Shapiro, S.M (2011) *Best Practices Are Stupid: 40 Ways to Out-Innovate The Competition*, Portfolio/Penguin, New York, NY.

130 Grau, R. (2015) "The Life Cycle of an Initiative", *Lean, Agile, Literature and Sport*, http://rainergrau.blogspot.be/2015/06/the-life-cycle-of-initiative-step-4.html/, Website Accessed October 30th, 2017.

Quotes

"In this era of digitalization, the cultural and managerial paradigms obtained through education and years of work experience are severely challenged.

Managers are confronted with the non-effectiveness of the traditional management models in the new digital environment. They are left in despair as few viable alternatives are provided.

With the "six batteries of change", Peter De Prins, Geert Letens and Kurt Verweire were able to capture the delicate balance between cultural aspects of change and the remaining need for direction and structure, which still characterizes any successful change and go-to-market strategy."

JOHAN THIJS | CEO of KBC Group

"I have waited patiently for the publication of *Six Batteries of Change* and recommend this book wholeheartedly. There are many books proposing models for organizational change, but this one is refreshing, and it is based on rigorous research and validation.

I love the way it is organized, it is easy to read, the illustrations are helpful, and the inclusion of the Spark for Reflection in each chapter provides great examples of each battery of change.

This work can be used as a handbook to successfully lead change in your organization, with step-by-step instructions including guidance on how to get an overall energy snapshot of your organization. Get started on your journey now!"

KIM LASCOLA NEEDY | Dean of the Graduate School and International Education, University of Arkansas

"The difference between *Six Batteries of Change* and just another book about change, is the real-life experience of the authors. But the real knock-out is this: when you finish this book, it's hard not to wonder how it has never been around before. Get your batteries fully loaded."

KOEN HOFFMAN | CEO at Values Square (and former CEO at KBC Securities)

"This book stands out among the many on organizational change. The sources of energy provides a powerful image and leads to practical applications to help you move forward toward your vision."

JEFFREY K. LIKER | Author of *The Toyota Way*

"If you want to succeed in leading change, this is the book for you. You will learn how you can energize your organization by employing six principles that are all too often ignored by CEOs stuck in the outdated command-and-control style of leadership."

MICHAEL BEER | Professor Emeritus, Harvard Business School

"The strength of this book is that it brings the "hard" and "soft" side of change together in one framework with incredible intuitive appeal. Any leader who is transforming his or her organization will find immediately applicable insights in it."

MARION DEBRUYNE | Dean of Vlerick Business School